PIE
LOVE

PIE LOVE

Inventive Recipes for Sweet and
Savory Pies, Galettes, Pastry
Creams, Tarts, and Turnovers

WARREN BROWN

Photography by Joshua Cogan

Stewart, Tabori & Chang

New York

Published in 2013 by Stewart, Tabori & Chang

An imprint of ABRAMS

Cataloging-in-Publication Data has been applied for and may be obtained from the Library of Congress.

ISBN: 978-1-58479-895-8

Editor: Jennifer Levesque

Designer: Alissa Faden

Production Manager: Tina Cameron

The text of this book was composed in Gotham, Lubalin Graph, Bullion, and Archive Kludsky.

Printed and bound in China

10 9 8 7 6 5 4 3 2 1

ABRAMS
THE ART OF BOOKS SINCE 1949

115 West 18th Street
New York, NY 10011
www.abramsbooks.com

3 3988 10116 1112

To Leonie

You are my Mountain

contents

INTRODUCTION

ENTER

the

I have this distinct memory of walking home from school sometime in the fourth or fifth grade. It was hot, and there was a hill, two streets to cross, and one yard before I was at my front door. The keys for the front door always got a little stuck, but I put up with that because it was faster than going around to the back. It was a straighter path to the kitchen—to the fridge—where the leftover pie was kept, waiting to become my after-school snack. Most of the time, there was enough for my sisters and me. But this lingering memory ends with an empty pie tin left out on the counter. I'll never know who got to it first; it was probably my mom. She loves apple pie and always has it à la mode with Breyer's vanilla ice cream. ("Made with real vanilla bean," she would proudly say.) She's the one who instilled in me my deep appreciation for real vanilla and all things gourmet. But that last slice, the delicious one I missed, I still want it.

There's a drive that comes from not getting what you want that never goes away. Apple pie will always be that dessert for me. Who knows if any of these recipes are as good as the slice that got away, but I'm having fun figuring it out. I hope you do too!

THE BASICS of PIE

INGREDIENTS

FLOUR

Unless otherwise noted, my flour of choice is General Mills brand unbleached all-purpose flour. Unlike with cakes, I don't bother to sift and weigh the flour; for crusts, we're aiming to mix a dense pastry anyway. If you have any of my other books or have seen me speak, you already know how strongly I feel about using a scale to get an accurate amount of flour for cake recipes. While a scale is your best bet for success when hedging against packing too much flour into a cup measure, it's okay to have a little more flour than called for when mixing pie dough. So if you don't have a scale or just want to keep the measuring simple, stick with the cup measures to scoop and level—*but only with pie dough*!

There are a range of other grains called for with the different piecrusts covered in the first chapter of this book. Baking with a mix of grains creates a lovely balance of flavors and textures in each bite.

- I especially like working with **whole-wheat flour**—either pastry flour or all-purpose whole-wheat flour—for the earthy bite it brings to a pie.

- **Flaxseed** is great and brings a distinctly nutty flavor to the dough, but be sure to grind it immediately before use to take advantage of the healthful omega-3s found in the oils. These will have evaporated from preground store-bought flaxseed flour.

- I dedicate a **kitchen coffee grinder** as a spice mill and gristmill for my grains.

- **Millet flour** is great as a substitute for wheat flour in limited quantities to lower the gluten content. If it's used exclusively in lieu of flour, the resulting crust will not have the same texture.

- **Polenta** is very finely ground cornmeal, which brings an oven-toasted crunch to the crusts.

SWEETENERS

Superfine granulated sugar is the default for each recipe. It's a little bit smaller than the standard "granulated" sugar and yields a finer texture with baked goods. Again, with pies, scooping the sugar works just as well as using a scale because we have a lot more fudge room. One cup weighs a little less than 8 ounces if you're using a very sensitive scale, but rounding up will do.

Occasionally, other sources of sweetness come into play. Here are a few alternatives to consider if you want to cut back on refined sugars in your baked goods.

Maple sugars and syrups are perfect substitutes for refined sugar. Note that the distinct maple flavor may compete with other ingredients, so choose this sweetener only if you're a real fan of maple syrup.

Agave nectar, or syrup, is produced from the sap of the agave plant. Both light and dark versions are available. The light has a taste closer to honey; the dark, which is simply less filtered, is closer to maple syrup. The carbohydrate in agave nectar has a low glycemic index, making it a natural option for people who need to manage their blood sugar. It will work as a near one-for-one substitute for maple syrup and corn syrup, but the exact results can't be guaranteed. When substituting for granulated sugar, add 1 tablespoon cornstarch per cup of agave (light or dark) and mix thoroughly in order to help thicken the syrup in the pie. Before you scoop the filling into the blind-baked piecrust, assess the texture of the filling. If it seems too runny, add more starch.

Cane syrups, known as *treacle* in the U.K., are made from refining cane sugars or boiling cane sugar with water. Golden Syrup is a popular brand that's also available here in the United States. Different viscosities and colors reveal varying levels of sweetness and flavors; the darker ones taste more like caramelized sugar syrups. They're suitable substitutes for corn syrup if that doesn't appeal to you.

Honey works well, but add it *after* cooking the filling on the stove, especially if you're using raw honey. The direct heat breaks down the sugars a bit, which dulls the sweetness and creates a slightly bitter flavor.

Corn syrups—both light and dark—have a role in pies that is difficult to replace with other syrups. Pecan pie just isn't the same without it. Of course, pie is made with sugar, so we're not going to fuss about whether or not we should eat sugars derived from corn, but there is no need for the high-fructose variety.

Molasses isn't something I recommend using as the main sweetener in your pie, unless you're making shoofly pie, such as the one on page 110. Its flavor and characteristics are not interchangeable with cane sugar, maple sugar, or honey. And a little molasses goes a long way, so it can be added as a flavor accent by the teaspoon.

Unrefined brown sugars, muscovado and turbinado, are hard to beat in terms of flavor. Neither is essential to make a wonderful pie, but both can add a depth of flavor if swapped in for one quarter to one third of the cane sugar called for in the recipe.

BUTTER AND OTHER FATS

Piecrust requires a healthy dose of fat. As always, unsalted butter is my go-to option for baking. Piecrust made with butter tastes homemade and has flavor notes that you just can't mistake for anything else. We don't have to be so exact with measuring here, either, so a scale isn't necessary. An extra teaspoon or so of butter will just mean a slightly flakier crust. But temperature matters a great deal. If the butter isn't cold and in small pieces when it's added, it won't disperse properly into the dry ingredients, and everything will become soggy—a catastrophe for piecrust. For the best results, use cold butter; cut it and rechill it before mixing it into the dough.

I prefer 82 percent milk fat unsalted butter. I'm not particular to a specific brand; just be sure it's not watery—some generic brands have an unhelpful amount of water.

Vegetable shortening lends a great dynamic to piecrust. The only thing it lacks is taste. When I tried a crust with 50 percent butter and 50 percent shortening, it was as flaky as my heart's desire, but I just didn't taste much. Not until I tipped the scale with a 60 percent butter and 40 percent shortening mix did I find what I was looking for. The 60/40 Crust (page 52) is a reliable workhorse that does well with certain cream and nut pies. When starting with a pound of flour, the best combination I found is four ounces butter to three ounces vegetable shortening, roughly 60 percent butter to 40 percent shortening.

Vegan crusts are entirely feasible, whether made with plain vegetable shortening or a **vegan shortening blend**, but for the sake of taste, I highly recommend using a vegan shortening blend. The mix of oils helps create a background of flavors that gives the crust a better taste profile.

Other vegetable sources of fat can be used to keep the piecrusts tender, including **coconut oil** and **cocoa butter**. For the most part, they're experimental—more to have fun with in the kitchen. They certainly work, but if you don't have the ingredient on hand and want to make that crust, just substitute in unsalted butter or vegetable shortening, and you'll be on your way.

Lard always has a place in pie making. There was a time when that place was probably first, but lard was eventually displaced with clever marketing ads promoting vegetable shortening and emphasizing the "ick" factor of baking with rendered pork fat. It makes a very tender, flaky crust that's suitable for use with most pie fillings and doesn't carry a detectable off flavor. Look for leaf lard, which is the highest quality, in international markets if it's not available at your local grocer.

FRUITS AND VEGETABLES

Choose the best-looking, freshest fruits and vegetables for pies and tarts. Natural, organic, or pesticide-free foods look and taste better. Plus, it's worth paying a little more for ingredients

when you've made the choice to spend time in the kitchen. And when you can, shop locally so you can ask the farmers at local markets about their practices. Make sure that your efforts in the kitchen are matched with equally hardworking hands on the farms where they grow crops and raise livestock naturally, with your family's health in mind. It may not be possible to shop entirely locally for everything you need to make the perfect pie, but source as much as you can from reputable vendors, and you won't be let down.

For ripening fruits, it's always helpful to keep at least two of a kind in an enclosed space. I place fresh fruits under a cake dome. This way fruit flies don't become a problem, the fruits have plenty of air to breathe, and gases that facilitate ripening can be passed between them. Placing fruit in a brown paper bag works just as well. For tarts, it's best to start with fruits at the peak of their ripeness and not much beyond that. Ripe fruit will taste best, especially berries, but handle them carefully, since they can bruise easily. Most fruit will be fine in a pie, even if it's a little past its prime—especially where a double crust is indicated. Just watch for a total breakdown of very fragile fruit, like peaches, that shouldn't be cooked down after they've ripened.

Thoroughly rinse your fruits and vegetables to remove as much dirt, debris, microbial pathogens, and chemicals used during cultivation as you can. Probably the best method for washing foods is to make a solution of three parts water and one part white vinegar. For fruits with lots of nooks and crannies, just soak them for a few minutes in the solution, then rinse them with cold water.

ESSENTIAL EQUIPMENT

Pies are fantastic because they're really simple: a great filling covered in a tasty pastry. Roll out the dough, line a pan with it, fill it, and bake. So long as there's enough filling and it's not watery, not much can go wrong. But there are a few things that will help you to achieve that simplicity every time.

When we're talking about pies and equipment, it's important to note that while traditional tools are great to have, they're not essential. No matter what tools you use, making crust and filling is remarkably fast and easy. I like to turn to whatever is already on hand. For example, if you don't have a rolling pin, grab a wine bottle or a straight-sided soda bottle. No food processor to cut the butter into the flour? No problem. It's just a matter of about five to seven minutes to cut the butter in using a fork or your fingers. It's more time consuming, but it's not impossible.

PANS AND SMALL TOOLS

Pie pans: I regularly bake with 9- to 10-inch pie pans that are 1 to 1½ inches deep; that's the standard depth. I like to use deep-dish pans for savory pies—they make a dramatic presentation. If you're working with a smaller pan, simply save a portion of the crust or filling. If you have a larger pan, then double the recipe and save any unused crust or filling. Pie dough keeps very well in the freezer—for weeks—if well sealed. (And finish off small amounts of leftover filling in a ramekin as a mini pie just for yourself!)

I don't really have a preference for one kind of pie pan material over another. Heatproof glass, metal, or ceramic all work equally well. Glass pie pans can be helpful because you can see whether the crust appears browned and well baked, but I also use disposable aluminum pans all the time and find they're just as reliable.

Tart pans: I use regular tin tart pans with removable bottoms and fluted edges. I don't use nonstick pans. The shiny surface of the tin is better suited for baking the crust to a nice golden brown. These pans rust easily, so don't let them drip dry; instead, dry them in a warm oven.

Bench scraper: This is a totally helpful tool to have on hand. We use the bench scraper all the time at the bakery, and I keep one at home to cut cold butter, cut through dough, help form shapes, and assist with cleanup. I've even used it as a chisel on blocks of chocolate!

Pastry brush: Another helpful tool. I prefer natural hair bristles over nylon, but both work. I'm not a fan of the silicone bristle brushes—they don't absorb anything and end up being a sloppy way to apply a wash. If you're in a pinch, loosely wad up a paper towel, dip it in your egg (or other) wash, then dab it on the piecrust—the effect will be the same.

Pie weights: Actually, I don't use pie weights or dry beans to prevent the crust from tenting during blind baking. When I used beans, they'd sink into the crust and then it was work to pluck them out. Heavier weights cratered the crust. I find that simply lining the crust with a round of parchment paper cut to fit and lightly pressing in a disposable pie pan works perfectly.

Parchment paper: This is one of those essential items; you just have to have it to keep life simple. Baking without parchment paper is like walking in the rain without an umbrella—totally doable, but life is so much nicer when you have one. Rolling out dough between sheets of parchment paper means nothing will stick to the rolling pin or the counter, and will easily transfer into the pie pan—all of which makes production remarkably easy.

Rolling pin: This item performs an essential pie-making function, but there are other items you can use instead. Broomsticks or wine bottles work as substitutes. If you do a lot of baking, though, you may want to buy one: I keep a few different rolling pins at home—I prefer French-style pins because their convex shape helps to form the dough into a nice, tight circle.

Rasp or plane zester: This is good for making very fine zest, grating cheese, or grating spices like nutmeg. Its versatile application makes it essential.

Sturdy forks, paring knives, peelers, baking sheets, and measuring cups and spoons are all must-have items, too.

LARGE TOOLS

Food processor: If you're serious about cooking, then you probably already have a food processor. If you've been making do without one, consider changing your ways. A food processor makes short work out of mixing piecrust and does it better than a standing mixer. The steel blade is the only attachment we'll use for making dough.

Standing mixer: They mix well, but I find that dough made with a standing mixer can be just a bit tougher than that mixed in a food processor or by hand. Most doughs—notably the Flaky Butter Crust (see page 32)—also require about 1 tablespoon more water. Use the paddle attachment for mixing pie dough.

Saucepans: High-quality saucepans are always helpful when making a delicate sauce, such as the béchamel for the Chicken Pot Pie (page 175) or the custards for the cream pies. A heavy pan is not necessarily high quality just because of its weight, but the best ones I've used are all heavy. My wife hates lugging the pots from the stove to the sink, but we never burn anything!

WHAT GOES ON IN A PIE?

Pies are a wonderfully simple way to showcase ingredients we treasure and enjoy. Their importance is revealed in the pride and passion bakers display when presenting them. Since they're beautiful to look at and are greeted with eager anticipation, it's critical that the dish live up to expectations. The first step in making sure that happens is to understand exactly what you're doing when you assemble a pie.

Piecrusts are a great domain in and of themselves. There's no shortage of recipes available to make the "perfect" crust. Generally a crust is made of grain ground into flour, butter, or vegetable shortening, or some of both, a dash or two of salt, and enough water to bring it all together. My recipes tend to include sugar—I guess that's my background in cakes showing through. I think a little sugar helps to tenderize the crust and keeps it from becoming too doughy. But the key thing to understand about crust is the purpose of the fats and the ideal way to blend them into the grains.

Aside from adding great flavor, the fats manage the gluten proteins by making the crust flaky. They keep a tight lid on their formation by shortening the length of the gluten strands—hence the term "shortening." When we add water to wheat flour and stir, gluten proteins develop to give the dough its characteristic stickiness. While we need the gluten proteins to be activated in order to shape the dough, it's important to maintain control over their formation, or the gluten will grow too strong and make the crust—or any pastry—tough and chewy. Cutting very cold butter into the flour distributes mini pieces of fat through the flour, which results in a very tender crust.

Since piecrust has very little liquid, that tenderness manifests as flakiness.

Many other fats are suitable for using alone or in combination with butter to manipulate the character of a crust's flakiness. Vegetable shortening melts at a higher temperature than butter and, when used in combination with it, increases the tenderness of the pastry. I like to experiment, so I've also toyed around with exotic fats like coconut oil, cocoa butter, and, of course, lard.

Keeping the ratios of flour and shortening in balance are critical starting points, but that's not all we can do. Minimizing the amount of pure water added to the flour also helps. Ice-cold vodka or vinegar mixed with cold water are both good options for liquids that make the dough come together with less activation of the gluten. I've had success with swapping 50 percent of the water for vodka or vinegar. You shouldn't find either necessary if you follow recipes closely, but it can be helpful if you have persistent problems with tough crusts.

HOMEMADE AND READY TO GO

If you are really organized, you can always make the crust ahead of time and freeze the raw or blind-baked shells in the pans. It's exactly what you'll find at the grocery store and will greatly reduce your prep time for the final bake off!

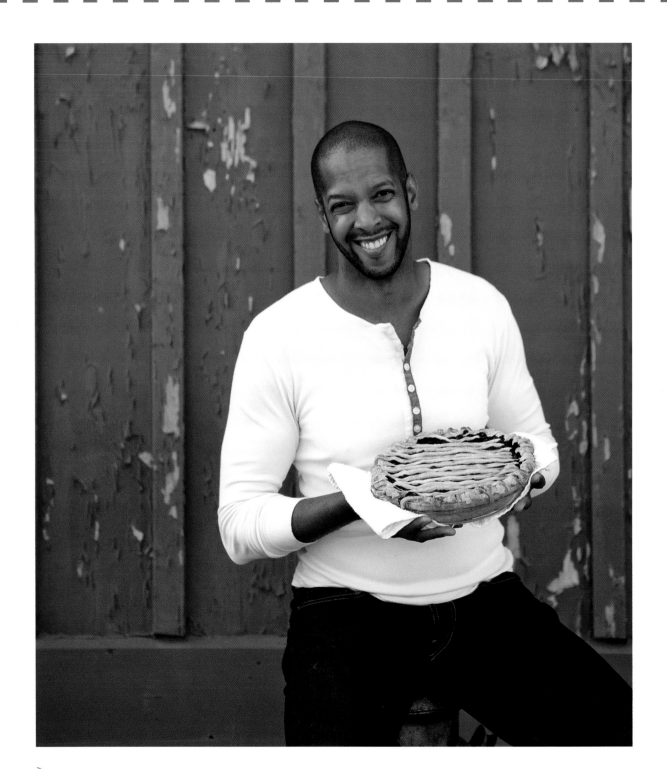

The last thing to consider for crusts is that they are a great canvas with which to experiment. Discovering flavors that pair well with the fats, starches, and proteins in piecrust can be very satisfying. I'm a particular fan of working freshly ground flaxseed into a dough. The nuttiness of the flax meal is a great way to deepen the overall flavor without introducing nut oils, which could harm the final texture of your crust.

For sweet pies, any added sugars must complement the filling. I like working with lots of different sweeteners, often together, in order to round out the flavor of the pie's star ingredient. A blend of honey, cane sugar, and a touch of maple is my favorite triumvirate—perfect for sweet potato pie. When you need to, feel free to cut back on the amount of added sweeteners. Also consider lower glycemic-index sweeteners, such as agave syrup. Pies are a lot more forgiving than cakes, cookies, and scones, and the texture isn't gravely affected by removing sweetness. But the end result will taste different. Let others know about the changes—those who need it will appreciate the consideration, and so long as you begin with great ingredients, the final result will be delectable.

PREP IT AND FORGET IT

Pie dough can be frozen without negative effect for months at a time. Simply portion off rounds in amounts to make a double-crust pie and wrap them tightly in plastic film. Add an identifying label and date, and you're all set. When you want to use the dough, simply thaw it on your counter. Wipe it clear of condensation before unwrapping it to roll out. If it's too soft, refrigerate it for up to 30 minutes and proceed.

The fillings for a pie run the gamut and are covered in detail within each recipe. A lot of your work is completed before the pie goes into the oven. Fruits are cooked down with sweeteners and starch on the stove top. Custard fillings are whisked until they simmer on the stove, and some sugar syrup–based fillings (like pecan pie) are just mixed and poured into the blind-baked shell. The flavor of the filling doesn't change all that much in the oven, so taste often and make whatever adjustments you like as you assemble the ingredients. Fillings tend to thicken as they cool, so don't be misled by a loose syrup. Plus, a pie is just a messy affair. Don't try to overcorrect—it won't seem homemade.

And one more thing: In each recipe, I suggest pairing specific crusts and fillings, but don't let that stifle your creative side. The whole idea of being in the kitchen is to express yourself. By all means, mix and match fillings with crusts that sound appealing.

CHAPTER ONE

PIE
CRUSTS

For a lot of people, a pie is all about the crust. Baking a pie usually begins with making dough, which ultimately, of course, becomes the crust. But that makes me wonder: When does dough become crust? Once it's no longer soft, but instead crusty? If that makes sense, then why don't we describe piecrust as "crusty" instead of "flaky"? After all, we don't call it pieflake. I like crusty edges on a lot of foods, such as pizzas, pound cakes, and scones, but I especially like crusty piecrust. Please read this tutorial on making dough all the way through for my hints on how to make it crusty!

MAKING PIE DOUGH

Making pie dough is not nearly as difficult as I once thought. Even after I opened CakeLove, I was intimidated by the process, and as a result, we didn't carry pies for years. But, as with most fears in life, eventually you have to face them. So I did, and here are a few of the lessons I learned.

Making crust by hand is entirely possible, but difficult and tiring. I highly recommend investing in a food processor or standing mixer to achieve results that you can enjoy without cramping forearms. My instructions are *not* based on mixing by hand.

Piecrust comes together very quickly. The ratios of the ingredients are, of course, critical, but effectively blending them depends on proper prep. One thing I realized is that it's not just about the weight of the flour, it's also about the size of the butter chunks. A ¼- to ½-inch dice will incorporate faster and much better than a tablespoon-size or larger hunk of butter. So cut the butter smaller—even if you're scaling up the recipe for multiple crusts.

Unlike with cakes, I don't bother to sift the flour. A crust should be dense, and the processor will break the flour up enough for that. Stir to blend the flour, sugar, spices, and salt in a bowl or blend them with the steel blade in a processor or flat paddle in a mixer.

Add the butter to the work bowl all at once. Dropping it in a little at a time just allows some of the butter to work too far into the flour. With the processor, pulse for brief bursts, 3 to 5 seconds at a time. With the mixer, lock down the tilt head and mix on low speed. Mixers will take longer—up to 1 minute—to crumble the butter

sufficiently and change the flour mix into a coarse-looking meal. Don't fully blend in the butter; keep some large chunks, as this will create pockets of crunch and crispiness during baking.

Don't get distracted during this next, important step: Slowly drizzle ice water in a thin, steady stream into the work bowl while pulsing the processor or turning the mixer off and on. Get the water into the dough quickly, but without rushing. Try to keep to the specified amounts, adding 1 extra tablespoon if you're using a mixer. The water takes time to expand into the flour's starch, transforming the crumbly looking meal into dough.

The dough will come to life. It will come off the sides of the work bowl and ride on top of the steel blade or stick to the flat paddle. It will be lightly tacky and stick to itself but, thankfully, not much else. Divide the dough—generally I use two thirds for the bottom and one third for the top crust.

I normally bake with pans that are about 1½ inches deep. If you're working with a deep-dish pan, which will measure about 2 inches in depth, you will need to increase the amount of filling by half; the dough recipe need not be changed, although the crusts will need to be rolled thinner. You can wrap each piece in plastic film and hold them in the fridge for up to 7 days, or in the freezer for several months, or roll them out right away.

The crust demonstrated here is the Flaky Butter Crust (page 32). It's a very clean crust that is easy to use. It's a bit wet, but not sticky, and is ideal for handling. I like to use parchment paper in

Unless the dough is losing shape and sticking to surfaces, it's not necessary to chill it before rolling it out. Plus, when it's cold, it's very difficult to crimp without breaking. I move right from making the dough to rolling it out and crimping. When I do chill it, I wait until after crimping so the egg wash won't break the crimped edges. One benefit to chilling the rolled-out crust is that cold butter bakes off better when introduced into a hot oven.

my kitchen and roll out the dough between two sheets. A very light dusting of flour helps prevent sticking, but go light. Dumping flour on the counter makes for messy cleanup.

If you're making a standard-size pie, begin with two sheets of parchment large enough to allow for a 10- to 11-inch circle of dough. Firmly shape the dough ball for the bottom crust into a 1-inch-thick disk. Smooth out the edges and any cracks by gently pressing the dough together.

Handle the dough as little as possible to prevent unnecessary development of the gluten and to avoid warming the butter with your hands. Lightly dry brush or dust the disk with flour and place it in the middle of one sheet of parchment. Cover it with the other sheet and begin rolling with the pin.

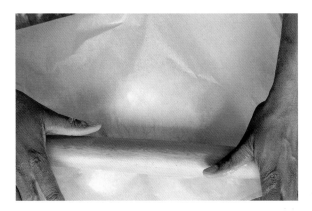

Rolling out the dough to form a perfect circle takes practice, but a few things help. Imagine that the disk is the face of a clock and your rolling pin is at rest in the center. Roll away from your body toward twelve o'clock, all the way off the edge of the dough. Turn the entire sandwich of parchment and dough about 5 minutes in either direction and do the same thing again. Always roll directly away from your body, toward twelve o'clock. The small turns between each roll help ensure a uniform spread of the dough. Eliminating the cracks in the disk's edge before rolling it out helps reduce the chances you'll end up with a jagged edge, too.

After one full rotation of the dough round, flip it and lift it off the bottom paper to release any creases in the parchment, which interfere with spreading. Lightly dust with flour and repeat.

Size up the dough with the pan: The crust should extend 1 to 2 inches beyond the rim.

Remove both pieces of parchment and gently transfer the dough to the pan. The dough is sturdy and won't tear easily, as long as it's not too thin. You can also consider transferring it with the parchment still attached on the top. This makes the transfer easier, but removing the paper can be a little tricky once the dough begins to droop into the pan. Trim the edges, if necessary.

Forming the edge of a piecrust is a matter of style and taste. I like to keep it rustic and simple with a finger roll or simply mash it with a fork.

If you're blind baking the crust: Dock the dough—prick the dough on the bottom of the pan all over with a fork—before placing the parchment paper and disposable pie pan on top.

To blind bake the crust, line the bottom with a round of parchment paper cut to size and a disposable pie pan placed on top.

If you'll be filling and baking the whole pie later, partially bake the crust in a 375°F oven for 5 to 7 minutes or until the pastry toasts to a light brown color. If you'll be using a filling that doesn't require baking, you will fully bake the crust now; this generally takes 10 to 12 minutes. Set the crust aside to cool, then remove the disposable pie pan and parchment paper.

Once the pie is filled with your choice of an exciting filling, it's time to proceed with the top crust.

TOP CRUST STYLES

Crumb topping: There's nothing wrong with a simple crumble sprinkled across the top (see the Dutch Crumb Topping on page 88). You'll pulse together a mixture of ingredients—nearly always some combination of butter, sugar, flour, and spices. Then just sprinkle the mixture liberally across the top to a depth of about ½ inch, or more if you like.

Traditional top crust with steam vents: Simply roll out the dough reserved for a top crust to a depth of about ⅛ to ¼ inch to make a round that matches the size of the pie pan and lay it across the top. Be sure the crust doesn't get too thin, or it will break when you brush it with the egg wash or during baking. Using your fingers, gently press the perimeter of the top crust into the crimped edge of the bottom crust. Some gaps are fine, but try to keep them to a minimum and no larger than ⅛ inch. Gently cut three to five steam vents in the center of the pie in a decorative manner.

Traditional top crust with decorations: Adding decorative accent pieces with leftover crust is a nice way to jazz up the presentation of your work of art! Just cover the pie with the top crust. Then use a cookie cutter or paring knife and press out fun complete or partial shapes from rerolled scraps. Apply the same egg wash, but then dredge or sprinkle the shapes heavily with sugar or spices to create a contrasting color with the rest of the dough.

Lattice top: Making a lattice top for a pie is not as difficult as it appears, but it does take practice.

FORMING A LATTICE CRUST

1. Roll out the top crust.

2. Using the rolling pin as a straight edge, cut the dough into strips, keeping the width consistent.

3. Transfer every other strip to the pie, placing them equal distances apart.

4. Fold back every other strip and place a new strip perpendicular to the folded ones.

5. Return all the folded strips to their original position and then fold back the alternate strips.

6. Repeat step 4.

7. Continue in this way until the lattice is complete.

MAKING THE CRUST CRUSTY: THE EGG WASH

After you've completed all the work of putting your pie together, the last stop is dressing it up so it'll get nice and golden on the outside and crisp and crusty to the bite. Blend an egg with a splash (less than ¼ teaspoon) of vanilla extract or any liqueur that you prefer and dab the mixture onto the edges and top using a pastry brush.

Sprinkle on a dusting of granulated sugar, cinnamon, nutmeg, or any other aromatic spice for color.

CRUST RECIPES

flaky BUTTER CRUST

Unbleached all-purpose flour	2 cups (10 ounces)
Superfine granulated sugar	1 teaspoon
Sea salt	½ teaspoon
Unsalted butter, very cold	¾ cup (1½ sticks), cut into small pieces
Ice water	3 tablespoons
Egg wash of choice or as specified in recipe	

This crust is reliable, easy to work with, and delicious. The ratio of butter to flour and water makes it a dense but very flaky crust. I also like it because there's nothing particularly tricky about making this dough. It's my default crust and can be used for any recipe in this book.

MAKES 18 OUNCES, ENOUGH FOR ONE 9- TO 10-INCH DOUBLE-CRUST PIE

1. Preheat the oven to 375°F.

2. Add the flour, sugar, and salt to the work bowl of a food processor and run it for at least 30 seconds.

3. Stop the processor and add the butter all at once.

4. Pulse in the butter until the mixture resembles fine crumbs; pulse in the water, 1 tablespoon at a time, until the dough comes together and rides on top of the S blade.

5. Turn the dough out onto lightly floured parchment, remove one third of it, and wrap it in plastic film to keep it from drying out. If you're not making a double-crust pie, hold this dough in the fridge or freezer for another use.

6. Shape the remaining dough into a disk, place a second sheet of parchment on top, and roll it out into a large round, approximately 12 inches in diameter and ⅛ inch thick.

7. Gently fit the dough into a 9- to 10-inch pie pan, fold the excess to form the edge, and crimp. Chill the crust for 15 to 30 minutes. Meanwhile, if you are making a double-crust pie, roll out the reserved dough between two sheets of parchment to a round approximately 10 inches across. Set it aside, keeping it between the parchment sheets to prevent it from drying out.

8. Brush the bottom crust edges with egg wash.

9. Dock the crust and weight it with a circle of parchment paper cut to size and a disposable pie pan resting gently above the pastry to prevent it from puffing up while toasting. If your pie filling will be baked, blind bake the crust for 5 to 7 minutes. If you'll be using the crust for a custard pie where baking isn't required, blind bake for 10 to 12 minutes—checking often after 10 minutes.

10. Set the blind-baked crust aside to cool while you prepare the filling of your choice. Top and finish the pie as desired or as directed in your recipe.

3:2:1 CRUST

The traditional ratios for flour to butter to water for pie crusts is 3:2:1. This will result in a very buttery crust, which is usually wonderful, but can get a little soggy if mixed incorrectly. Be sure the butter is very cold. The ratios are always easy to remember and the dough is a cinch to mix.

Unbleached all-purpose flour	2½ cups (12 ounces)
Sea salt	½ teaspoon
Unsalted butter, very cold	8 ounces, cut into small pieces
Water	4 tablespoons, very cold

Follow the same method as the Flaky Butter Crust.

This crust is used for
the Blueberry Maple
Pie on page 79.

cinnamon-
BUTTER PIECRUST

A hint of cinnamon makes this a nice option for apple pie, but this crust is versatile enough for any sweet pie. The spice has a very subtle presence—in fact, some say they don't even notice it. That's probably true, but I like the idea of added cinnamon, and it gives a bit of color while the flour is mixing, which helps you to know that the dry mix is well blended before you add the butter.

This is a sturdy crust that is very easy to roll out and crimp, but it's a bit wet and will feel a tad odd to experienced bakers. The full amount of water called for will usually be necessary. Start by adding 1 tablespoon at a time, up to 5 tablespoons; dry days or climates may call for the sixth.

Unbleached all-purpose flour	2 cups (10 ounces)
Superfine granulated sugar	3 tablespoons
Cinnamon	½ teaspoon
Sea salt	1 teaspoon
Unsalted butter, very cold	10 tablespoons (1¼ sticks), cut into small pieces
Ice water	5 to 6 tablespoons

MAKES 18 OUNCES, ENOUGH FOR ONE 9- TO 10-INCH
DOUBLE-CRUST PIE

1. Preheat the oven to 375°F. Lightly grease a 9- to 10-inch pie pan with butter and lightly sprinkle it with sugar.

2. Add the flour, sugar, cinnamon, and salt to the work bowl of a food processor and mix for at least 30 seconds.

3. Stop the processor and add the butter all at once.

4. Pulse in the butter until the mixture resembles fine crumbs; pulse in the water, 1 tablespoon at a time, until the dough forms into a ball and rides on top of the S blade.

5. Turn the dough out onto a lightly floured piece of parchment. Set aside one third of the dough. If you're not making a double-crust pie, wrap it in plastic film and freeze or refrigerate it for another use.

6. Form the remaining dough into a disk, place a second piece of parchment on top, and roll it into a large round about 12 inches in diameter and ⅛ inch thick.

MINI PIES

It takes 1½ to 2 ounces of dough to make a 1-cup mini pie; a typical large ramekin is the perfect size for this. Mini pies make a great presentation—and it's a windfall for anyone who loves crust! You can use any dough, but Flaky Butter Crust (page 32) works particularly well.

Roll out the dough on very lightly floured parchment to make a round large enough to line the ramekin. Place the ramekin on the dough, slide your hand under the parchment, and invert the round so that it falls into the ramekin. Gently tuck the dough into place with your fingers. Scoop in the filling to the brim and decoratively crimp the edges, adding a top crust if you wish. Brush on egg wash, sprinkle the little pie with sugar, and place it on a parchment-lined baking sheet. Bake at 375°F for 15 to 20 minutes until the juices bubble and the top is golden brown. Allow the mini pies to rest for 15 to 20 minutes before serving.

7. Gently fit the rolled dough into the pie pan, fold the excess underneath, crimp the edge, and chill the crust for 10 minutes. Meanwhile, if you are making a double-crust pie, roll out the reserved dough between two sheets of parchment to a round approximately 10 inches across. Set it aside, keeping it between the parchment sheets to prevent it from drying out.

8. Dock the bottom crust and cover it with a circle of parchment paper cut to size and a disposable pie pan resting gently above the crust to prevent it from puffing up while toasting. If your pie filling will be baked, blind bake the crust for 5 to 7 minutes. If you'll be using the crust for a custard pie where baking isn't required, blind bake it for 12 to 15 minutes—checking often after 10 minutes.

9. Set the blind-baked crust aside to cool while you prepare the filling of your choice. Top it as desired and bake it as directed in your recipe.

über BUTTER CRUST

Much more butter relative to the flour and water make this a heavier crust with much more flakiness. It's more difficult to handle and roll out due to the overall dryness of the dough, but it performs well when baked and has an undeniable buttery flavor. Be prepared to use a fair amount of flour when rolling out and move gingerly when transferring to the pie pan or the dough will easily tear.

In order to get even greater flakiness from the crust, I rolled it out, then folded it back onto itself and rolled it out again—in the spirit of croissants. The result was nice large, flaky sheets of crust in each slice.

Unbleached all-purpose flour	1⅔ cups (8 ounces)
Superfine granulated sugar	4 tablespoons (2 ounces)
Sea salt	1 pinch
Unsalted butter, very cold	¾ cup (1½ sticks), cut into small pieces
Ice water	1½ tablespoons

MAKES 16 OUNCES, ENOUGH FOR ONE 9- TO 10-INCH
DOUBLE-CRUST PIE

In a food processor, pulse the flour, sugar, salt, and butter to blend, then drizzle in the water and pulse until it comes together. Wrap in plastic film and let rest in the fridge for 30 minutes, or store in the freezer for up to 2 weeks. Roll out and blind bake as with the Cinnamon-Butter Piecrust, using care not to roll too thin.

This crust is used for the Strawberry-Peach Galette on page 121.

vanilla bean
PIECRUST

Vanilla bean	½
Unbleached all-purpose flour	2½ cups (12½ ounces)
Whole wheat flour	2 teaspoons
Superfine granulated sugar	1½ teaspoons
Sea salt	¾ teaspoon
Unsalted butter, very cold	¾ cup (1½ sticks), cut into small pieces
Ice water	5 to 6 tablespoons
Egg wash of choice or as specified in recipe	

The delicious flavor of vanilla doesn't have to be saved for ice cream when it comes to serving pie! Adding vanilla to the crust wraps a wonderful bouquet of flavor around the filling and is very close to the palate in a way that's different from cold ice cream or when it's bound up in the business of a cake. This is one of my favorite recipes for its simplicity and big yet subtle flavor.

◇◇
MAKES 20 OUNCES, ENOUGH FOR ONE 9- TO 10-INCH DOUBLE-CRUST PIE
◇◇

1. Preheat the oven to 375°F.

2. Flatten the vanilla bean with the side of a paring knife. Slice it open lengthwise and scrape out the seeds with the back of the knife. (Reserve the pod to flavor milk, brandy, or sugar.)

3. Add the flours, sugar, salt, and vanilla seeds to the work bowl of a food processor and mix for at least 30 seconds.

4. Stop the processor and add the butter all at once.

5. Pulse in the butter until the mixture resembles fine crumbs; pulse in the water, 1 tablespoon at a time, until the dough comes together and rides on top of the S blade.

6. Turn the dough out onto lightly floured parchment; remove one third of it and wrap it in plastic film to keep it from drying out. If you're not making a double-crust pie, hold it in the fridge or freezer for another use.

7. Form the remaining dough into a disk, place a second piece of parchment on top, and roll it into a large round approximately 12 inches in diameter and ⅛ inch thick.

8. Gently fit the dough into a 9- to 10-inch pie pan, fold the excess to form the edge, and crimp. Chill the crust for 15 to 30 minutes. Meanwhile, if you are making a double-crust pie, roll out the reserved dough between two sheets of parchment to a round approximately 10 inches across. Set it aside, keeping it between the parchment sheets to prevent it from drying out.

9. Brush the bottom crust edges with egg wash.

10. Dock the crust and weight it with a circle of parchment paper cut to size and a disposable pie pan resting gently above the crust to prevent it from puffing up while toasting. If your pie filling will be baked, blind bake the crust for 10 minutes. If you'll be using the crust for a custard pie where baking isn't required, blind bake for 12 to 15 minutes—checking often after 10 minutes.

11. Set the blind-baked crust aside to cool while you prepare the filling of your choice. Top the pie as desired and bake as directed in your recipe.

anise and mace
SPICED PIECRUST

Unbleached all-purpose flour	2 cups (10 ounces)
Superfine granulated sugar	2 teaspoons
Aniseed, crushed	¼ teaspoon
Mace, ground	¼ teaspoon
Sea salt	½ teaspoon
Unsalted butter, very cold	10 tablespoons (1¼ sticks), cut into small pieces
Bourbon	2 tablespoons
Ice water	3 to 5 tablespoons
Egg wash of choice or as specified in recipe	

Despite the individual intensities of anise and mace, this is a nice, buttery crust that offers a pleasant, mild flavor and doesn't overwhelm.

MAKES 18 OUNCES, ENOUGH FOR ONE 9- TO 10-INCH DOUBLE-CRUST PIE

1. Preheat the oven to 375°F.

2. Add the flour, sugar, spices, and salt in the work bowl of a food processor and mix for at least 30 seconds.

3. Stop the processor and add the butter all at once.

4. Pulse in the butter until the texture resembles fine crumbs; pulse in the bourbon, followed by the water, 1 tablespoon at a time, until the dough comes together and rides on top of the S blade.

5. Turn the dough out onto lightly floured parchment. Set aside one third of the dough and wrap it in plastic film to keep it from drying out. If you're not making a double-crust pie, hold it in the fridge or freezer for another use.

6. Shape the remaining dough into a disk, place a second piece of parchment on top, and roll it out into a round approximately 12 inches in diameter and ⅛ inch thick.

7. Gently fit the round into a 9- to 10-inch pie pan, fold the excess to form the edge, and crimp. Chill the crust for 15 to 30 minutes. Meanwhile, if you are making a double-crust pie, roll out the reserved dough between two sheets of parchment to a round approximately 10 inches across. Set it aside, keeping it between the parchment sheets to prevent it from drying out.

8. Brush the bottom crust edges with egg wash.

9. Dock the crust and weight it with a circle of parchment paper cut to size and a disposable pie pan resting gently above the crust to prevent it from puffing up while toasting. If your pie filling will be baked, blind bake the crust for 5 to 7 minutes. If you'll be using the crust for a custard pie where baking isn't required, blind bake it for 12 to 15 minutes—checking often after 10 minutes.

10. Set the blind-baked crust aside to cool while you prepare the filling of your choice. Top and finish the pie as desired or as directed in your recipe.

british SHORT-CRUST PASTRY

Sugar	for sprinkling
Unbleached all-purpose or pastry flour	2 cups (10 ounces)
Unsalted butter, very cold	¾ cup (1½ sticks), cut into small pieces
Egg	1
Ice water	1 tablespoon

This versatile, easy-to-make dough is extra rich because of the whole egg. Straight from across the pond, this classic British recipe shows up in both sweet and savory pies.

◇◇◇◇◇◇◇◇◇◇◇◇◇◇◇◇◇◇◇◇◇◇◇◇◇◇◇◇◇◇◇◇◇◇◇◇
MAKES 18 OUNCES, ENOUGH FOR ONE 9- TO 10-INCH
DOUBLE-CRUST PIE
◇◇◇◇◇◇◇◇◇◇◇◇◇◇◇◇◇◇◇◇◇◇◇◇◇◇◇◇◇◇◇◇◇◇◇◇

1. Preheat the oven to 400°F. Grease a 9- to 10-inch pie pan with butter and lightly sprinkle it with sugar.

2. Add the flour and butter to the work bowl of a food processor and pulse together until a crumbly meal forms.

3. Add the egg, and then the water, and pulse to combine until the dough forms a ball.

4. Remove one third of the dough and wrap it in plastic film; wrap the remaining piece of dough in plastic. Chill both pieces for 30 minutes before rolling them out. If you are not making a double-crust pie, hold the smaller ball in the fridge or freeze it until you are ready to use it.

5. Turn the larger portion of the chilled dough out onto lightly floured parchment, shape it into a disk, cover it with a second piece of parchment, and roll it into a round about 12 inches in diameter and ⅛ inch thick. Gently fit the rolled dough into the pie pan, fold the excess underneath, crimp the edge, and chill the crust for 10 minutes. Meanwhile, if you are making a double-crust pie, roll out the reserved dough between two sheets of parchment to a round approximately 10 inches across. Set it aside, keeping it between the parchment sheets to prevent it from drying out.

6. Dock the bottom crust and weight it with a circle of parchment paper cut to size and a disposable pie pan resting gently above the crust to prevent it from puffing up while toasting. If your pie filling will be baked, blind bake the crust for 5 to 7 minutes. If you'll be using the crust for a custard pie where baking isn't required, blind bake it for 10 to 12 minutes—checking often after 10 minutes.

7. Set the blind-baked crust aside to cool while you prepare the filling of your choice. Top the pie as desired and finish it as directed in your recipe.

whole wheat PIECRUST

Whole wheat pastry flour	2 cups (10 ounces)
Superfine granulated sugar	2 teaspoons
Sea salt	1 teaspoon
Unsalted butter, very cold	1 cup (2 sticks), cut into small pieces
Ice water	2 to 3 tablespoons
Cornmeal	as needed for dusting

If you want the goodness of whole grain in your piecrust, I recommend using whole wheat pastry flour. Like traditional pastry flour, it is lower in protein and, because it is softer, it produces a more tender, crispier crust, with a finer texture than you would get with regular whole wheat flour.

Truthfully, I use this crust because I like the way it tastes. It's delicious with pumpkin pie or sweet potato pie or any dessert you want to give a little more wholesome flavor to. Whole wheat flour is very prone to sticking; use cornmeal to dust the work surface as needed.

MAKES 19 OUNCES, ENOUGH FOR ONE 9- TO 10-INCH DOUBLE-CRUST PIE

1. Preheat the oven to 375°F.

2. Add the flour, sugar, and salt in the work bowl of a food processor and mix for at least 30 seconds.

3. Stop the processor and add the butter all at once.

4. Pulse in the butter until the texture resembles fine crumbs; pulse in the water 1 tablespoon at a time until the dough comes together and rides on top of the S blade (keep in mind that whole wheat dough tends to be very sticky).

5. Turn the dough out onto a piece of parchment dusted with cornmeal. Remove about one third and set it aside. If you are not making a double-crust pie, hold the smaller ball in the fridge or freeze it until you are ready to use it.

6. Shape the remaining dough into a disk and cover it with a second piece of parchment. Roll it out into a large round, about 12 inches in diameter and ⅛ inch thick.

This crust is used for the Boiled Sweet Potato Pie on page 95.

7. Gently fit the rolled dough into a 9- to 10-inch pie pan, fold the excess underneath, crimp the edge, and chill the crust for 10 minutes. Meanwhile, if you are making a double-crust pie, roll out the reserved dough between two sheets of parchment to a round approximately 10 inches across. Set it aside, keeping it between the parchment sheets to prevent it from drying out.

8. Dock the bottom crust and weight it with a circle of parchment paper cut to size and a disposable pie pan resting gently above the crust to prevent it from puffing up while toasting. If your pie filling will be baked, blind bake the crust for 5 to 7 minutes. If you'll be using the crust for a custard pie where baking isn't required, blind bake it for 10 to 12 minutes—checking often after 10 minutes.

9. Set the blind-baked crust aside to cool while you prepare the filling of your choice. Top and finish the pie as desired or as directed in your recipe.

multigrain PIECRUST

Unbleached all-purpose flour	1½ cups plus 3 tablespoons (8½ ounces)
Flaxseed, ground	1 teaspoon
Whole rolled oats	2 tablespoons
Sea salt	1 teaspoon
Cinnamon	¼ teaspoon
Ginger	¼ teaspoon
Superfine granulated sugar	3 tablespoons
Unsalted butter, very cold	10 tablespoons (1¼ sticks), cut into small pieces
Ice water	6 tablespoons or more, as necessary
Egg wash of your choice or as directed in your recipe	

This is another option when you're looking for a healthier crust that offers different flavor profiles from alternative grains: oats and flax.

MAKES 18 OUNCES, ENOUGH FOR ONE 9- TO 10-INCH DOUBLE-CRUST PIE

1. Preheat the oven to 375°F.

2. Add the flour, flaxseed, oats, salt, spices, and sugar in the work bowl of a food processor and mix for at least 30 seconds.

3. Stop the processor and add the butter all at once.

4. Pulse in the butter until the texture resembles fine crumbs; pulse in the water 1 tablespoon at a time until the dough comes together and rides on top of the S blade.

5. Turn the dough out onto lightly floured parchment; remove one third of the dough, then wrap both that piece and the larger dough piece in plastic film to keep them from drying out. Refrigerate the dough for 15 minutes. If you're not making a double-crust pie, hold the smaller piece in the fridge or freezer for another use.

6. Shape the larger dough ball into a disk, place a second sheet of parchment on top, and roll it into a round approximately 12 inches in diameter and ⅛ inch thick.

7. Gently fit the rolled dough into a 9- to 10-inch pie pan, fold the excess to form the edge, and crimp. Chill the crust for 15 to 30 minutes. Meanwhile, if you are making a double-crust pie, roll out the reserved dough between two sheets of parchment to a round approximately 10 inches across. Set it aside, keeping it between the parchment sheets to prevent it from drying out.

8. Brush egg wash onto the edges of the bottom crust.

9. Dock the crust and weight it with a circle of parchment paper cut to size and a disposable pie pan resting gently above the crust to prevent it from puffing up while toasting. If your pie filling will be baked, blind bake the crust for 5 to 7 minutes. If you'll be using the crust for a custard pie where baking isn't required, blind bake it for 10 to 12 minutes—checking often after 10 minutes.

10. Set the blind-baked crust aside to cool while you prepare the filling of your choice. Top and finish the pie as desired or as directed in your recipe.

gluten-free PIECRUST

Golden flaxseeds	3 tablespoons
Brown or white rice flour	2 tablespoons
Tapioca flour	2 tablespoons
Millet flour	2⅓ cups (9¼ ounces)
Superfine granulated sugar	1 tablespoon
Sea salt	½ teaspoon
Unsalted butter, very cold	1 cup (2 sticks), cut into small pieces
Egg white	1
Ice water	2 to 3 tablespoons

This gluten-free crust is inspired by the very popular gluten-free cakes we've baked at CakeLove for years. Here, I've added freshly ground golden flaxseeds, which add a wonderful, nutty aroma and taste to the dough. The rice flour lends sweetness, and millet is a good substitute for the starch component in flour, but it doesn't do much in the way of binding. That task is left to the tapioca and egg white, which help hold the dough together as you roll it out.

MAKES 18 OUNCES, ENOUGH FOR ONE 9- TO 10-INCH DOUBLE-CRUST PIE

1. Thoroughly soak and scrub all your equipment and work surfaces to remove any trace of wheat flour. Be sure to clean underneath the blade mechanism in the food processor and in between the grooves of any tools to free any crusty debris.

2. Grind the flaxseeds in a coffee grinder or spice mill. Add the flax with all three flours, the sugar, and salt in the work bowl of a food processor and pulse to combine.

3. Remove the lid for the processor's work bowl and sprinkle the butter across the top. Pulse until the texture resembles coarse crumbs.

4. Pulse in the egg white, and then add the water, 1 tablespoon at a time, until the dough comes together.

5. Remove the dough from the work bowl (it will be crumbly at this point) and gently knead it on a work surface or parchment paper lightly dusted with millet flour.

6. Remove one third of the dough so that you have two pieces. Wrap both pieces of dough in plastic film and chill them in the refrigerator for 60 minutes or up to 3 days before using. If you are not making a double-crust pie, hold the smaller disk in the freezer for another use.

7. Preheat the oven to 350°F. Place the larger disk of dough between two sheets of parchment lightly dusted with millet flour and roll it into a round 12 inches in diameter and $\frac{1}{8}$ inch thick.

8. Gently fit the rolled dough into a 9- to 10-inch pie pan, then crimp and shape the edges. Refrigerate the crust for 30 minutes. Meanwhile, if you are making a double-crust pie, roll out the other piece of dough between two sheets of parchment to a round approximately 10 inches across. Set it aside, keeping it between the parchment sheets to prevent it from drying out.

9. Dock the bottom crust and weight it with a circle of parchment paper cut to size and a disposable pie pan resting gently above the crust to prevent it from puffing up while toasting. If your filling will be baked, blind bake the crust for 5 to 7 minutes. If you'll be using the crust for a custard pie where baking isn't required, blind bake it for 12 to 15 minutes—checking often after 10 minutes.

10. Set the blind-baked crust aside to cool while you prepare the filling of your choice. Top and finish the pie as desired or as directed in your recipe.

vegan
PIECRUST

Unbleached all-purpose flour	2½ cups (12½ ounces)
Sea salt	1 teaspoon
Vegetable shortening, very cold	10 tablespoons, cut into small pieces
Ice water	4 to 5 tablespoons
Vanilla extract	¼ teaspoon

We traditionally think of butter or lard as being necessary ingredients for a successful piecrust, but vegan crusts are entirely feasible—just use vegetable shortening and brush on alternative sugars like agave syrup or maple syrup. Be sure to use a shortening that has a blend of oils and preferably one that is marketed as a "butter-flavored" product. Straight palm kernel oil isn't unappetizing, but it lacks a discernable flavor, so anything made with it can taste similarly bland.

MAKES 20 OUNCES, ENOUGH FOR ONE 9- TO 10-INCH DOUBLE-CRUST PIE

1. Preheat the oven to 375°F.

2. Combine the flour and salt in the work bowl of a food processor and mix for at least 30 seconds.

3. Stop the processor and add the shortening all at once.

4. Pulse in the shortening until the texture resembles fine crumbs; pulse in the water 1 tablespoon at a time, until the dough comes together and rides on top of the S blade.

5. Turn the dough out onto lightly floured parchment, remove one third of it, and wrap it in plastic film to keep it from drying out. If you're not making a double-crust pie, hold this piece in the fridge or freezer for another use.

6. Shape the remaining dough into a disk, place a second sheet of parchment on top, and roll it into a round approximately 12 inches in diameter and ⅛ inch thick.

7. Gently fit the rolled dough into a 9- to 10-inch pie pan, fold excess to form the edge, and crimp. Chill the crust for 15 to 30 minutes. Meanwhile, if you are making a double-crust pie, roll out the reserved dough between two sheets of parchment to a round approximately 10 inches across. Set it aside, keeping it between the parchment sheets to prevent it from drying out.

8. Brush the edges of the bottom crust with the vanilla.

9. Dock the crust and weight it with a circle of parchment paper cut to size and a disposable pie pan resting gently above the crust to prevent it from puffing up while baking. If your pie filling will be baked, blind bake the crust for 5 to 7 minutes. If you'll be using the crust for a custard pie where baking isn't required, blind bake it for 10 to 12 minutes— checking often after 10 minutes.

10. Set the blind-baked crust aside to cool while you prepare the filling of your choice. Top and finish the pie as desired or as directed in your recipe.

60/40 CRUST

Unbleached all-purpose flour	3 cups (15 ounces)
Sea salt	¾ teaspoon
Superfine granulated sugar	2 teaspoons
Unsalted butter, very cold	½ cup (1 stick), cut into small pieces
Vegetable shortening, very cold	6 tablespoons (3 ounces), cut into small pieces
Ice water	up to ½ cup
Egg wash of your choice or as directed in recipe	

PALM KERNEL OIL:

This is a naturally occurring saturated fat that is solid at room temperature. It works just as well as hydrogenated vegetable shortening, but with fewer health concerns. I prefer using palm kernel oil whenever shortening is called for.

Vegetable shortening and butter are an excellent pair in piecrust. Each has a different melting point, and this creates a dough that's easy to handle and bakes up with pockets of air and crunchiness that bring extra goodness to any filling. Artificially hydrogenated vegetable shortening performs best—a drawback, for sure, but not one that will ruin your health in and of itself. If you ask me, moderation, exercise, and honesty are a better approach to a healthful lifestyle than categorically forgoing delicious treats.

MAKES 24 OUNCES, ENOUGH FOR ONE 9- TO 10-INCH DOUBLE-CRUST PIE

1. Preheat the oven to 375°F.

2. Combine the flour, salt, and sugar in the work bowl of a food processor and pulse until blended.

3. Add the butter and shortening to the bowl. Pulse until the mixture resembles coarse crumbs.

4. Pulse in the water 1 tablespoon at a time.

5. This dough won't ball up in the processor—it remains rather crumbly. After all the water is in, gather it from the work bowl and gently knead it together on a lightly floured work surface or parchment paper.

6. Remove one third of the dough and wrap it in plastic film. If you're not making a double-crust pie, hold this piece in the fridge or freezer for another use. (At this point, you can also wrap everything tightly and refrigerate it for up to 2 weeks.)

7. Flatten the larger piece of dough into a disk 1 inch thick and place it between two sheets of very lightly floured parchment paper. Roll it out into a round approximately 12 inches in diameter and ⅛ inch thick.

This crust is used for the Traditional Cherry Pie on page 84.

8. Gently fit the rolled dough into a 9- to 10-inch pie pan, fold the excess to form the edge, and crimp. Chill the crust for 15 to 30 minutes. Meanwhile, if you are making a double-crust pie, roll out the reserved dough between two sheets of parchment to a round approximately 10 inches across. Set it aside, keeping it between the parchment sheets to prevent it from drying out.

9. Brush egg wash onto the edges of the bottom crust.

10. Dock the crust and weight it with a circle of parchment paper cut to size and a disposable pie pan resting gently above the crust to prevent it from puffing up while toasting. If your pie filling will be baked, blind bake the crust for 5 to 7 minutes. If you'll be using the crust for a custard pie where baking isn't required, blind bake it for 10 to 12 minutes—checking often after 10 minutes.

11. Set the blind-baked crust aside to cool while you prepare the filling of your choice. Top and finish the pie as desired or as directed in your recipe.

chocolate PIECRUST

Unbleached all-purpose flour	2 cups minus 2 tablespoons (9 ounces)
Unsweetened cocoa powder	2 tablespoons
Superfine granulated sugar	¼ cup
Sea salt	1 teaspoon
Unsalted butter, very cold	10 tablespoons (1¼ sticks), cut into small pieces
Ice water	4 to 5 tablespoons
Egg wash of your choice or as directed in your recipe	

This crust is used for the Chocolate Cream Pie on page 117.

Looks can be deceiving with this piecrust. You might think you are filling a big chocolate cookie, but it's actually not very sweet. Not every filling makes a good partner (I tried pumpkin, and the results were not very tasty), but I do like this filled with Vanilla or Coffee Pudding Cream (page 146) and topped with Whipped Cream (page 118).

This dough is one that requires a little more attention. It seems that the cocoa powder absorbs a lot of the moisture, perhaps before it reacts with the flour to activate the glutens. In drier climates or on less humid days, it may take up to double the amount of water called for. But don't rush through it; add the water 1 tablespoon at a time and watch how the dough comes together.

MAKES 18 OUNCES, ENOUGH FOR ONE DOUBLE-CRUST 9- TO 10-INCH PIE

1. Preheat the oven to 375°F.

2. Add the flour, cocoa powder, sugar, and salt to the work bowl of a food processor; pulse for 30 seconds to combine.

3. Stop the processor and add the butter all at once.

4. Pulse in the butter until the texture resembles fine crumbs; pulse in the water 1 tablespoon at a time, until the dough comes together and rides on top of the S blade.

5. Turn the dough out onto lightly floured parchment, remove one third of it and wrap it in plastic film to keep it from drying out. If you're not making a double-crust pie, hold this piece in the fridge or freezer for another use.

6. Shape the remaining dough into a disk, place it between two sheets of very lightly floured parchment paper, and roll it into a round approximately 12 inches in diameter and ⅛ inch thick.

7. Gently fit the rolled dough into a 9- to 10-inch pie pan, fold the excess to form the edge, and crimp. Chill the crust for 15 to 30 minutes. Meanwhile, if you are making a double-crust pie, roll out the reserved dough between two sheets of parchment to a round approximately 10 inches across. Set it aside, keeping it between the parchment sheets to prevent it from drying out.

8. Brush egg wash onto the edges of the bottom crust.

9. Dock the crust and weight it with a circle of parchment paper cut to size and a disposable pie pan resting gently above the crust to prevent it from puffing up while toast-ing. If your pie filling will be baked, blind bake the crust for 10 minutes. If you'll be using the crust for a custard pie where baking isn't required, blind bake it for 10 to 12 minutes—checking often after 10 minutes.

10. Set the crust aside to cool as you prepare the filling of your choice. Top and finish the pie as desired or as directed in your recipe.

lard CRUST

Unbleached all-purpose flour	10 ounces (2 cups)
Lard	5 ounces
Superfine granulated sugar	1 teaspoon
Sea salt	¼ teaspoon
Ice water	4 tablespoons

Lard is enjoying a well-deserved comeback and once again taking its rightful place in kitchens across the country. It's a superb shortening for baking. The texture and flavor it yields are better than butter. Lard used to be preferred to butter but it lost ground to vegetable shortening, which was successfully marketed as a new baking ingredient after the electric lightbulb rendered wax candles made with vegetable fats obsolete.

MAKES 19 OUNCES, ENOUGH FOR ONE 9- TO 10-INCH DOUBLE-CRUST PIE

1. Preheat the oven to 375°F.

2. Add the flour, lard, sugar, and salt to the work bowl of a food processor and run it for 30 seconds.

3. Pulse in the water, 1 tablespoon at a time, until the dough comes together and rides on top of the S blade.

4. Turn the dough out onto a lightly floured parchment, remove one third of it, and wrap it in plastic film to keep it from drying out. If you're not making a double-crust pie, hold this dough in the fridge or freezer for another use.

5. Shape the remaining dough into a disk, place a second sheet of parchment on top, and roll it out into a large round, approximately 12 inches in diameter and ⅛ inch thick.

6. Gently fit the dough into a 9- to 10-inch pie pan, fold the excess to form the edge, and crimp. Chill the crust for 15 to 30 minutes. Meanwhile, if you are making a double-crust pie, roll out the reserved dough between two sheets of parchment to a round approximately 10 inches across. Set it aside, keeping it between the parchment sheets to prevent it from drying out.

7. Brush the bottom crust edges with egg wash.

8. Dock the crust and weight it with a circle of parchment paper cut to size and a disposable pie pan resting gently above the pastry to prevent it from puffing up while toasting. If your pie filling will be baked, blind bake the crust for 5 to 7 minutes. If you'll be using the crust for a custard pie where baking isn't required, blind bake for 10 to 12 minutes—checking often after 10 minutes.

9. Set the blind-baked crust aside to cool while you prepare the filling of your choice. Top and finish the pie as desired or as directed in your recipe.

cheese PIECRUST

Unbleached all-purpose flour	2¾ cups (14 ounces)
Superfine granulated sugar	1 teaspoon
Hard aged cheese, finely grated, very cold	½ cup
Sea salt	¼ teaspoon
Unsalted butter, very cold	¾ cup (1½ sticks), cut into small pieces
Ice water	6 tablespoons
Egg wash of your choice or as directed in your recipe	

This crust is used for the Meatball Pie on page 170.

This crust is a very nice surprise for either a sweet or savory pie. Be sure to use a good-quality aromatic, aged hard cheese that you can grate very fine; otherwise, the crust will be gritty. I particularly like pecorino Romano or Parmesan, but whatever you choose, avoid those with a high moisture content because they will make the crust oily and chewy. The meatball (page 170) is the best filling for this crust, but the Chicken Pot Pie (page 175) and the lemon apple (page 76) are really good options too.

◇◇
MAKES 24 OUNCES, ENOUGH FOR ONE 9- TO 10-INCH DOUBLE-CRUST PIE
◇◇

1. Preheat the oven to 375°F.

2. Add the flour, sugar, cheese, and salt to the work bowl of a food processor and pulse for at least 30 seconds to combine.

3. Stop the processor and add the butter all at once.

4. Pulse in the butter until the texture resembles fine crumbs; pulse in the water 1 tablespoon at a time until the dough comes together and rides on top of the S blade.

5. Turn the dough out onto lightly floured parchment, remove one third of it, and wrap it in plastic film to keep it from drying out. If you're not making a double-crust pie, hold this piece in the fridge or freezer for another use.

6. Shape the remaining dough into a disk, place a second sheet of parchment on top, and roll it into a round approximately 12 inches in diameter and ⅛ inch thick.

7. Gently fit the rolled dough into a 9- to 10-inch pie pan, fold the excess to form the edge, and crimp. Chill the crust for 15 to 30 minutes. Meanwhile, if you are making a double-crust pie, roll out the reserved dough between two sheets of parchment to a round approximately 10 inches across. Set it aside, keeping it between the parchment sheets to prevent it from drying out.

8. Brush egg wash onto the edges of the bottom crust.

9. Dock the crust and weight it with a circle of parchment paper cut to size and a disposable pie pan resting gently above the crust to prevent it from puffing up while baking. If your pie filling will be baked, blind bake the crust for 5 to 7 minutes. If you'll be using the crust for a custard pie where baking isn't required, blind bake it for 10 to 12 minutes—checking often after 10 minutes.

10. Set the blind-baked crust aside to cool while you prepare the filling of your choice. Top and finish the pie as desired or as directed in your recipe.

paprika BUTTER CRUST

Unbleached all-purpose flour	3 cups (15 ounces)
Sweet paprika	2 tablespoons
Sea salt	1 teaspoon
Nutmeg, freshly grated	1 teaspoon
Flaxseeds, whole	2 teaspoons
Unsalted butter, very cold	1¼ cups (2½ sticks), cut into small pieces
Ice water	2 tablespoons

This dough takes on a fabulous red-orange color that suggests it will be fiery hot, but it's a nice, mild flavor that holds up beautifully with the Chicken Pot Pie filling (page 175).

MAKES 24 OUNCES, ENOUGH FOR ONE DOUBLE-CRUST DEEP-DISH POT PIE

1. Preheat the oven to 375°F. Combine the flour, paprika, salt, nutmeg, and flaxseeds to the bowl of a food processor and pulse to thoroughly combine. Stop and add the butter all at once. Pulse to blend it in until the mixture sticks together when lightly pinched.

2. Pulse in the water, 1 tablespoon at a time, until the dough comes together.

3. Gather the dough into a ball, remove one third, and wrap it in plastic film. If your pie will not have a top crust, hold this piece in the refrigerator or freezer for another use. Shape the remaining dough into a disk, place it between two sheets of parchment paper, and roll it out into a round about 12 inches across and ⅛ inch thick.

4. Gently fit the dough round into a 9- to 10-inch pie pan. Chill the crust for 10 minutes. Meanwhile, if you are making a double-crust pie, roll out the reserved dough between two sheets of parchment to a round approximately 10 inches across. Set it aside, keeping it between the parchment sheets to prevent it from drying out.

5. Crimp the edges of the bottom crust and weight it with a circle of parchment paper cut to size and a disposable pie pan resting gently above the crust to prevent it from puffing up while baking. Blind bake the crust for 5 to 7 minutes. Allow it to cool before pouring in the filling and proceeding as your recipe directs.

This crust is
used for the
Chicken Pot Pie
on page 175.

coconut butter
PIECRUST

Unbleached all-purpose flour	1⅔ cups (8 ounces)
White rice flour	½ cup (2 ounces)
Sea salt	½ teaspoon
Superfine granulated sugar	1 teaspoon
Nutmeg, freshly grated	1 teaspoon
Cloves, ground	¼ teaspoon
Coconut oil, very cold	¼ cup (2 ounces), cut into small pieces
Vegetable shortening, very cold	¼ cup (2 ounces), cut into small pieces
Unsalted butter, very cold	2 tablespoons, cut into small pieces
Ice water	3 tablespoons
Egg wash of your choice or as directed in your recipe	

This crust is filled with the delicate flavor of coconut and has the tender texture that coconut oil and rice flour bring to the party. It's a particularly nice pairing for Banana, Chocolate, and Coconut Cream Pie (page 108). The crust has a lot of fat and not much water, so it will be very crumbly.

MAKES 15 OUNCES, ENOUGH FOR ONE 9- TO 10-INCH DOUBLE-CRUST PIE

1. Preheat the oven to 375°F.

2. Add the flours, salt, sugar, and spices to the work bowl of a food processor and mix for at least 30 seconds.

3. Stop the processor and add the coconut oil, shortening, and butter all at once.

4. Pulse the water into the work bowl 1 tablespoon at a time, until the dough begins to come together and rides on top of the S blade. Work slowly to avoid overheating the coconut oil.

5. Turn the dough out onto lightly floured parchment, remove one third of it, and wrap it in plastic film to keep it from drying out. If you're not making a double-crust pie, hold this piece in the fridge or freezer for another use. Chill both pieces of dough for 10 minutes before rolling them out if the dough is very loose.

6. Shape the larger piece of dough into a disk, place it between two sheets of very lightly floured parchment paper, and roll it into a round approximately 12 inches in diameter and ⅛ inch thick.

7. Gently fit the rolled dough into a 9- to 10-inch pie pan, fold the excess to form the edge, and crimp. Chill the crust for 15 to 30 minutes. Meanwhile, if you are making a double-crust pie, roll out the remaining dough between two sheets of parchment to a round approximately 10 inches across. Set it aside, keeping it between the parchment sheets to prevent it from drying out.

8. Brush egg wash onto the edges of the bottom crust.

9. Dock the crust and weight it with a circle of parchment paper cut to size and a disposable pie pan resting gently above the crust to prevent it from puffing up while toasting. If your pie filling will be baked, blind bake the crust for 5 to 7 minutes. If you'll be using the crust for a custard pie where baking isn't required, blind bake it for 10 to 12 minutes— checking often after 10 minutes.

10. Set the blind-baked crust aside to cool while you prepare the filling of your choice. Top and finish the pie as desired or as directed in your recipe.

citrus zest
PIECRUST

Unbleached all-purpose flour	2¾ cups (14 ounces)
Superfine granulated sugar	1 teaspoon
Lemon or orange zest, finely grated	1 tablespoon
Sea salt	¾ teaspoon
Unsalted butter, very cold	¾ cup (1½ sticks), cut into small pieces
Ice water	3 to 4 tablespoons
Egg wash of your choice or as directed in your recipe	¼ cup (2 ounces), cut into small pieces

So much attention is paid to the texture of a piecrust that I find people tend to overlook the flavor. Adding just a bit of citrus zest gives an unexpected burst of sunshine to each bite, one that works particularly well with fillings such as apple, lemon meringue, or pecan. Make sure you're using organic fruit, and finely grate only the surface of the peel, avoiding the bitter, white pith.

MAKES 22 OUNCES, ENOUGH FOR ONE 9- TO 10-INCH DOUBLE-CRUST PIE

1. Preheat the oven to 375°F.

2. Add the flour, sugar, zest, and salt to the work bowl of a food processor and mix for at least 30 seconds.

3. Stop the processor and add the butter all at once.

4. Pulse in the butter until the texture resembles fine crumbs; pulse in the water 1 tablespoon at a time, until the dough comes together and rides on top of the S blade.

5. Turn the dough out onto lightly floured parchment, remove one third of it, and wrap it in plastic film to keep it from drying out. If you're not making a double-crust pie, hold this piece in the fridge or freezer for another use.

6. Shape the remaining dough into a disk, place a second sheet of parchment on top, and roll it into a round approximately 12 inches in diameter and ⅛ inch thick.

7. Gently fit the rolled dough into a 9- to 10-inch pie pan, fold the excess to form the edge, and crimp. Chill the crust for 15 to 30 minutes. Meanwhile, if you are making a double-crust pie, roll out the reserved dough between two sheets of parchment to a round approximately 10 inches across. Set it aside, keeping it between the parchment sheets to prevent it from drying out.

8. Brush egg wash onto the edges of the bottom crust.

9. Dock the crust and weight it with a circle of parchment paper cut to size and a disposable pie pan resting gently above the crust to prevent it from puffing up while baking. If your pie filling will be baked, blind bake the crust for 5 to 7 minutes. If you'll be using the crust for a custard pie where baking isn't required, blind bake it for 10 to 12 minutes—checking often after 10 minutes.

10. Set the blind-baked crust aside to cool while you prepare the filling of your choice. Top and finish the pie as desired or as directed in your recipe.

This crust is used
for the Peach Pie
on page 83.

ginger CRUST

I made this on a whim while searching for something to jazz up a peach pie. The ginger really adds a depth of flavor without detracting from the filling it holds. There's lots of room to play with flavor in pies, and the crust is a fantastic place to start.

MAKES 25 OUNCES, ENOUGH FOR ONE 9- TO 10-INCH DOUBLE-CRUST PIE

Unbleached all-purpose flour	2½ cups (12½ ounces)
Whole wheat flour	½ cup (2½ ounces)
Sea salt	¾ teaspoon
Superfine granulated sugar	1 teaspoon
Ginger	2 tablespoons
Cloves, ground	¼ teaspoon
Mace or nutmeg, freshly grated	⅛ teaspoon
Vegetable shortening, very cold	¼ cup (2 ounces), cut into small pieces
Unsalted butter, very cold	¾ cup (1½ sticks), cut into small pieces
Ice water	5 to 6 tablespoons
Egg wash of your choice or as directed in your recipe	

1. Preheat the oven to 350°F.

2. Add the flours, salt, sugar, and spices to the work bowl of a food processor and mix for at least 30 seconds.

3. Stop the processor and add the shortening and butter all at once.

4. Pulse until the texture resembles fine crumbs; pulse in the water 1 tablespoon at a time, until the dough comes together and rides on top of the S blade.

5. Turn the dough out onto lightly floured parchment, remove one third of it, and wrap it in plastic film to keep it from drying out. If you're not making a double-crust pie, hold this piece in the fridge or freezer for another use.

6. Shape the remaining dough into a disk, place a second sheet of parchment on top, and roll it into a round approximately 12 inches in diameter and ⅛ inch thick.

7. Gently fit the rolled dough into a 9- to 10-inch pie pan, fold the excess to form the edge, and crimp. Chill the crust for 15 to 30 minutes. Meanwhile, if you are making a double-crust pie, roll out the reserved dough between two sheets of parchment to a round approximately 10 inches across. Set it aside, keeping it between the parchment sheets to prevent it from drying out.

8. Brush egg wash onto the edges of the bottom crust.

9. Dock the crust and weight it with a circle of parchment paper cut to size and a disposable pie pan resting gently above the crust to prevent it from puffing up while baking. If your pie filling will be baked, blind bake the crust for 5 to 7 minutes. If you'll be using the crust for a custard pie where baking isn't required, blind bake it for 10 to 12 minutes— checking often after 10 minutes.

10. Set the blind-baked crust aside to cool while you prepare the filling of your choice. Top and finish the pie as desired or as directed in your recipe.

graham cracker CRUST

The classic crust for so many custard-filled pies couldn't be simpler. This is also an easily adaptable crust: Consider adding spices such as cinnamon, or using chocolate graham crackers as your base.

Graham crackers	10 full crackers (5 ounces)
Superfine granulated sugar	3 tablespoons
Unsalted butter	6 tablespoons (¾ stick), melted
Sea salt	⅛ teaspoon

MAKES ONE 9- TO 10-INCH PIECRUST

1. Preheat the oven to 300°F and place the rack in the middle position.

2. Crush the graham crackers in a bowl or food processor into very fine crumbs. Line the bottom of a 9- to 10-inch pie plate with parchment.

3. Using a fork, toss the crumbs, sugar, butter, and salt in a bowl until evenly combined. Press the mixture firmly into the prepared pan.

4. Bake until the crust is fragrant, 10 to 12 minutes. Set it aside to cool while you prepare the filling of your choice. Top and finish the pie as desired or as directed in your recipe.

This crust is used for the Lemon Meringue Pie on page 101.

CHAPTER TWO

SWEET PIE FILLINGS

A lot of things surprised me about pies as I got down to working through recipes for this book, but the one major surprise was cornstarch. I hardly ever use cornstarch in cakes, but it's just about everywhere in this book. And I've been surprised at how much I like the results from this easy-to-find, inexpensive ingredient—the way cornstarch hugs the tongue in fruit pie fillings, how it softens and smooths out vanilla pudding custard or adds to the crispiness in shortbread tart crusts.

When it comes to baking a perfect pie, controlling the liquid in the filling is most of the battle. Adding starch is the most common solution—but at what point and by what method? This is just as critical as how much. Flour plays a part with pie fillings, but it's more for flavor, and its role is minor compared to the star, cornstarch. The reason my shopping list for cakes rarely includes cornstarch is that it tends to need a higher temperature than the other ingredients to bake fully, so its starchy taste is more likely to linger. But that handicap with cakes becomes a real advantage on the stove top, where pie fillings are cooked. In fact, cornstarch withstands direct heat so well it seems to shine when used this way. Once the starch is cooked through and absorbs the liquid it's swimming in, it turns clear, glistens a bit, and takes on that silky texture that's so appealing to the tongue and palate. This is a great effect that flour won't achieve.

There isn't a universal ratio of starch to fruit that works for all pies. Each filling will behave a little differently. But if you observe these basic principles when precooking your fillings, your pie should come out well.

Never mix cornstarch with anything hot. The heat activates the absorption properties of the starch too soon and produces pesky clumps that ruin any filling, no matter how small they are or how hard you try to whisk them out. I prefer to whisk the cornstarch into my other dry ingredients in a bowl before tossing them lightly with the fruit or stirring them into a custard base. Once the starch is well mixed with everything else, I'll move it all to the stove top to cook it down.

Use a heat-resistant spatula and stir the whole time. If you stop stirring, hot spots will develop that can give you the false impression the syrup is thoroughly cooked. Pies with fillings that were taken off the stove too soon are marred by their starchy mouthfeel. Continuous stirring keeps the heat distribution nice and even, so that once the liquid begins to be absorbed in one place, it's happening everywhere.

Don't rush the process. You'll start with lightly simmering syrup and uncooked starch. The liquid will flow quickly among the fruit pieces, especially as the pot gets hotter and water is drawn from the fruit. But once the starch hits temperature and reacts to absorb and hold the water, the viscosity of the syrup quickly changes, and the simmer rate slows considerably. Rather than remove the pan from the heat, at this point I advise you to stir faster, move the saucepan around the burner to prevent scorching, and simmer for another 20 to 30 seconds to be sure the starch is fully cooked. Don't rely on the pie's time in the oven to eliminate the starchy taste in the filling. Carefully taste-test the syrup to see if it's lost the starchy mouthfeel before you take the filling off the stove top.

Let it cool. Once the filling is cooked, allow it to cool slightly before transferring it to a pie shell. The consistency of the partially cooled filling is pretty much what you'll end up with after baking, so make sure it's not runny. If necessary, return it to the stove to cook down a bit more. For proper cooling, custard pie fillings should always be transferred to a shallow container, covered with plastic film placed directly on the surface, and set in a shallow bowl of ice water for rapid cooling. For fruit fillings, I just cover the pot with a lid to let the condensation act as a shield against the development of a skin.

MOM'S *(traditional)* APPLE PIE

Granny Smith apples, peeled, cored, and cut horizontally into ¼-inch slices	7½ cups (2 pounds)
Superfine granulated sugar	1 cup (8 ounces), plus additional for sprinkling
Sea salt	¼ teaspoon
Unbleached all-purpose flour	2 tablespoons
Cornstarch	3 tablespoons
Cinnamon	¾ teaspoon, plus additional for sprinkling
Nutmeg, freshly grated	½ teaspoon
Allspice	¼ teaspoon
Unsalted butter	4 tablespoons (½ stick)
Flaky Butter Crust (page 32)	1 recipe, bottom crust blind baked
Egg	1
Vanilla extract	¼ teaspoon

The pie I grew up with was baked by Mom, but made by Howard Johnsons. After music practice on Tuesday afternoons, we'd pick up a few frozen pieces from the local HoJos. They were delicious hot out of the oven, but I enjoyed the leftovers even more as an after-school snack. It might not have been homemade, but this is the flavor that reminds me of home.

Like anything worthwhile in life, this takes a bit of time to prepare, but the effort is worth it. About 3 pounds of whole apples will yield 2 pounds of peeled and cut apple for the pie (although that will vary slightly based on the size of the apples). Be sure to stir continuously while cooking the fruit until it simmers, so you don't end up with an underdone filling that tastes of starch.

There is nothing better than bringing an apple pie to a table full of guests for dessert. Everyone sits in anticipation of something they know well and most look forward to. I *love* apple pie. It's one of those desserts that just makes me forget everything else and focus on what's on my plate.

MAKES ONE 9- TO 10-INCH PIE

1. Preheat the oven to 350°F.

2. Place the apple slices in a 6-quart pot.

3. Mix the sugar, salt, flour, cornstarch, and spices in a bowl. Combine the mixture with the apples, add the butter, and cook over medium heat, stirring continuously, until the juices bubble and thicken.

4. Set the filling aside to cool a bit.

5. Place 1 tablespoon of the apple liquid into a small bowl and set it aside. Scoop the filling into the cooled crust.

6. Cover the pie with the top crust of your choice and style (see page 29). Whisk together the reserved apple liquid, the egg, and vanilla to make an egg wash. Brush the crust with the wash and lightly sprinkle the top of the pie with sugar and cinnamon.

7. Bake the pie for 45 to 50 minutes. When finished, the juices should simmer around the edges and the top crust should be golden brown.

8. Allow the pie to cool for 1 hour to let the filling set before slicing.

VARIATIONS

Lemon Apple Pie—I love the way lemon zest imparts a brilliant bouquet of flavor that surrounds each bite of apple. Just add the zest of 2 lemons (organic, please)—about 1½ tablespoons—to the filling of Mom's Apple Pie.

Dried Cranberry Apple Pie—There's nothing better than getting a nice bite of crust filled with apples and sweetened dried cranberries. The berries add great color and texture, along with a sweetness that's distinct. Add ¾ cup dried cranberries along with the apple slices.

Apple Cheddar Pie—Unusual but delicious, especially when served hot so the cheese is melted and stringy. Slice 8 to 12 ounces of extra-sharp cheddar cheese into 1-inch slices and spread them throughout the apple filling while assembling the pie. I prefer a yellow cheddar, so that it's easily distinguished from the apples.

heirloom APPLE PIE

This is my go-to apple pie. It's simple, classic, and easy to make all year long. If heirloom apples aren't available, just substitute Granny Smiths, which work well in baking and have a consistent flavor year-round. My colleague at CakeLove suggested prepping the apples as cubes, which seemed weird, but in the end, I really like them that way. Assembling the pie is much faster, the apple cubes retain a nicer texture after baking than slices, and I love the way they spill out of the slice when it's served.

My goal with this filling was just a touch of sweetness in the syrup; the natural sugars of the apples should be center stage. You'll notice a bit of juice pooling on top of the crust at the edges toward the end of the baking time, but this recedes and blends back into the pie once it cools. I like the Cinnamon-Butter Piecrust, with its nuance of spice, for this pie and extra dough cookies across the top crust (see Note, page 78).

MAKES ONE 9- TO 10-INCH PIE

Heirloom apples, peeled, cored, and cut into ½- and ¼-inch cubes	7½ cups (2 pounds)
Superfine granulated sugar	½ cup (4 ounces), plus additional for sprinkling
Light brown sugar	2 tablespoons, packed
Sea salt	¼ teaspoon
Unbleached all-purpose flour	2 tablespoons
Cornstarch	2 tablespoons
Cinnamon	½ teaspoon, plus additional for sprinkling
Nutmeg, freshly grated	½ teaspoon
Allspice (optional)	¼ teaspoon
Unsalted butter	4 tablespoons (½ stick)
Honey	1 tablespoon
Cinnamon-Butter Piecrust, Flaky Butter Crust, or Whole Wheat Piecrust (page 35, 32, or 44)	1 recipe, bottom crust blind baked
Egg (optional)	1
Vanilla extract (optional)	¼ teaspoon

1. Preheat the oven to 375°F.

2. Place the apple cubes in a 6-quart pot.

3. Mix both sugars, the salt, flour, cornstarch, and spices in a bowl. Combine this mixture with the apples, add the butter, and cook over medium heat, stirring occasionally, until the juices bubble and thicken.

4. Remove the pot from the heat, stir in the honey, and allow the filling to cool a bit.

5. Scoop the filling into the cooled crust.

6. Cover with the top crust of your choice and style (see page 29). If desired, whisk together the egg and vanilla to make an egg wash. Brush the crust with the wash and lightly sprinkle the top of the pie with sugar and cinnamon.

7. Bake the pie for 40 to 45 minutes. When finished, the juices should simmer around the edges and the top crust should be golden brown.

8. Allow the pie to cool for 1 hour to let the filling set before slicing.

Note: Crust cookies are especially festive pie decorations. To make them, ball up any extra dough and roll it in granulated sugar. Roll the dough out to $\frac{1}{8}$ inch thick and cut it with cookie cutters into the desired shapes. Press the cookies onto the top crust of the pie in a decorative pattern and brush with egg wash, then bake as directed in step 7.

BLUEBERRY MAPLE PIE

Apple may have been my first pie, but once I tasted blueberry pie, it became and remains my favorite over any other flavor. My oldest sister, Lenora, makes an ingenious version of blueberry pie sweetened exclusively with maple syrup. Packed with wild berries between a flaky, buttery crust, she combined two of my favorite foods into my favorite form of dessert and now has a fan for life! This isn't her exact recipe, but it's close. (Okay, full disclosure: She couldn't bear to part with her recipe, so I had to improvise!)

I prefer using wild blueberries because they're smaller and much more flavorful. They also don't seem to leak out as much liquid, which can be a serious problem with blueberry pie. I also recommend using organic berries to reduce your exposure to pesticides, which are used in fairly large quantities on conventional blueberries.

Organic frozen wild blueberries, thawed	2½ pounds (2½ packages, such as Trader Joe's Wild Blueberries; about 8 cups)
Grade-A maple syrup, cold	1 cup
Cornstarch	¼ cup
Cinnamon	½ teaspoon, plus additional for sprinkling
Nutmeg, freshly grated	½ teaspoon
Sea salt	¼ teaspoon
Unsalted butter	4 tablespoons (½ stick)
Cinnamon-Butter Piecrust (page 35)	1 recipe, bottom crust blind baked
Egg	1
Vanilla extract	¼ teaspoon
Superfine granulated sugar	for sprinkling

◇◇
MAKES ONE 9- TO 10-INCH PIE
◇◇

1. Preheat the oven to 375°F.

2. Place the fully thawed blueberries in a colander to drain for 15 minutes, and discard the liquid.

3. Pour the berries into a large, heavy-bottomed pot and stir in the maple syrup.

4. Stir together the cornstarch, spices, and salt, then stir the mixture into the berries with a heatproof spatula or wooden spoon.

5. Add the butter.

6. Turn on the heat to medium. Cook, stirring slowly but continuously, until the juices bubble slowly and thicken, 5 to 8 minutes. Allow the filling to cool slightly.

7. Scoop the filling into the prepared piecrust. Cover the pie as desired (see page 29).

8. If using a top crust, whisk the egg and vanilla together and brush this wash over the pie; lightly sprinkle with sugar and cinnamon.

9. Bake the pie for about 30 minutes, until the berries begin to lightly bubble and the crust has a golden color. Allow the pie to cool for 1 hour to let the filling set before slicing.

PEACH PIE

Fresh peaches make a fabulous pie. When they're ripe, it's time to bake. But if you're stuck or just want to make peach pie off-season, frozen organic peaches can look and taste just as good as fresh ones.

I like using honey with peach pie because it brings out the best flavors of the peaches. Honey, whether creamed or a filtered specialty variety or ordinary clover, lends sweetness that lingers. Add honey only *after* cooking down the fruit, or what was sweet can turn bitter. I stay away from waxy, raw honey altogether for peach pies.

Fresh or thawed, well-drained frozen peaches	3 pounds, peeled and quartered
Superfine granulated sugar	¾ cup (6 ounces)
Cornstarch	2 tablespoons plus 1 teaspoon
Nutmeg, freshly grated	1 teaspoon, plus additional for sprinkling
Sea salt	¼ teaspoon, plus additional for sprinkling
Unsalted butter	4 tablespoons (½ stick)
Honey	2 tablespoons
Cinnamon-Butter Piecrust or Ginger Crust (page 35 or 67)	1 recipe, bottom crust blind baked
Egg	1
Vanilla extract	¼ teaspoon
Cinnamon	for sprinkling

∞∞∞∞∞∞∞∞∞∞∞∞∞∞∞∞∞∞∞∞∞∞∞∞∞∞∞∞
MAKES ONE 9- TO 10-INCH PIE
∞∞∞∞∞∞∞∞∞∞∞∞∞∞∞∞∞∞∞∞∞∞∞∞∞∞∞∞

1. Preheat the oven to 375°F and position one rack in the middle of the oven and one rack at the top.

2. Put the peaches in a large, heavy-bottomed pot. Add the sugar, cornstarch, nutmeg, and salt. Stir the mixture into the peaches.

3. Add the butter and cook the peaches over medium heat, stirring slowly but continuously, until the juices lightly simmer.

4. Remove the pot from the heat, stir in the honey, and allow the filling to cool slightly. Scoop it into the cooled piecrust.

5. Cover with the crust of your choice (see page 29). Whisk together the egg and vanilla and brush this wash over the pie.

6. Place the pie on a parchment-lined baking sheet.

7. Sprinkle a dash of cinnamon, nutmeg, and salt across the top. Place an empty sheet pan on the top oven rack to prevent excessive browning.

8. Bake the pie on the middle rack for 45 to 50 minutes, until the juices on the edges simmer rapidly and the crust turns golden brown. Let the pie cool completely before serving.

traditional
CHERRY PIE

Pitted fresh or frozen cherries	2 pounds (6 cups)
Molasses	½ teaspoon
Lemon juice	1 tablespoon
Sea salt	⅛ teaspoon
Superfine granulated sugar	¾ cup (6 ounces), plus additional for sprinkling
Cornstarch	3 tablespoons
60/40 Crust, Flaky Butter Crust, or Cinnamon-Butter Piecrust (page 52, 32, or 35)	1 recipe, blind baked
Egg	1
Vanilla extract	½ teaspoon
Cinnamon	for sprinkling

The success of a cherry pie depends on the quality of the cherries—and it might take a few tries until you get it right. Most people recommend using sour cherries for a pie, but I like to use juicy sweet Bings or a combination of sweet and sour. No matter which type you choose, there's no question of what to do when you get your hands on two pounds of ripe, juicy cherries—make a pie! Once you work through pitting them, the rest is easy.

MAKES ONE 9- TO 10-INCH PIE

1. Preheat the oven to 375°F.

2. Place the cherries in a large, heavy-bottomed pot and add the molasses, lemon juice, and salt.

3. Combine the sugar and cornstarch and then stir the mixture into the cherries. Cook over medium heat for 5 to 8 minutes, until the juices thicken and lightly simmer. Stir slowly but continuously.

4. Remove the pot from the heat and allow the filling to cool a bit. Scoop it into the cooled crust, scraping all the juices out of the pan.

5. Whisk together the egg and vanilla to make an egg wash. Lay the dough round for the top crust over the pie, crimp the edges, and brush it with the egg wash. Sprinkle sugar and a touch of cinnamon on top.

6. Bake the pie for 30 to 35 minutes, or until the juices bubble and the top crust is golden brown.

7. Allow it to cool to room temperature before serving.

spiced CHERRY PIE

Sour cherries, pitted	1 pound (3 cups)
Sweet cherries, pitted	1 pound (3 cups)
Light brown sugar	½ cup, packed (4 ounces)
Cornstarch	¼ cup
Fresh mint leaves	1 tablespoon, minced
Lemon juice	1 tablespoon
Sea salt	⅛ teaspoon
Aniseed	½ teaspoon, crushed, plus additional for sprinkling
Honey	1 tablespoon
60/40 or Flaky Butter Crust (page 52 or 32)	1 recipe, bottom crust blind baked
Egg	1
Cherry liqueur (optional)	¼ teaspoon
Milk	splash
Superfine granulated sugar	for sprinkling
Cinnamon	for sprinkling

There's a wonderful new direction in which we can take cherry pie just by adding a touch of herbs and spices. I like fresh mint combined with aniseed hand-crushed in a mortar and pestle. Together, they make a more adventurous cherry pie.

MAKES ONE 9- TO 10-INCH PIE

1. Preheat the oven to 375°F.

2. Place the cherries in a large, heavy-bottomed pot.

3. Combine the brown sugar and cornstarch, then stir the mixture into the cherries and add the mint, lemon juice, salt, and aniseed. Cook over medium heat for 5 to 8 minutes, until the juices thicken and lightly simmer. Stir slowly but continuously.

4. Remove the pot from the heat, stir in the honey, and allow the filling to cool a bit. Scoop the filling, including all of the thickened juices, into the cooled crust. Cover the pie with the rolled-out top crust and crimp the edges.

5. Whisk together the egg, liqueur if using, and milk and apply this wash generously with a pastry brush. Sprinkle some superfine sugar and a pinch of crushed aniseed and cinnamon over the top of the crust.

6. Bake the pie for 45 to 50 minutes, or until the juices bubble and the top crust is golden brown.

7. Allow it to cool to room temperature before serving.

Note: For an extra-special touch, before adding the crust to the pan, sprinkle a sugar-and-spice blend onto the pie pan. Combine 2 tablespoons superfine granulated sugar with ½ teaspoon crushed aniseed, ¼ teaspoon crushed sea salt, and ¼ teaspoon cinnamon. Use about 1½ tablespoons of this for the pie pan, and sprinkle the remainder on top of the assembled pie before baking.

BLACKBERRY PIE

Blackberries make a delicious pie filling that shouldn't be missed, especially if you have access to them locally and in season. They're sweeter than raspberries, but have more of a bite than blueberries. Let the berries do all the work here—they're special enough to stand alone.

Fresh blackberries	1½ pounds (6 cups)
Superfine granulated sugar	¾ cup
Cornstarch	¼ cup
Unsalted butter, cold	3 tablespoons
Vanilla extract	2 tablespoons
Flaky Butter Crust (page 32)	¾ recipe, rolled into a bottom crust and blind baked
Dutch Crumb Topping (page 88)	1 recipe

◇◇◇◇◇◇◇◇◇◇◇◇◇◇◇◇◇◇◇◇◇◇◇◇◇◇◇◇
MAKES ONE 9- TO 10-INCH PIE
◇◇◇◇◇◇◇◇◇◇◇◇◇◇◇◇◇◇◇◇◇◇◇◇◇◇◇◇

1. Preheat the oven to 375°F.

2. Rinse and drip-dry the berries to remove any excess water. Place them in a large bowl.

3. Combine the sugar and cornstarch in a small bowl. Pour the mixture over the berries and gently fold it in.

4. Transfer the berries to a large, heavy-bottomed pot, add the butter, and cook over low to medium heat for 5 to 8 minutes, stirring constantly, until the juices lightly simmer and thicken. Add the vanilla.

5. Remove the pot from the heat and allow the filling to cool a bit, then scoop it into the cooled piecrust.

6. Cover the filling with the Dutch Crumb Topping.

7. Bake the pie for 35 minutes, until the berries are bubbling and the crust is golden brown. Allow it to cool completely before serving.

make it first
DUTCH CRUMB TOPPING

Dark brown sugar	¼ cup, packed (2 ounces)
Unbleached all-purpose flour	¼ cup (1¼ ounces)
Superfine granulated sugar	1 tablespoon
Cinnamon	¼ teaspoon
Aniseed, crushed	⅛ teaspoon
Unsalted butter, cold	3 tablespoons

Simple and quick, this is a great topping for berry pies or whenever you have enough leftover dough for only a bottom crust and don't want to spend time making more.

MAKES ENOUGH TO TOP ONE 9- TO 10-INCH PIE

Pulse all the ingredients in a food processor until the mixture resembles coarse meal. Pinch pieces of it firmly into clumps and sprinkle them across the top of the pie to any depth you like.

RED BERRY PIE

Strawberries and/or raspberries	2½ pounds
Superfine granulated sugar	1 cup (8 ounces)
Cornstarch	6 tablespoons (1½ ounces)
Sea salt	¼ teaspoon
Unsalted butter	4 tablespoons (½ stick)
Vanilla extract	2 teaspoons
Lemon zest	1 tablespoon
Flaky Butter Crust (page 32)	1 recipe, bottom crust blind baked
Dutch Crumb Topping (page 88); optional	1 recipe

If you have a bumper crop of berries and don't have to time to put up preserves, here's a wonderful option for using them before they spoil. It doesn't really matter whether it's all strawberries, raspberries, or a combination of both.

MAKES ONE 9- TO 10-INCH PIE

1. Toss the berries and sugar together, then place them in a colander set over a bowl to catch the juices.

2. Combine the juices with the cornstarch and salt in a small saucepan; whisk well. Cook over low to medium heat, stirring constantly, until the juice thickens and simmers.

3. Add the butter, vanilla, and lemon zest to the syrup.

4. Toss to combine this syrup with the berries.

5. Scoop the filling into the blind-baked piecrust.

6. Top the pie as desired, with either the second round of dough or the Dutch Crumb Topping.

7. Bake the pie for 45 to 55 minutes, until the berries are bubbling and the crust is golden brown. Allow it to cool for 1 hour before serving.

PECAN PIE

One of my pet peeves in life is the faux pecan pie. You come to the end of a fantastic meal, order a slice of pecan pie, and all you get is a single layer of pecans sitting atop a mattress of corn syrup and egg custard. It leaves everyone oh so unfulfilled.

Not this pie. It's the real deal, and the best way to enjoy it is with a little peach or cinnamon ice cream!

One of the more trying aspects of baking pecan pie is getting the filling to set without baking off all the moisture. Keep the oven temperature low—and place a baking sheet on the rack above the pie to deflect some of the heat. If you still have problems—place a small pan of water on the bottom rack to keep the air moist.

Eggs	4
Dark brown sugar	½ cup, packed (4 ounces)
Cornstarch	2 tablespoons
Sea salt	1 teaspoon
Vanilla extract	1 teaspoon
Dark corn syrup	¾ cup
Light corn syrup	¾ cup
Cinnamon	¼ teaspoon
Nutmeg, freshly ground	½ teaspoon
Cloves, ground	⅛ teaspoon
Pecans	2½ cups (8 ounces)
Whole Wheat Piecrust, Flaky Butter Crust, or 60/40 Crust (page 44, 32, or 52)	bottom crust only, blind baked
Peach or cinnamon ice cream (optional)	for serving

MAKES ONE 9- TO 10-INCH PIE

1. Preheat the oven to 325°F and position racks in the middle and top positions.

2. Combine the eggs, brown sugar, cornstarch, salt, vanilla, corn syrups, and spices in a large bowl. Whisk well. Fold in the pecans, then pour the filling into the cooled piecrust.

3. Bake the pie for 30 to 35 minutes, until the filling bubbles around the perimeter. Cool the pie completely before serving.

VARIATIONS

Pecan Chocolate Pie—Sprinkle ¼ cup of coarsely chopped bittersweet chocolate across the bottom of the crust, add the pecan filling, then dot the top of the pie with ¼ cup more chocolate.

Pecan Sweet Potato Chocolate Pie—Peel 1 large sweet potato, dice it into ¼-inch cubes. Melt 2 ounces (¼ stick) unsalted butter over medium heat and add the potatoes, 2 tablespoons superfine granulated sugar, and 2 tablespoons orange juice; braise until the potatoes are soft when pierced, about 15 minutes. Allow the potatoes to cool, then fold them into the pecan filling. Layer the chocolate and fillings as described above.

boiled SWEET POTATO PIE

All through law school, I entertained friends with dinner parties and brunches, but dessert was an afterthought at best. The only dessert in my repertoire in those days was sweet potato pie—which I made because my mom had sent me a greeting card with a sweet potato pie recipe on the back. Over time, I improvised my way to a pie that's pretty easy to throw together and extremely good. (You can make this with store-bought piecrusts. Because they're shallower, this amount of filling is enough for two pies.)

This recipe is for a fairly traditional—sweet—sweet potato pie, made rich with evaporated milk. If you're looking for something less sweet and a bit lighter all around, Roasted Sweet Potato Pie (page 96) is a good option.

MAKES ONE 9- TO 10-INCH PIE

Sea salt	1 tablespoon plus ¼ teaspoon
Superfine granulated sugar	2 tablespoons plus ½ cup (5 ounces)
Cinnamon stick (optional)	1
Sweet potatoes	3 to 4 (2½ pounds)
Dark brown sugar	¼ cup, packed (2 ounces)
Unsalted butter	4 tablespoons (½ stick)
Evaporated milk	½ cup
Vanilla extract	1 teaspoon
Rum (optional)	1 teaspoon
Honey	1 tablespoon
Cinnamon, ground	¼ teaspoon
Nutmeg, freshly grated	¼ teaspoon
Allspice	⅛ teaspoon
Egg	1
Flaky Butter Crust or Whole Wheat Piecrust (page 32 or 44)	bottom crust only, blind baked

1. Bring 3 quarts water to a rolling boil and add 1 tablespoon of the salt, 2 tablespoons of the superfine sugar, and the cinnamon stick, if using.

2. Scrub the sweet potatoes and add them whole to the boiling water. Cook until soft, about 35 minutes. Meanwhile, prepare a large bowl of ice water and preheat the oven to 350°F.

3. Remove the potatoes from the pot and plunge them into the ice water. Pat them dry and remove the skins. Place the potatoes in the bowl of a standing mixer fitted with the paddle attachment. Add the remaining ½ cup superfine sugar, the brown sugar, butter, evaporated milk, vanilla, rum (if using), honey, spices, and remaining ¼ teaspoon salt. Beat until smooth.

4. Loosely beat the egg and fold it into the sweet potato mixture.

5. Fill the cooled piecrust to the rim and bake for 50 to 60 minutes, checking frequently after 50 minutes, or until the center is set. Cool to room temperature before serving.

roasted SWEET POTATO PIE

Roasted Sweet Potato Puree (see facing page)	2 cups
Superfine granulated sugar	½ cup (4 ounces)
Dark brown sugar	½ cup (4 ounces), packed
Unsalted butter	4 tablespoons (½ stick), melted
Vanilla extract	1 teaspoon
Evaporated milk	¾ cup
Cinnamon	1 teaspoon
Cloves, ground	¼ teaspoon
Eggs, lightly beaten	2
Flaky Butter Crust, Whole Wheat Piecrust, or 60/40 Crust (page 32, 44, or 52)	2 bottom crusts, unbaked

This is a lighter version of the classic, taking its flavor and richness more from the roasted potatoes than brown sugar and evaporated milk. Don't get me wrong—it's still a sweet pie, but there's a depth of flavor that comes from preparing the potatoes this way that's unique.

◇◇
MAKES TWO 9- TO 10-INCH PIES
◇◇

1. Preheat the oven to 350°F.

2. In the work bowl of a food processor, combine all the ingredients except the eggs and crusts and pulse to combine. Lightly beat the eggs, add them to the food processor, and pulse to combine.

3. Pour the pie filling into blind-baked piecrusts. Do not use egg wash.

4. Bake the pies for 45 to 50 minutes. The filling will puff—that's okay. You'll know they're done when a skewer poked into the center comes out clean. If the pies begin to brown too quickly, place a baking sheet on the upper oven rack to shield the pies from the heat.

5. Let the pies cool before serving.

make it first
ROASTED SWEET POTATO PUREE

Use fresh Jewel yams here (they are actually sweet potatoes, not yams, but that's a long story).

Sweet potatoes	20 ounces

ENOUGH FOR TWO 9- TO 10-INCH PIES

1. Preheat the oven to 400°F and position a rack in the bottom position.

2. Wash the sweet potatoes well, but don't peel them. Place the scrubbed, whole sweet potatoes on a baking sheet lined with parchment paper. Roast them on the bottom oven rack until they are soft all the way through when poked with a bamboo skewer, approximately 1 hour, 15 minutes. Their juices may begin to weep and burn a bit before they're done.

3. Let the sweet potatoes cool, then peel them and place them in the bowl of a food processor and puree them until they're smooth—this will take at least 2 minutes—before measuring them out for the recipe. Any extra puree will keep in the fridge for up to 3 days.

PUMPKIN PIE

Pure pumpkin puree	1 (15-ounce) can
Superfine granulated sugar	1 cup (8 ounces)
Half-and-half	1 cup
Orange blossom honey	2 tablespoons
Cinnamon	½ teaspoon
Nutmeg, freshly grated	½ teaspoon
Sea salt	½ teaspoon
Allspice	¼ teaspoon
Vanilla extract	1¼ teaspoons
Eggs	3
Flaky Butter Crust (page 32)	bottom crust only, blind baked

When the *TODAY* show asked if I had any great Thanksgiving recipes, I developed and brought this recipe with me to New York City for the taping. This style of pie is easy to bake, but it's also easy to mess up with the wrong ingredients or proportions, so bake it once as written before you begin working to personalize it. Make sure you start with pure canned pumpkin, not pumpkin pie filling.

MAKES ONE 9- TO 10-INCH PIE

1. Preheat the oven to 350°F. In a large bowl, combine the pumpkin, sugar, half-and-half, honey, cinnamon, nutmeg, salt, allspice, and 1 teaspoon of the vanilla. Slowly stir, using a spoon, to mix all the ingredients without incorporating air. Lightly beat 2 of the eggs and fold them into the filling.

2. Make the egg wash by whisking together the remaining egg and ¼ teaspoon vanilla and brush the mixture onto the edges of the crust. Pour in the pie filling.

3. Bake the pie for 75 to 90 minutes, until the filling doesn't jiggle and a skewer poked into the center comes out clean. Let it cool completely before serving.

lemon
MERINGUE PIE

This recipe is a tribute to my sister Liz. Back in the 1980s, when my mom dragged me to the mall with my sisters, we would ask for a treat from the bakery. It might really have been only one time, but I seem to remember Liz always choosing lemon meringue pie. How we marveled at its height and airiness! I don't even know if I had any idea what the pie was made of. It was just beautiful—and really, really sweet.

〰〰〰〰〰〰〰〰〰〰〰〰〰〰〰〰〰〰〰
MAKES ONE 9- TO 10-INCH PIE
〰〰〰〰〰〰〰〰〰〰〰〰〰〰〰〰〰〰〰

Lemon juice	1 cup (from about 8 lemons)
Lemon zest, finely grated	2 tablespoons
Cornstarch	3 tablespoons
Superfine granulated sugar	1½ cups (12 ounces)
Eggs	4
Egg yolks	4
Unsalted butter	½ cup (1 stick)
Sea salt	⅛ teaspoon
Graham Cracker Crust or Flaky Butter Crust (page 69 or 32)	bottom crust only, blind baked
Uncooked or Cooked Meringue (page 103 or 105)	1 recipe

1. Combine the lemon juice and zest, cornstarch, sugar, eggs, egg yolks, butter, and salt in a medium-size, heavy-bottomed saucepan and whisk slowly and continuously over medium to high heat until the mixture begins to thicken and yield large, slow-forming bubbles that vent a lot of steam. This takes about 12 minutes. Do not walk away from the stove once you begin cooking the mixture—the contents can scorch easily.

2. Strain the custard through a fine-mesh sieve to capture any egg proteins and pieces of lemon zest.

3. Pour the custard into the cooled piecrust. Cover it with plastic film placed directly on the surface to prevent a skin

BE PATIENT—COOK THOROUGHLY

This lemon curd recipe has a little extra cornstarch to help the custard stay put once it's sliced. The taste isn't compromised, but be sure to cook it all the way through to cook off the starch. Don't stop stirring prematurely; continuous, steady stirring until the curd burps steam from large bubbles is absolutely necessary.

from forming and refrigerate the pie until it is thoroughly chilled, about 2 hours. Meanwhile, make the meringue of your choice.

4. Remove the plastic film from the filled pie. Fill a piping bag fitted with a tip of your choice (the open star looks nice and is easy to control) and pipe on the meringue in a design of your liking. Don't add a lot of layers of height when piping on the meringue; it acts as an insulator, so if it's piped on too thick, the center won't heat when baked.

5. If you choose the Uncooked Meringue, preheat the oven to 400°F and set a rack in the middle. Set the pie on a large baking sheet to make handling easy and bake it for 5 to 7 minutes, until the top is browned. For dramatic coloring, use a kitchen torch to highlight a few edges.

6. If you choose the Cooked Meringue, toast the peaks of the meringue to the desired color using a kitchen torch.

7. Allow the pie to come to room temperature before serving. To cleanly cut through the meringue, dip a knife in a clean pitcher of warm water before slicing. Wipe the blade clean and dip it back into the water between slices.

UNCOOKED MERINGUE

Making a meringue is not the easiest job. The bowl must be totally clean. The egg whites free of yolks. The meringue shouldn't be overwhipped. The sugar (superfine only) must be added slowly. And the air bubbles can burst, reducing the volume, if you fuss too much over forming the perfect peaks on the pie. There's a lot that can go wrong, and that's all before it goes in the oven! And remember, this meringue must be baked because it incorporates raw egg.

Don't fret. Each step is easy enough to handle when the ingredients are prepared and set out. And the pitfalls are easy to avoid. Just go natural when styling the meringue on the pie—tall peaks are great if you can get them, but soft peaks are fine too. Lemon meringue pie looks best when served immediately after you've toasted the meringue. If you have to wait too long, the sugars and proteins in the meringue can begin to break down where they are in contact with the acid in the lemon custard, and a gap will develop between them that's watery and unappetizing.

Egg whites	5
Superfine granulated sugar	½ cup (4 ounces)

ENOUGH FOR ONE 9- TO 10-INCH PIE

1. Preheat the oven to 400°F and set a rack in the middle.

2. Whip the egg whites to stiff peaks using a standing mixer fitted with the wire whip and set to high speed.

3. Slowly sprinkle the sugar into the whites and continue to whip for 2 minutes, then lower the speed to medium and run for another 2 minutes.

4. Meanwhile, remove the plastic film from the custard-filled pie.

5. Add the meringue with a spatula or pipe it on. If using a piping bag, fit it with a tip of your choice—the open star looks nice and is easy to control—and pipe on the meringue, but keep it to one layer. Don't make a mound or multiple passes with the meringue or the lower layers won't bake.

6. For dramatic coloring, use a kitchen torch to highlight a few edges.

7. Set the pie on a large baking sheet to make handling easy and place in the oven to bake for 5 to 7 minutes.

8. Remove and serve immediately.

COOKED MERINGUE

The cooked meringue—also known as Italian meringue—is very stable and easy to work with. It has a wonderful marshmallow-like texture that complements the satin-smooth texture of the lemon custard. There is no need to bake a cooked meringue; just brown the peaks as you like with a kitchen torch, then serve immediately.

Superfine granulated sugar	1 cup (8 ounces)
Water	¼ cup
Egg whites	6
Vanilla extract	1 teaspoon

ENOUGH FOR ONE 9- TO 10-INCH PIE

1. In a small, heavy-bottomed saucepan, combine the sugar with the water, stir, and heat to 245°F (it's best to use a candy thermometer to get an accurate read of the syrup's temperature).

2. Add the egg whites to the bowl of a standing mixer fitted with the whip attachment and, using high speed, whip the egg whites to stiff peaks.

3. Pour the sugar syrup into the beaten egg whites, and add the vanilla immediately after.

4. Add the meringue with a spatula or pipe it on. If using a piping bag, fit it with a tip of your choice—the open star looks nice and is easy to control—and pipe on the meringue. It's okay to pipe on a lot because this meringue is already cooked and doesn't require baking.

5. For dramatic coloring, use a kitchen torch to highlight a few edges.

6. Serve immediately.

mango MERINGUE PIE

Mango, fresh or frozen, peeled and cut into ½-inch chunks	2 cups (from 4 to 5 whole fruits)
Superfine granulated sugar	1½ cups (12 ounces)
Eggs	4
Egg yolks	4
Cornstarch	2 tablespoons
Unsalted butter	½ cup (1 stick)
Cinnamon-Butter Piecrust (page 35)	bottom crust only, blind baked for a custard filling
Uncooked or Cooked Meringue (page 103 or 105)	1 recipe

Why not make a delicious custard base from one of the world's best fruits and then top it with a delightful, airy meringue? Mango meringue pie is a perfect combination, if you ask me. Buy frozen mangos or use fresh ones when they're in season and readily available.

MAKES ONE 9- TO 10-INCH PIE

1. Combine the mango chunks and sugar in a medium-size, heavy-bottomed saucepan and bring the mixture to a light simmer over medium heat. Cook for about 5 minutes. Set the pan aside to cool.

2. Transfer the mango and its juices to a deep mixing bowl and puree them using a stick blender or blender. Measure out 1½ cups of puree and return it to the same saucepan. Reserve any remaining puree for another use.

3. Add the eggs, egg yolks, cornstarch, and butter to the pot and whisk to blend over medium heat. Continue whisking gently and constantly until slow-forming bubbles appear and release a lot of steam.

4. If desired, strain the filling through a fine-mesh sieve and allow it to cool a bit.

5. Pour the filling into the cooled piecrust. Cover the pie with plastic film placed directly on the surface to prevent a skin from forming and refrigerate until thoroughly chilled, about 2 hours. Meanwhile, make the meringue of your choice.

6. When the pie is fully chilled, top it with Uncooked Meringue and toast it in a 400°F oven for 10 minutes or top it with Cooked Meringue and toast it with a kitchen torch.

BANANA, CHOCOLATE, and COCONUT CREAM PIE

Coco López (or other brand) cream of coconut	1½ cups
Milk	1½ cups
Vanilla bean	½ pod
Superfine granulated sugar	1¼ cups (10 ounces)
Bittersweet chocolate, chopped into small pieces	8 ounces
Egg yolks	5
Cornstarch	¼ cup
Unbleached all-purpose flour	1 tablespoon
Sea salt	pinch
Lard Crust or Coconut Butter Piecrust (page 56 or 62)	bottom crust only, blind baked for a custard filling
Banana	½, sliced
Whipped Cream (page 118)	1 recipe
Shredded, sweetened coconut	for garnish

Cold pie was one of my favorite things when three o'clock meant school was out and a snack was dead ahead. Even though those days are long gone, biting into a cold pie—any cold pie—takes me back. I especially like biting into all three of these flavors in a pie that has come straight from the fridge. Use the coconut butter crust for an added hit of coconut in each bite. The coconut oil in the crust will melt quickly in the mouth, whereas the vegetable shortening gives form to the crust when working the dough and baking.

MAKES ONE 9- TO 10-INCH PIE

1. Combine the cream of coconut, milk, vanilla bean, and 1 cup of the sugar in a medium saucepan and bring the mixture to a simmer over medium heat.

2. Place the chocolate in a heatproof bowl and set it aside.

3. Meanwhile, in a large bowl, briskly whisk to combine the egg yolks, cornstarch, flour, salt, and remaining ¼ cup sugar. Once the milk mixture begins to simmer, slowly pour it into the yolk mixture.

4. Return the mixture to the pan and cook, stirring constantly, over medium heat until slow-forming "lava" bubbles appear.

5. Reduce the heat to the lowest possible setting and continue to cook for another 30 seconds, stirring constantly. Remove the vanilla bean.

6. Pour the custard into the bowl of chocolate, scraping as much as you can out of the pot with a flexible spatula. Stir to combine the custard and chocolate.

7. Pour some custard into the cooled piecrust, then arrange banana slices over the custard. Add the remaining custard and spread it evenly over the banana slices. Gently press any leftover banana slices into the top of the custard and cover the pie with plastic film placed directly on the surface to prevent a skin from forming. Refrigerate the pie until it is completely cool, at least 3 hours.

8. Cover generously with whipped cream and garnish with coconut. Serve immediately.

SHOOFLY PIE

Unbleached all-purpose flour	¾ cup (4 ounces)
Dark brown sugar	½ cup, packed (4 ounces)
Superfine granulated sugar	2 tablespoons
Cinnamon	⅛ teaspoon
Ginger	⅛ teaspoon
Nutmeg, freshly grated	⅛ teaspoon
Cloves, ground	⅛ teaspoon
Unsalted butter, very cold	5 tablespoons
Molasses, light or dark corn syrup, treacle, or Golden Syrup	1½ cups
Honey	1 tablespoon
Eggs	2
Water	½ cup
Vanilla extract	2 teaspoons
Baking soda	¾ teaspoon
Flaky Butter Crust, 60/40 Crust, or Cinnamon-Butter Piecrust (page 32, 52, or 35)	bottom crust only, blind baked
Whipped Cream (page 118)	for serving

This favorite of Pennsylvania Dutch country and the Southern states is easy to make, and yet the pie itself often reflects how serious its maker is about baking. That's because the typical shoofly recipe allows for a lot of creativity, whether in the spices used in the crumb topping or the layering of the crumb and sugary filling. Although molasses is the traditional syrup for shoofly pie, it packs quite a punch, so use a different sweetener if you like. Have fun with changing up the spices in the topping and keep your fly swatter close by—whether to keep away the pests or to shoo away hungry fingers before dessert is served! Try this crumble topping on fruit pies too. It's quick to put together and comes in handy when time is short and there's a lot of baking to do.

MAKES ONE 9- TO 10-INCH PIE

1. Preheat the oven to 400°F.

2. In a large bowl, whisk together the flour, both sugars, and the spices. Cut in the butter, using a fork or pastry cutter, until the mixture resembles a fine meal.

3. In another large bowl, whisk together the molasses, honey, eggs, water, vanilla, and baking soda.

4. Sprinkle one third of the crumble into the cooled crust, then pour in half of the filling. Repeat, then finish with the last third of the crumble topping. Be sure to reserve enough crumble for the top layer.

5. Bake the pie for 15 minutes, then reduce the oven temperature to 350°F and continue baking for another 20 minutes. Let the pie cool completely before serving. Add a large dollop of whipped cream to each slice.

BOURBON PIE

This is a great dessert that's essential for any Kentucky Derby party but is also easy to make any time of year. Just about any crust will do, but I'd go all the way and pair it with the lard crust. There's a ton of tradition that comes with this pie, but it all boils down to walnuts hugged by a healthy dose of sugar, butter, chocolate, and bourbon. With that list of ingredients, how could you have a bad outcome?

MAKES ONE 9- TO 10-INCH PIE

1. Preheat the oven to 350°F.

2. In a large bowl, combine both sugars, the corn syrup, eggs, vanilla, and bourbon. Whisk briskly until the mixture is frothy.

3. In another large bowl, combine the flour, salt, chocolate chips, and walnuts. Fold in the sugar mixture with a rubber spatula.

4. Fold in the butter.

5. Pour the filling into the cooled piecrust. Bake for 45 to 50 minutes, until the filling lightly bubbles and the top is golden brown. Let the pie cool completely before serving.

Light or dark brown sugar	¾ cup, packed (6 ounces)
Superfine granulated sugar	6 tablespoons (3 ounces)
Light corn syrup or Golden Syrup	1 cup
Eggs	4
Vanilla extract	1½ teaspoons
Bourbon	6 tablespoons
Unbleached all-purpose flour	¼ cup (1¼ ounces)
Sea salt	¼ teaspoon
Bittersweet or semisweet chocolate chips	1⅓ cups (8 ounces)
Walnuts	1⅓ cups, chopped
Unsalted butter	6 tablespoons (¾ stick), melted
Lard Crust (page 56)	bottom crust only, blind baked

SUGAR CREAM PIE

Heavy cream	1½ cups
Milk	½ cup
Unsalted butter	2 tablespoons, melted
Superfine granulated sugar	1½ cups (12 ounces)
Cornstarch	¼ cup
Unbleached all-purpose flour	1 tablespoon
Sea salt	¼ teaspoon
Vanilla extract	2 teaspoons
Flaky Butter Crust or Cinnamon-Butter Piecrust (page 32 or 35)	bottom crust only, blind baked
Cinnamon	for sprinkling

Like the Shoofly and the Bourbon (pages 110 and 111), this is another pie with strong regional associations, this time to Indiana. You'll sometimes see it referred to as a Hoosier pie in older recipe books, but versions are also found wherever there is a large Amish population. Pies don't get much simpler than this—created from the most common pantry ingredients combined with farm-fresh cream, milk, and butter. This one is sweet enough to satisfy the most serious sugar craving.

This is a solid recipe that makes a great dessert any time of year, and especially during the summer months because it's best served chilled. Recipes vary on whether to bake it or precook the filling on the stove top. I like to be sure the starch is fully cooked before it's chilled, so I prefer to make the filling in a saucepan.

MAKES ONE 9- TO 10-INCH PIE

1. Preheat the oven to 350°F. In a heavy-bottomed saucepan over medium heat, bring the cream, milk, butter, and 1 cup of the sugar to a light simmer. Meanwhile, in a large stainless-steel bowl, whisk together the remaining ½ cup sugar with the cornstarch, flour, and salt.

2. Briskly whisk the mixture from the saucepan into the bowl and return the mixture to the pan. Continue whisking rapidly while the liquid thickens and slowly bubbles, 3 to 4 minutes.

3. Remove the pan from the heat and add the vanilla.

4. Pour the filling into the cooled piecrust and sprinkle on cinnamon—as much as you like for color.

5. Cover the pie with plastic film placed directly on the surface to prevent a skin from forming and refrigerate it until it is completely cool. It won't appear firm until it cools.

6. Before serving, add more cinnamon to refresh the appearance of the pie.

Brûléed Sugar Cream Pie—Instead of sprinkling on more cinnamon before you serve the pie, top it with a layer of sugar and caramelize it with a kitchen torch, as if you're making crème brûlée.

Molasses Sugar Cream Pie—Try this luscious version of the simple sugar cream pie: Reduce the sugar by ½ cup and substitute 1 cup molasses for 1 cup of the heavy cream.

Make It a Maple Cream Pie—Increase the flour to ¼ cup and swap ¼ cup of grade-A maple syrup for the same amount of sugar; add the syrup at the same time as the vanilla.

MAPLE-WALNUT PIE

Light brown sugar	¾ cup, packed (6 ounces)
Maple syrup	1⅓ cups
Eggs	3
Vanilla extract	1 tablespoon
Unbleached all-purpose flour	¼ cup plus 1 teaspoon
Sea salt	¼ teaspoon
Walnuts	1¾ cups, chopped
Unsalted butter	½ cup (1 stick), melted
Cinnamon-Butter Piecrust (page 35)	bottom crust only, blind baked

More of a late-winter, early-spring flavor, this offshoot of the Bourbon Pie (page 111) makes a great presentation served warm and à la mode. I always use grade-A maple syrup—it's what I prefer, and it's simpler to keep one bottle in the pantry. It won't matter if you have grade-B, though—you just need to use real maple syrup.

MAKES ONE 9- TO 10-INCH PIE

1. Preheat the oven to 350°F.

2. In a large bowl, combine the brown sugar, maple syrup, eggs, and vanilla. Whisk briskly until the mixture is frothy.

3. In another large bowl, combine the flour, salt, and walnuts. Fold the maple mixture into the flour with a rubber spatula. Fold in the butter.

4. Pour the filling into the cooled piecrust. Bake for 45 to 60 minutes until the filling lightly bubbles and the top is golden brown. Let the pie cool completely before serving.

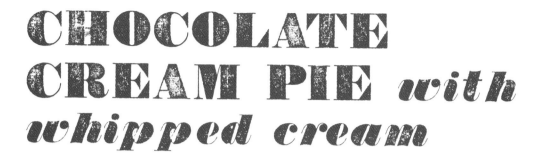

CHOCOLATE CREAM PIE *with whipped cream*

This pie is like a flourless brownie batter that's just loaded with chocolate. It's a must-have for chocoholics. Chocolate pastry cream isn't difficult to make, but it is delicate, so give it your complete attention. Keep the custard moving in the saucepan, stirring constantly to prevent scorching. Once it simmers lightly, reduce the heat to the lowest possible setting and swirl briskly for another 30 seconds to finish cooking. Note that there is a lot of liquid left in this custard because it relies on the chocolate to keep it firm once it cools.

◇◇
MAKES ONE 9- TO 10-INCH PIE
◇◇

Milk	2 cups
Superfine granulated sugar	¾ cup (6 ounces)
Unsalted butter	4 tablespoons (½ stick)
Bittersweet chocolate, chopped	12 ounces
Egg yolks	6
Cornstarch	1 tablespoon
Chocolate Piecrust (page 54)	bottom crust only, blind-baked for a custard filling
Whipped Cream (page 118)	1 recipe
Chocolate chips	about 1 ounce, for garnish

1. Combine the milk and ½ cup of the sugar in a medium saucepan and bring the mixture to a simmer over medium heat.

2. Place the butter and bittersweet chocolate in a heatproof bowl and set it aside.

3. Meanwhile, add the egg yolks, cornstarch, and remaining ¼ cup sugar to a mixing bowl and briskly whisk to combine. Slowly pour in the heated milk and stir.

4. Return the mixture to the saucepan and cook, stirring constantly, over medium heat until slow-forming bubbles appear. Reduce the heat to low and continue to cook for another 30 seconds.

5. Using a flexible spatula, scrape the custard into the bowl of butter and chocolate. Stir to combine the custard, chocolate, and butter. The chocolate must be completely melted before you go on to the next step.

6. Pour the custard into the cooled piecrust. Cover the custard with plastic film placed directly on the surface to prevent a skin from forming and refrigerate the pie for at least 3 hours.

7. Cover the surface of the pie generously with whipped cream and garnish with chocolate chips.

make it second WHIPPED CREAM

ENOUGH TO COVER ONE 9- TO 10-INCH PIE

Heavy cream, cold	2½ cups
Vanilla extract	2 teaspoons
Superfine granulated sugar	2 tablespoons

1. Using a mixer bowl and whisk chilled in the fridge for 20 to 30 minutes, whip the cream, vanilla, and sugar to soft peaks.

2. Stop the mixer and whip by hand with a wire whisk to medium peaks.

3. It's best to stop before you reach the desired texture because a few whips just prior to serving is usually necessary.

HICKORY PIE

Hickory wood is great fuel for grilling and smoking meats, but the nuts are terrific in pies, too. They have a special flavor and texture that is similar to pecans but distinctive enough that anyone who is wild about pies should try it sometime. Unfortunately, the shells are very, very hard so they're not easily found in stores, but you can find them online. Special thanks to Mark and Diane Theyeryl outside of Milwaukee for sharing their special recipe.

Eggs, lightly beaten	3
Dark corn syrup	1 cup
Superfine granulated sugar	1 cup
Unsalted butter	2 tablespoons, melted
Vanilla extract	1 teaspoon
Sea salt	⅛ teaspoon
Hickory nuts, coarsely chopped	1 cup
Cinnamon-Butter Piecrust (page 35)	bottom crust only, blind baked

MAKES ONE 9- TO 10-INCH PIE

1. Preheat the oven to 400°F.

2. In a large bowl, beat together the eggs, corn syrup, sugar, butter, vanilla, and salt. Add the nuts and stir.

3. Pour the filling into the cooled crust. Bake the pie for 15 minutes, then reduce the oven temperature to 350°F and bake for another 30 to 35 minutes.

4. The filling should be slightly less set in the center than around the edges. Allow the pie to cool completely before serving.

GALETTES

Galettes are a welcome reprieve from the work required when crimping piecrusts. Simply roll out the dough, place a fruit filling in the middle, and fold in the sides, covering some of the fruit, but leaving the center of the filling exposed. Making a decorative edge is always an option, but it's not necessary with this rustic version of a pie. It's easiest to bake it in a pie pan, but if you're a purist, then bake it on a sheet pan lined with parchment paper—this makes a dramatic presentation. A galette has a wonderfully crispy edge and a beautiful, rustic look that is sometimes even prettier than a perfect pie.

strawberry-peach GALETTE

I like this combination of fruits because they taste great and look very pretty together. Both are fairly watery, though, so bake and serve this on the same day. It won't hold that well overnight.

MAKES ONE 9- TO 10-INCH GALETTE

Dough for Flaky Butter Crust or Über Butter Crust (page 32 or 37)	1 recipe
Fresh or frozen peaches, peeled, pitted, and sliced	2 pounds
Strawberries	10 ounces
Superfine granulated sugar	¾ cup (6 ounces), plus additional for sprinkling
Cornstarch	2 tablespoons plus 1 teaspoon
Sea salt	⅛ teaspoon, plus additional for sprinkling
Unsalted butter	3 tablespoons
Egg	1
Vanilla extract	¼ teaspoon
Cinnamon	for sprinkling
Nutmeg, freshly grated	for sprinkling

1. Preheat the oven to 350°F and position racks in the middle and at the top of the oven.

2. If you're using frozen peaches, thaw them completely and drain off all the liquid. Place the peaches in a large, heavy-bottomed pot.

3. Set aside 3 or 4 whole strawberries, then cut the remainder into ¼-inch slices and add them to the pot with the peaches. Combine the sugar, cornstarch, and salt in a bowl, then stir the mixture into the fruit. Add the butter and cook the filling over medium heat, stirring slowly but continuously until it lightly simmers. Allow it to cool slightly.

4. Roll the pie dough into one large round about ⅛ inch thick and place it loosely in a 9- to 10-inch pie pan (don't crimp the edges); set the pan on a parchment-lined baking sheet. Alternatively, if you prefer the traditional method of assembling a galette, simply line a baking sheet with parchment.

5. Mound the filling onto the center of the prepared dough round. Fold the edges of the dough up over the filling to cover some of it, but leave the majority uncovered to reveal the fruit.

6. Cut the reserved strawberries into ⅛-inch slices and arrange them decoratively on the fruit filling.

7. Whisk together the egg and vanilla and brush the crust with this wash. Sprinkle sugar on the crust. Sprinkle a dash of cinnamon, nutmeg, and salt across the top of the whole galette.

8. Bake the galette for 35 to 45 minutes. Place an empty sheet pan on the rack above the pie to prevent excessive browning, especially to protect the strawberries.

9. Cool the galette completely before serving.

TURN-OVERS

Turnovers are a fun way to make individual servings of just about any fruit pie. You can bake them in the oven or fry them on the stove top; the baked kind are easier and cleaner to make—and probably a lot healthier—but the crispy edges that frying offers can be a real treat every once in a while. Precook the fruit a bit so the dough and filling will finish cooking at the same time.

APPLE TURNOVERS

This is the simplest possible filling you can make—just some apples cooked down with butter and sugar. If you want something apple-oriented but a little fancier, use Mom's Apple Pie filling (page 74). And if you're ready for more than just apples, see the variations on page 126.

◇◇◇◇◇◇◇◇◇◇◇◇◇◇◇◇◇◇◇◇◇◇◇◇◇◇◇◇◇◇◇◇◇◇◇
MAKES 12 TURNOVERS
◇◇◇◇◇◇◇◇◇◇◇◇◇◇◇◇◇◇◇◇◇◇◇◇◇◇◇◇◇◇◇◇◇◇◇

Granny Smith apples, peeled, cored, and chopped	5
Superfine granulated sugar	¼ cup
Unsalted butter	2 tablespoons
Dough for Cinnamon-Butter Piecrust (page 35)	1 recipe
Egg (optional)	1
Vanilla extract (optional)	¼ teaspoon
Vegetable oil (optional)	for frying

1. If you plan to bake your turnovers, preheat the oven to 350°F. For fried turnovers, set the oven to a low warming temperature.

2. Place the apples, sugar, and butter in a medium-size saucepan and cook the mixture over medium-low heat for 5 to 10 minutes, until the fruit is softened and barely browned on the edges.

3. Roll the pie dough out into a large rectangle, about 12 by 16 inches.

4. Cut the dough into 4-inch squares. Place ¼ cup filling in the center of each square, fold the dough over to form a triangle, and crimp the edges with a fork.

5. For baked turnovers, use a sharp knife to cut a vent across the top of each one. Whisk together the egg and vanilla and dab this wash onto the crust with a pastry brush. Place the turnovers on a parchment-lined baking sheet and bake them for 25 to 30 minutes, until the edges are crispy and golden.

6. To deep fry the turnovers, do not cut vents or use the egg wash. Chill the assembled turnovers for 30 minutes. Add 2 inches of vegetable oil to a large, deep skillet and heat the oil for 5 minutes over medium heat. Add the turnovers, three to five at a time, and fry them for 4 to 5 minutes per side. Hold the turnovers in a warm oven (200°F to 225°F) until you're ready to serve.

Each of these filling options makes enough to fill one turnover.

Chocolate and Vanilla Pudding Cream Turnover—Combine ¼ cup Vanilla Pudding Cream (page 146) with 2 to 3 tablespoons bittersweet chocolate pieces.

Apple and Cream Filled Turnovers—Stir together ¼ cup Vanilla Pudding Cream (page 146) and 3 tablespoons Mom's Apple Pie filling (page 74) or ½ cup raw diced apples sautéed in 1 tablespoon unsalted butter until browned.

Nutella Turnover—Fill the turnover with ¼ cup of Nutella, fold, and crimp.

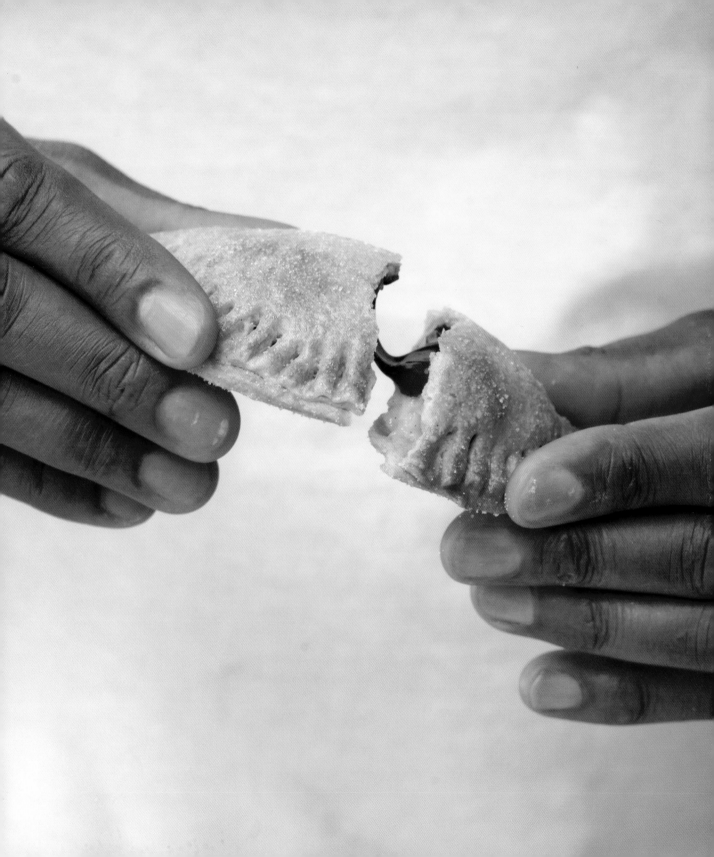

blueberry COBBLER

Fresh blueberries	8 cups (32 ounces)
Superfine granulated sugar	1 cup (8 ounces), plus additional for sprinkling
Unbleached all-purpose flour	1 cup (5 ounces)
Cornstarch	1 tablespoon
Baking powder	½ teaspoon
Sea salt	¼ teaspoon
Unsalted butter, very cold	½ cup (1 stick), cut into small pieces
Egg, lightly beaten	1
Vanilla extract	½ teaspoon
Cinnamon (optional)	for sprinkling
Nutmeg, freshly grated (optional)	for sprinkling
Vanilla ice cream (optional)	for serving

Way before I opened my first bakery, I volunteered at a few cooking classes—that's where I learned this simple recipe. After you've made this cobbler once or twice you'll be familiar enough with the recipe that you won't even need to measure. Immediately after this dish is pulled from the oven, the juices bubble rapidly and make the most pleasant sound.

MAKES ONE 13-BY-9-INCH COBBLER

1. Preheat the oven to 400°F.

2. Butter a 9-by-13-inch baking dish and lightly sprinkle sugar and a pinch of salt in the bottom.

3. Wash and pat the berries dry to remove excess liquid.

4. Combine the sugar, flour, cornstarch, baking powder, and salt in a large bowl. Toss 2 to 3 tablespoons of this mixture with the blueberries. Pour the berries into the prepared baking dish.

5. Cut the butter into the remaining flour mixture with a fork or pastry cutter.

6. Stir together the egg and vanilla. Drizzle the egg into the dough while turning constantly with a fork. The dough will slowly come together—it should be damp, not wet.

7. Lightly press the dough into disks the size of silver dollars about ¼ inch thick. Lay these across the berries, leaving some gaps between them.

8. Lightly sprinkle sugar (and spices, if desired) across the top.

9. Bake the cobbler for 45 to 50 minutes, or until the fruit juices bubble rapidly and the crust is golden brown.

10. Cool the cobbler completely before serving, ideally with vanilla ice cream.

CHAPTER THREE

TART CRUSTS

Tarts are their own domain. At one time, I thought of them as minimalist pies, but they're really quite different. Perhaps the most important distinction is the crust. The typical crust is a shortbread, which would never make it as a piecrust. The bottom-release tart pan is ideal for working with shortbread crusts and really can't be replaced by a traditional pie pan. Nut crusts, of which I'm a big fan, are an alternative to shortbread crust—but don't put them in the oven. Try them topped with custards and fresh fruit to create no-bake desserts.

buttery shortbread TART CRUST

Even though she married a baker, my wife doesn't really indulge in sweets. When I bring home experiments, she looks at them matter-of-factly, nibbles, and gently pushes them away. So you can imagine my surprise when she commented about this shortbread crust, "It's a little tough to cut, but that's okay because it's really good."

Crispy and buttery—that's what this crust is all about. I always use the food processor to prepare shortbread crust. The paddle attachment of a standing mixer just doesn't cut the butter into the flour well enough, which leads to a lot of clumping and uneven baking. Generally shortbread crust does not need to be baked with a parchment liner or nonstick spray. The copious amount of butter in the dough makes it pretty nonstick.

Unsalted butter, very cold	½ cup (1 stick), cut into small pieces
Confectioners' sugar	⅔ cup (2½ ounces)
Unbleached all-purpose flour	1½ cups (7 ounces)
Sea salt	½ teaspoon
Cornstarch	¼ cup

MAKES ONE 9- TO 10-INCH TART CRUST

1. Preheat the oven to 325°F.

2. Add the butter, confectioners' sugar, flour, salt, and cornstarch to the work bowl of a food processor. Process for 8 to 10 seconds to combine the ingredients, then pulse three times more, until the mixture resembles coarse meal.

3. Press the dough firmly into the tart pan. Bake it for 20 minutes until it is golden brown. Set the crust aside to cool completely while you prepare the filling of your choice.

Tamp down
the crust.

It should
form an
even layer.

pecan caramel TART CRUST

Every nut is a little different, and pecans make a crust that is quite a bit looser than one made with almonds or peanuts. Extra sugar and less caramel compensate for the oils in pecans. This crust is ideally suited for a custard-filled tart with no baking required.

Toasted pecans	2 cups (8 ounces)
Confectioners' sugar	¾ cup (3 ounces)
Sea salt	¼ teaspoon
Caramel Sauce (page 149)	2 to 3 tablespoons

MAKES ONE 9- TO 10-INCH TART CRUST

1. Combine the pecans, confectioners' sugar, and salt in the work bowl of a food processor. Process into a fine meal, about 20 seconds.

2. Remove the work bowl lid and add the Caramel Sauce 1 tablespoon at a time. Process until the mixture gathers together into a dough.

3. Press the dough into a tart or pie pan so that it's about ¼ inch deep—or higher if desired. No need to chill or bake the crust before filling it.

VARIATION

Pecan Caramel Chocolate Tart Crust— Adapt the pecan and caramel crust into a more decadent carriage for any sweet tart. Add 2 to 3 tablespoons of mini chocolate chips after the caramel and just before the nut mixture comes together into a dough.

almond caramel
TART CRUST

Roasted, unsalted almonds	2 cups (6 ounces)
Confectioners' sugar	½ cup (2 ounces)
Superfine granulated sugar	2 tablespoons
Sea salt	¼ teaspoon
Unsalted butter	1 ounce, softened
Caramel Sauce (page 149)	¼ cup, plus additional if needed
Cornstarch (optional)	for dusting

Nuts and caramel form a rich tart base that's best set off by a coating of ganache or Vanilla Pudding Cream (page 146) and fruit.

MAKES ONE 9- TO 10-INCH TART CRUST

1. Line the bottom of a 9-inch tart pan with a circle of parchment paper.

2. Combine the almonds, both sugars, and the salt in the work bowl of a food processor. Process for about 20 seconds into a fine meal.

3. Add the butter and Caramel Sauce. Process until the meal forms into a dough. Add more caramel if necessary to make the dough pliable (but not loose). At this point, the dough will keep, well wrapped in plastic film, for up to a month in the fridge.

4. Press the dough flat into the tart pan so that it's about ¼ inch deep. If you want to, go ahead and press it up the sides of the pan. If the dough seems too sticky, lightly dust it with cornstarch. No need to chill or bake the crust before filling it.

lemon shortbread TART CRUST

This crust is buttery, with a hint of lemon freshness. Be sure to shave only the zest from the whole fruit, avoiding the bitter white pith.

<><><><><><><><><><><><><><><><><><><><><><><><><><><><><><>
MAKES ONE 9- TO 10-INCH TART CRUST
<><><><><><><><><><><><><><><><><><><><><><><><><><><><><><>

Unsalted butter, very cold	½ cup (1 stick), cut into small pieces
Confectioners' sugar	⅔ cup (3¼ ounces)
Unbleached all-purpose flour	1½ cups (7 ounces)
Sea salt	¼ teaspoon
Cornstarch	¼ cup
Lemon zest, finely grated	1 tablespoon

1. Preheat the oven to 325°F.

2. Add the butter, confectioners' sugar, flour, salt, cornstarch, and lemon zest to the work bowl of a food processor. Process for 8 to 10 seconds to combine the ingredients, then pulse three times, until the mixture resembles coarse meal.

3. Press the dough firmly into the tart pan. Bake it for 20 minutes, until it is golden brown. Set the crust aside to cool completely while you prepare the filling of your choice.

VARIATION

Orange Shortbread Tart Crust—A delicious, if not unusual, tart crust that pairs nicely with chocolate as well as fruit or custard fillings. Replace the lemon zest with 2 tablespoons of orange zest. (In fact, you can replace the lemon zest in the original recipe with any citrus zest, adjusting the amounts up or down, according to your taste and mood.)

peanut
TART CRUST

Shelled, unsalted peanuts	2 cups (8 ounces)
Sugar Syrup (page 144)	¼ cup
Superfine granulated sugar	¼ cup
Sea salt	¼ teaspoon
Confectioners' sugar	½ cup (2 ounces)
Caramel Sauce (page 149)	5 tablespoons

This is a fantastic nut crust—delicious all on its own—that works with vanilla, chocolate, or coffee custard fillings. You must use roasted peanuts, and the extra step of making them into candied peanuts is well worth the effort. Simply adding sugar to roasted peanuts won't yield the same result. Make extra to have candied peanuts for snacking. They won't last long.

MAKES ONE 9- TO 10-INCH TART CRUST

1. Preheat the oven to 350°F. Line a baking sheet with parchment paper and set it aside.

2. In a bowl, toss to combine the nuts, Sugar Syrup, superfine sugar, and salt. Spread the sugar-coated peanuts on the prepared sheet and toast them in the oven for 10 minutes. Set the nuts aside to cool completely.

3. Combine the candied peanuts and confectioners' sugar in the work bowl of a food processor. Add the Caramel Sauce 1 tablespoon at a time and pulse to process into a dough.

4. Press the dough into a tart or pie pan so that it's about ¼ inch deep or higher if desired. No need to chill or bake the crust before filling it.

CHAPTER FOUR

SWEET TARTS

Tart shells can be filled with layers of creamy custards or pudding, or they can serve as a platform for fresh fruit. Only the ripest fruits without any blemishes are suitable for tarts. Berry tarts are the easiest to put together—when you use larger fruits, you'll want a very sharp knife for slicing them, and you may find that preparing a decorative pattern takes a little time. They're typically paired with some sort of pastry cream to anchor the fruits featured on top, but lemon curd or any other fruit puree that complements the other elements will work well. The glaze added in the final moments of baking should be cooked down from your favorite fruit preserve, not a commercial mirror gel like those we've all had the regrettable experience of biting into. I like my tarts with a touch of Vanilla Pudding Cream (page 146) as a base to showcase the fruit on top, but be prepared to store most of the cream because even half a recipe is more than enough for one tart.

CHOCOLATE-AMARETTO TART

I'm always looking for ways to work amaretto and almonds into desserts. I love the versatility of almonds, and the flavor of amaretto is so complex that it works in many desserts. Of course, when they're paired with chocolate the beauty of each is vividly amplified. The crisp shortbread crust makes it complete.

MAKES ONE 9- TO 10-INCH TART

Creamy Ganache, made with Amaretto (page 143)	1 recipe
Buttery Shortbread Tart Crust (page 133)	1 recipe, blind baked
Candied Almonds (page 144)	1 cup

1. Spoon the ganache into the prepared tart shell, smooth the surface with an offset spatula, and place the tart in the fridge to chill for 20 minutes.

2. Gently warm the sides of the tart pan to loosen any chocolate that may have stuck to the pan. (Apply a warm dish towel or just let the tart rest at room temperature for up to 30 minutes.) Release the bottom from the sides of the pan.

3. Gently apply the Candied Almonds to the sides of the tart, then slide the tart off the pan bottom and onto a serving platter. Serve at room temperature.

make it first
CREAMY GANACHE

I doubled the cream called for in the ganache I use for cakes to create this version. It is loose and soft to the bite when served chilled—as is recommended.

MAKES 3 CUPS

Heavy cream	2 cups
Bittersweet chocolate, chopped	1 cup (6 ounces)
Frangelico or other liqueur (optional)	¼ cup

Bring the cream to a simmer, pour it over the chocolate, and add the liqueur. Whisk to combine, stirring until the chocolate is melted and the mixture is smooth. Allow to cool without setting before using.

make it first
CANDIED ALMONDS

MAKES 1 CUP

Sliced almonds blanched	1 cup (6 ounces)
Sugar Syrup (see below)	¼ cup
Superfine granulated sugar	1 tablespoon
Sea salt	¼ teaspoon

1. Preheat the oven to 350°F.

2. Toss all the ingredients together in a large mixing bowl.

3. Spread the sugared nuts on a baking sheet lined with parchment or a silicone baking mat.

4. Roast the almonds for 7 to 10 minutes, or until they're golden brown.

SUGAR SYRUP

Combine ½ cup water and 1 cup superfine granulated sugar in a small, heavy-bottomed saucepan. Stir the mixture over medium heat until it reaches 245°F (it's best to use a candy thermometer to get an accurate read of the syrup's temperature). This will yield 1 cup and will keep in a covered jar in the fridge for up to 30 days.

vanilla PUDDING CREAM

Vanilla extract or vanilla bean	2 tablespoons or ½ bean
Milk	2 cups
Heavy cream	1 cup
Superfine granulated sugar	1½ cups (12 ounces)
Egg yolks	5
Unbleached all-purpose flour	2 tablespoons
Cornstarch	¼ cup

This pudding cream is well suited for custard pies because it tends to hold its shape when cut into slices. Cooking the cream to the point of ridding it of a starchy taste or texture is critical. Don't pull it off the heat just because it has bubbled once or twice. Taste often to determine whether the starch has cooked off.

<><><><><><><><><><><><><><><><><><><><><><><><><>
MAKES 3 TO 4 CUPS
<><><><><><><><><><><><><><><><><><><><><><><><><>

1. If you're using a vanilla bean, flatten it with the side of a paring knife, then slice it open lengthwise. Use the back of the paring knife to scrape the seeds into a medium-size pot along with the milk, cream, and 1 cup of the sugar. (If you're using vanilla extract, add it as the final step.) Bring the mixture to a simmer.

2. Meanwhile, in a medium-size, heatproof bowl, whisk the remaining flour, sugar, and cornstarch into the egg yolks.

3. Once the milk mixture comes to a simmer, slowly whisk it into the egg yolk mixture. Immediately return everything to the pot and return it to the stove over medium to low heat. Slowly whisk continuously until large bubbles form.

4. Reduce the temperature to the lowest setting and whisk briskly for another 30 seconds to finish cooking the custard.

5. Scrape the custard into a heatproof bowl, stir in the vanilla extract, if using, and cover with plastic film. Press the plastic film directly onto the surface of the custard to prevent a skin from forming. Refrigerate or cool in an ice bath until you're ready to use. Refrigerated, the pudding cream will keep for 7 days.

VARIATION

Coffee Pudding Cream—Try this with the Buttery Shortbread or Almond Caramel Tart Crust (page 133 or 136). Follow the instructions for Vanilla Pudding Cream, but add ½ cup freshly ground coffee beans as well. After the cream is fully cooked, pour it through a very fine-mesh strainer to remove the coffee grounds.

This photograph shows the Coffee Pudding Cream variation.

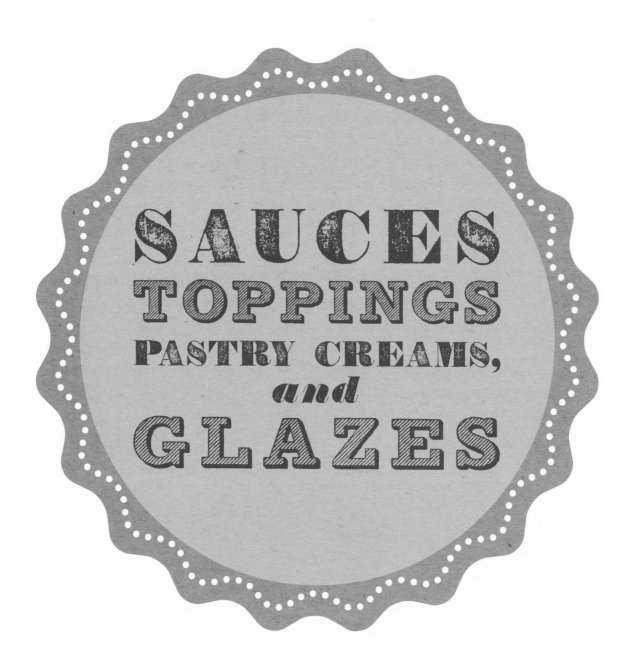

SAUCES
TOPPINGS
PASTRY CREAMS,
and
GLAZES

caramel SAUCE

Nothing is as simple as Caramel Sauce, and yet it will lift a serving of dessert from the ordinary to something gourmet and photoworthy. We make a ton of caramel in-house at CakeLove—and we do it without copper pots, so you can too.

MAKES 1¼ CUPS

Superfine granulated sugar	1¼ cups (10 ounces)
Water	⅓ cup
Heavy cream, at room temperature	1 cup
Vanilla extract	1 teaspoon
Sea salt	¼ teaspoon

1. Combine the sugar and water in a small, heavy-bottomed saucepan. Cook the mixture over low heat until it reaches 340°F (it's best to use a candy thermometer to get an accurate read of the mixture's temperature).

2. Using a wooden spoon or heat-resistant spatula, stir in the cream. Cook until the mixture turns a deep amber color.

3. Remove the pan from the heat and stir in the vanilla and salt. Let the caramel cool completely, then transfer it to a squeeze bottle. Caramel can be kept in the refrigerator for 2 to 3 weeks.

chocolate SAUCE

Of course, this sauce will taste just as good on ice cream—or any other dessert—as it does on a piece of pie or a tart!

MAKES 1 CUP

Bittersweet chocolate, chopped	½ cup
Heavy cream	¼ cup
Sugar Syrup (page 144)	½ cup, or to taste
Vanilla extract	½ teaspoon

1. Place the chocolate in a heatproof bowl and set it aside.

2. Pour the cream into a small, heavy-bottomed saucepan and bring it to a simmer over medium heat. Pour the hot cream over the chocolate pieces and whisk until the chocolate melts and the mixture is smooth. Whisk in the Sugar Syrup and the vanilla.

3. Taste and add more Sugar Syrup if desired. Store in a sealed container in the refrigerator for up to 2 weeks.

raspberry COULIS

Raspberries, fresh or frozen	1 cup
Superfine granulated sugar	¼ cup
Lemon juice	1 teaspoon
Water	½ cup
Sugar Syrup (page 144)	as needed

A beautiful accent for plating design, this is a great way to use frozen berries or fresh ones that are past their prime.

MAKES 1 CUP

1. Combine the berries, sugar, and lemon juice with the water in a heavy-bottomed saucepan. Bring the mixture to a light simmer over low to medium heat and cook until the berries have liquefied and the sugar has dissolved, about 7 minutes.

2. Strain the mixture through a fine-mesh sieve. Add Sugar Syrup as needed to bring it to a pourable consistency. Refrigerate the coulis between uses; it will keep for about a week.

mango COULIS

Mango chunks, fresh or frozen	1 cup (5 ounces)
Water	¼ cup
Superfine granulated sugar	½ cup (4 ounces)
Lemon Juice	2 teaspoons

Great for plating and a vegan option for filling a fruit tart, mango coulis is a must-have item for the well-stocked kitchen. Those who avoid refined sugar can use light agave syrup instead of the sugar and water.

MAKES 1¼ CUPS

1. Combine the mango, water, and sugar in a heavy-bottomed saucepan. Cook the mixture over low to medium heat until the liquid lightly simmers.

2. Transfer the coulis to a blender and add the lemon juice. Puree, taste, and add sugar as necessary.

3. Refrigerate coulis between uses; it will keep for up to a week.

honey sage
PASTRY CREAM

Two of my favorite ingredients to work with are honey and sage. I always prefer raw honey; it's thick, spreadable, and has a much bolder flavor and sweetness. Sage is the prized herb in my backyard garden. I favor it over everything else and tend to use a lot when cooking at home for my family. To me, fresh sage is unique—the waxy resin on the leaves carries wonderful flavor that gets a little lost in the dried or ground offerings. Try this pastry cream with any of the savory and nut crusts. Pair it with the Apple and Cream Filled Turnovers (page 126).

Milk	¾ cup
Sage	10 leaves
Cloves, ground	½ teaspoon
Superfine granulated sugar	1⅓ cups (11 ounces)
Vanilla bean	½ pod
Egg yolks	4
Unbleached all-purpose flour	1½ tablespoons
Sea salt	¼ teaspoon
Raw honey	1 tablespoon

MAKES 2 CUPS

1. Bring the milk, sage, and cloves to a simmer in a heavy-bottomed saucepan, then remove the pan from the heat and steep for 10 minutes. Strain the mixture through a colander and return the liquid to the pot.

2. Add 1 cup of the sugar and the vanilla bean to the pot with the milk and return it to a simmer. Meanwhile, whisk the egg yolks, flour, salt, honey, and remaining ⅓ cup sugar together in a large bowl. Slowly whisk the heated milk mixture into the yolk mixture.

3. Pour the cream back into the pot, place it over medium heat, and cook, whisking continuously, until the pastry cream thickens and large, steam-venting bubbles appear.

4. Pour the pastry cream into a heatproof bowl and cover with plastic film placed directly on the surface to prevent a skin from forming.

5. Refrigerate the pastry cream until you're ready to use it; it will keep for up to 7 days.

sugar GLAZE

Confectioners' sugar	½ cup
Water	3 to 4 tablespoons
Rum, brandy, or liqueur (optional)	1 teaspoon

For obvious reasons, this glaze—essentially the finishing touch in the two-step process that begins with the Fruit Preserve Glaze on page 153—is as neutral in flavor as possible. But adding a bit of rum or brandy can be a nice touch.

MAKES ¼ CUP

Put the sugar in a small mixing bowl, then add the water, 1 tablespoon at a time, stirring until the sugar is dissolved. The solution should be quite thin, but not watery. Stir in the liquor, if using. Lightly brush the sugar glaze onto the tart after applying Fruit Preserve Glaze. The glaze will keep, refrigerated in a covered container, for up to 5 days.

mint SYRUP

Honey	1 tablespoon
Superfine granulated sugar	6 tablespoons
Water	½ cup
Mint leaves, tightly packed	¼ cup

Mint is a lovely addition to a fruit tart—it highlights and brings out the flavors. Sprinkle this over the fruit prior to baking. It is a flavor enhancement, though, not a substitute for a glaze.

MAKES ½ CUP

Combine the honey, sugar, and water in a small saucepan. Bring the mixture to a simmer to dissolve the sugar. Add the mint leaves, cook for 1 minute, then turn off the heat and steep for 5 minutes. Pour the mixture through a fine-mesh strainer and discard the solids. Store the syrup in a squeeze bottle to use as necessary; it will keep in the fridge for up to 1 month.

fruit preserve GLAZE

Fruit tarts often look a little dull after baking. A glaze is commonly used to refresh the appearance and help preserve the fruit. The best method for glazing a tart is a two-step process of brushing on strained fruit preserves followed by a confectioners' sugar and water glaze (page 152). Generally apricot preserve is used—it's preferred for its neutral flavor. I've tried other fruits, and I agree that apricot does seem to work the best.

Apricot preserves	1 cup
Lemon juice	1 tablespoon

MAKES ¾ CUP

Combine the preserves and lemon juice in a small, heavy-bottomed saucepan and simmer the mixture over low heat until the preserves have melted. Strain the glaze through a fine-mesh sieve and discard any fruit pulp. Store the glaze in a covered container in the fridge for up to 3 days. Warm it gently in a water bath before applying a light coating to the tart surface with a clean pastry brush.

STRAWBERRIES AND CREAM TART

Vanilla Pudding Cream (page 146)	2 cups
Almond Caramel Tart Crust (page 136)	1 recipe, blind baked
Fresh strawberries	2 pints
Mint Syrup (page 152)	2 tablespoons
Fruit Preserve Glaze (page 153)	2 tablespoons, warmed
Sugar Glaze (page 152)	2 tablespoons

This luscious tart has the perfect combination of fruit and filling—there's just no better early-summer dessert. Choose fruit at the peak of the season and make sure the berries are ripe but still firm.

MAKES ONE 9- TO 10-INCH TART

1. Preheat the oven to 350°F.

2. Spoon the Vanilla Pudding Cream over the cooled crust and smooth it with an offset spatula, leaving a 1-inch border between the edge of the pastry cream and the tart rim.

3. Wash and hull the strawberries. Slice them in half lengthwise, or slice them at an angle for a more decorative presentation. Arrange them neatly in concentric circles on top of the pastry cream, leaving some space in between the berry halves. Alternatively, if your berries are all of similar size, you can leave them whole and place them on the cream stem side down.

4. Sprinkle the Mint Syrup over the top of the filling.

5. Place the pan on top of a baking sheet and bake for 25 minutes, until the tart is aromatic.

6. Gently brush on the warmed Fruit Preserve Glaze and Sugar Syrup with a pastry brush and bake for 5 minutes longer. Cool the tart completely before serving.

MANGO AND STRAWBERRY TART

Mango Coulis (page 150)	2 cups
Almond Caramel Tart Crust (page 136)	1 recipe
Fresh strawberries	2 pints
Mint Syrup (page 152)	2 tablespoons
Fruit Preserve Glaze (page 153)	2 tablespoons, warmed
Sugar Glaze (page 152)	2 tablespoons

Mango Coulis replaces vanilla cream in this totally vegan and gluten-free dessert that everyone will enjoy. Strict vegans should use turbinado sugar or agave syrup.

MAKES ONE 9- TO 10-INCH TART

1. Preheat the oven to 325°F.

2. Spoon the Mango Coulis into the tart crust and smooth it with an offset spatula leaving a 1-inch border between the edge of the puree and the tart rim.

3. Wash and hull the strawberries. Slice them in half lengthwise or slice them at an angle for a more decorative presentation. Arrange the strawberry halves so the cut sides are face down, staggering each row so they have an organized appearance.

4. Lightly sprinkle the Mint Syrup over the top of the filling.

5. Gently brush on the warmed Fruit Preserve Glaze and Sugar Glaze with a pastry brush and bake the tart for 5 minutes. Cool it completely before serving.

ORANGE AND CHOCOLATE TART

I'm a big fan of orange paired with chocolate. I experiment with these two flavors frequently at CakeLove. They complement each other very well, and this is especially apparent in a tart—it's just easier to appreciate their flavors without the dominance of cake or buttercream.

◇◇◇◇◇◇◇◇◇◇◇◇◇◇◇◇◇◇◇◇◇◇◇◇◇◇◇◇◇◇◇◇◇◇◇◇
MAKES ONE 9- TO 10-INCH TART
◇◇◇◇◇◇◇◇◇◇◇◇◇◇◇◇◇◇◇◇◇◇◇◇◇◇◇◇◇◇◇◇◇◇◇◇

Bittersweet chocolate, chopped	2 cups (12 ounces)
Vanilla extract	1 teaspoon
Orange liqueur, such as Cointreau or triple sec	¼ cup
Superfine granulated sugar	2 tablespoons
Heavy cream	1 cup
Orange Shortbread Tart Crust (page 137)	1 recipe, blind baked
Whipped Cream with Orange Segments (page 158)	1 recipe

1. Preheat the oven to 300°F and set a rack in the middle.

2. Place the chocolate in a heatproof bowl with the vanilla and liqueur.

3. Combine the sugar and cream in a small, heavy-bottomed saucepan and bring the mixture to a simmer over medium heat. Pour the cream over the chocolate and stir until the chocolate is melted and the mixture is smooth.

4. Allow the chocolate to cool for a few minutes so it won't splash, then pour it into the cooled crust. Even it out with an offset spatula if necessary, smoothing it all the way to the edges.

5. Place the tart on a baking sheet and bake it for 25 minutes, or until set. Let the tart cool completely, then spread Whipped Cream with Orange Segments on top and serve.

punched up
WHIPPED CREAM

Nothing makes an elegant statement more easily than freshly whipped cream. Add a little sauce to it and you've got even more thrills coming your way. Have fun!

MAKES 3 CUPS

Heavy cream, cold	1½ cups
Confectioners' sugar	1 tablespoon
Frangelico liqueur	1½ tablespoons

WITH FRANGELICO

Add the cream, sugar, and liqueur to the bowl of a standing mixer fitted with the whisk attachment. Whip the cream to medium peaks, then stop the mixer and use a balloon whisk to whip the cream by hand to the desired medium to stiff peaks. Immediately use the cream as a topping or an accompaniment to your dessert.

Navel orange	1
Heavy cream, cold	1½ cups
Confectioners' sugar	1 tablespoon

WITH ORANGE SEGMENTS

1. Peel and supreme the navel orange. Gently break apart the supremes to release the tiny little sacs of fruit. Set aside.

2. Combine the cream and confectioners' sugar in the bowl of a standing mixer fitted with the whisk attachment. Whip the cream to medium peaks, then stop the mixer and whisk by hand to medium to stiff peaks, so as not to overmix.

3. Fold in the orange and immediately use the cream as a topping or accompaniment to your dessert.

> ### SUPREME
> This is a method to release citrus fruit pulp from pith. Using a very sharp knife, cut off one end of the citrus fruit. Stand the fruit on the cut end so it stays level, then use the knife to cut away the rind all the way to the flesh, leaving no white pith behind. Next, cut along the side of each membrane until segments of fruit come free.

HAZELNUT TRUFFLE TART

Chocolate and hazelnut is a classic flavor combination. This luxurious tart is a sophisticated ending for a dinner party or a gathering of family and friends.

◇◇
MAKES ONE 9- TO 10-INCH TART
◇◇

Bittersweet chocolate, chopped	1½ cups (12 ounces)
Vanilla extract	1 teaspoon
Frangelico (optional)	1 tablespoon
Heavy cream	1 cup
Superfine granulated sugar	1½ tablespoons
Peanut Tart Crust (page 138)	1 recipe
Whipped Cream with Frangelico (page 158)	1 recipe
Candied peanuts (page 138; optional)	for garnish
Chocolate shavings (optional)	for garnish
Caramel Sauce (page 149; optional)	for garnish

1. Place the chopped chocolate in a heatproof bowl with the vanilla and Frangelico, if using.

2. Combine the cream and sugar in a small, heavy-bottomed saucepan and bring the mixture to a simmer over medium heat. Pour the cream over the chocolate and stir until the chocolate melts and the mixture is smooth.

3. Allow the chocolate to cool for a few minutes, so it won't splash, then pour it into the cooled crust. Even it out with an offset spatula if necessary, smoothing it all the way to the edges.

4. Allow the tart to cool to room temperature or refrigerate it for 1 hour. When it's completely cool, top it with Whipped Cream with Frangelico. Garnish with candied peanuts, chocolate shavings, and/or Caramel Sauce, as desired.

mixed FRUIT TART

Lemon Curd (page 163)	½ cup
Buttery Shortbread Tart Crust (page 133)	1 recipe, blind baked
Vanilla Pudding Cream (page 146)	½ cup
Kiwi	2
Strawberries	½ pint
Blackberries	½ pint
Blueberries	½ pint
Raspberries	1 pint
Fruit Preserve Glaze (page 153)	2 tablespoons, warmed
Sugar Glaze (page 152)	1 tablespoon

This is a beautiful tart that makes a perfect centerpiece for dessert. Although it will look as if you've planned far ahead, this is just the dessert to make when you have leftover lemon curd or pastry cream on hand, as well as plenty of ripe fruit that's ready to be used.

MAKES ONE 9- TO 10-INCH TART

1. Preheat the oven to 350°F and set the rack in the middle position.

2. Spread the lemon curd on top of the cooled tart crust. Smooth it with an offset spatula. Spread the pastry cream on top of the lemon curd and smooth it with an offset spatula.

3. Peel and thinly slice the kiwi. Hull all the berries, then wash and dry them. Assemble the fruit in concentric circles—I like to alternate the fruit with each row of circles.

4. Place the tart on a baking sheet and bake it for 25 minutes. Gently apply the Fruit Preserve Glaze and Sugar Glaze and bake for 5 minutes longer. Cool the tart completely before serving.

APRICOT TART

One of the first desserts I successfully made was an apricot tart I saw featured on the cover of *Bon Appétit* magazine in the late 1990s. I had never made anything with apricots before, but the picture was so beautiful I had to try it. It inspired me to believe in the creative side of baking.

Vanilla Pudding Cream (page 146)	1 to 2 cups
Pecan Caramel Tart Crust (page 135)	1 recipe, blind baked
Fresh apricots	6 to 8
Mint Syrup (page 152)	2 tablespoons
Fruit Preserve Glaze (page 153)	2 tablespoons, warmed
Sugar Glaze (page 152)	2 tablespoons

◇◇◇◇◇◇◇◇◇◇◇◇◇◇◇◇◇◇◇◇◇◇◇◇◇◇◇◇◇◇◇◇◇◇◇◇◇◇

MAKES ONE 9- TO 10-INCH TART

◇◇◇◇◇◇◇◇◇◇◇◇◇◇◇◇◇◇◇◇◇◇◇◇◇◇◇◇◇◇◇◇◇◇◇◇◇◇

1. Preheat the oven to 350°F.

2. Spoon the Vanilla Pudding Cream over the cooled crust to the depth you desire and smooth it out with an offset spatula, leaving a 1-inch border between the edge of the pastry cream and the tart rim.

3. Pit the apricots and cut them in half. Arrange the halves, cut side down, on top of the cream, leaving some room between them. Lightly sprinkle the Mint Syrup over the top of the filling.

4. Place the pan on top of a baking sheet and bake for 25 minutes, until the tart is aromatic. Remove the tart but leave the oven on. Allow tart to cool to room temperature.

5. Gently brush on the warmed Fruit Preserve Glaze and Sugar Glaze with a pastry brush and bake for 5 minutes longer. Cool the tart completely before serving.

RASPBERRY-LEMON TART

Make this tart when raspberries are in peak season and afford-able. It's a refreshing dessert that's as lovely to look at as to eat.

◇◇
MAKES ONE 9- TO 10-INCH TART
◇◇

Lemon juice	1 cup (from about 8 lemons)
Lemon zest, finely grated	2 tablespoons
Cornstarch	1 tablespoon
Superfine granulated sugar	1½ cups
Eggs	4
Egg yolks	4
Unsalted butter	½ cup (1 stick)
Sea salt	⅛ teaspoon
Lemon Shortbread Tart Crust (page 137)	1 recipe, blind baked
Fresh raspberries	1 pint
Fruit Preserve Glaze (page 153)	2 tablespoons, warmed
Sugar Glaze (page 152)	1 tablespoon

1. Preheat the oven to 350°F and set the rack in the middle position.

2. Combine the lemon juice and zest, cornstarch, sugar, eggs, egg yolks, butter, and salt in a small, heavy-bottomed sauce-pan and whisk slowly and continuously over medium to high heat until the mixture begins to simmer, 12 to 15 minutes. Do not walk away from the stove once you begin cooking the mixture—the contents can scorch easily. Strain the custard through a fine-mesh sieve into a heatproof bowl to capture any egg proteins and pieces of lemon zest. Place a piece of plastic film directly on the surface of the custard to prevent a skin from forming and refrigerate for at least 1 hour. Only about half the lemon curd will be used—store the remainder in an airtight container in the refrigerator for up to 2 weeks.

3. Spread 1 cup of the lemon curd onto the cooled tart crust, leaving a ½-inch border around the edge, so that the layer of curd is about ¼ inch high.

4. Place the raspberries, stem side down, on the curd begin-ning in the center and working outward in tight concentric circles.

5. Place the tart on a baking sheet and bake for 25 minutes.

6. Gently brush on the warmed Fruit Preserve Glaze and Sugar Glaze with a pastry brush and bake for 5 minutes longer. Allow the tart to cool completely before serving.

BLACK PLUM TART

Vanilla Pudding Cream (page 146)	1 cup
Buttery Shortbread Tart Crust (page 133)	1 recipe, blind baked
Black plums	8 to 10
Aniseeds, whole	1 tablespoon (optional)
Fruit Preserve Glaze (page 153)	3 tablespoons, warmed
Sugar Glaze (page 152)	1 tablespoon

Few desserts live forever in my mind, but the combination of black plums and anise shown to me in a simple tart well before I opened CakeLove has lingered in my memory. I can't even remember where I had it, but my longing for the flavor is still with me. Sadly, I don't get a chance to serve it often since most people don't really care for anise. It's optional, but if it was just for you and me, I would include it.

I recommend using the shortbread crust. Because plums are very wet, the shortbread is better suited to absorb some of the juices that run off during baking. The tricks to a beautiful presentation of the fruit are to use a very sharp paring knife and have lots of patience.

MAKES ONE 9- TO 10-INCH TART

1. Preheat the oven to 350°F and set the rack in the middle position.

2. Spread the Vanilla Pudding Cream on top of the cooled tart crust. Smooth with an offset spatula.

3. Cut the plums in half and remove the stones. Thinly slice the plum halves evenly and arrange them in neat rows on top of the cream. Sprinkle the aniseeds over the fruit if using.

4. Place the tart on a baking sheet and bake for 25 minutes. Gently apply the Fruit Preserve Glaze and Sugar Glaze and bake for 5 minutes longer. Cool the tart completely before serving.

CHAPTER FIVE

SAVORY PIES

I've enjoyed cooking my whole life, but cakes and pies have not always been the center of my focus in the kitchen. The first recipe I can remember following was a barbeque sauce for pork ribs. I love cooking savory foods—probably a little bit more than baking—but sharing baked goods is always a lot more fun.

Because pies have a versatility that's distinctly different than cakes, I wanted to take this opportunity to share just a few of the recipes I make at home with my family so you can share them with yours.

Ever since I started cooking I've dreamed up recipes that tend to be a little on the elaborate side. I enjoy mixing flavors from a variety of sources, and the lengthy ingredient lists reflect my passion for flavors. Sometimes drawing out the right flavors just takes certain steps, not all of which can be simplified to a short, carefree process. It's a labor of love, and the wonderful smells and sensations that come from a commitment to cooking from scratch are always worthwhile.

APPLE LASAGNA

One of my good friends and longtime colleagues at CakeLove brought me this recipe. Cynthia is known for working all day at CakeLove, then turning right around and catering events for her friends and family. She's always combing the culinary landscape for what's new and unusual. This is one of her favorite surprises, and it gets rave reviews wherever she brings it. Any lasagna noodle will work here—no boil or the traditional type. This also presents well as individually sized dishes.

Sea salt	to taste
Superfine granulated sugar	for sprinkling
Granny Smith or other tart, crisp apples	2 pounds
Unsalted butter	2 tablespoons
Dark brown sugar	2 tablespoons, packed
Water	1 tablespoon
Dried cranberries or raisins	¼ cup
Cinnamon	¼ teaspoon
Nutmeg, freshly grated	⅛ teaspoon
Lasagna noodles	1 pound, cooked according to package directions
Honey Sage Pastry Cream (page 151)	1 recipe
Walnuts, chopped	¼ cup

MAKES ONE 9-BY-13-INCH CASSEROLE

1. Preheat the oven to 350°F and place a rack in the bottom position. Butter a 9-by-13-inch baking dish and sprinkle it with salt and sugar.

2. Peel, core, and slice the apples ¼ inch thick. Put them in a medium-size, heavy-bottomed saucepan with the butter, brown sugar, and water. Cook the mixture over low heat for 5 minutes. Stir in the cranberries and spices and set the pan aside.

3. Cover the bottom of the prepared dish with a single layer of lasagna noodles. Spread a layer of the apple mixture over the noodles. Repeat twice more for a total of three layers.

4. Spoon the pastry cream over the top layer of apples and sprinkle with walnuts.

5. Bake the casserole for 20 to 25 minutes. Allow it to cool before serving.

MEATBALL PIE

Mozzarella cheese, freshly shredded	8 ounces, or more as desired
Parmesan cheese, freshly grated	4 to 6 ounces
Egg	1
Dough for Cheese Piecrust (page 58)	1 recipe
Homemade Meatballs (page 173)	10 to 12 (2-ounce) meatballs
Homemade Tomato Sauce (page 174)	4 cups
Sea salt	to taste
Black pepper, freshly ground	to taste
Dried or minced herbs (any combination of thyme, basil, rosemary, or oregano)	for sprinkling

This extravaganza was inspired by a holiday meal of fresh pasta, meatballs, and marinara made by my friend Jay. Meatballs are one of those foods I senselessly stayed away from for years when I left red meat for a lighter lifestyle. With kids it's hard to be that selective, so now that I've come back, it's remarkable how delicious they can be! I don't follow the Italian tradition of mixing ground beef, veal, and pork—my meatballs are a mixture of beef and turkey, which makes them lighter.

There are a lot of steps to this one, so don't worry if you need to take a shortcut or make life more simple by using jarred red sauce. If you have the time to make all three parts from scratch, then by all means, pour yourself a glass of wine and enjoy it. The recipes should yield enough meatballs and sauce for one Meatball Pie. Don't hold back on the cheese, either. A cheesy filling really makes this dish complete, so add more if you want it.

MAKES ONE DEEP-DISH PIE TO SERVE 8,
OR ABOUT 15 MINI PIES

1. Preheat the oven to 375°F.

2. Combine the mozzarella and Parmesan in a bowl and set it aside. Whisk together the egg and wine and set aside.

3. To make mini pies, for each pie place a 2-ounce piece of dough between two sheets of parchment paper and roll it into a 4-inch round.

4. A little off center, add 1 to 2 meatballs, ¼ cup sauce, and ½ cup of the mixed cheeses.

5. Fold the dough over the filling and crimp the edges. Place the pies on a parchment-lined baking sheet.

6. Brush the pies with the egg wash and sprinkle them with salt, pepper, and dried or minced herbs.

7. To make a family-size casserole, take about two thirds of the dough, place it between two sheets of parchment, and roll it into an 11- to 12-inch round; gently fit it into a deep-dish pie pan.

8. Spread a thin layer of tomato sauce in the bottom of the crust, about ¼ cup, followed by a single layer of meatballs, the mixed cheeses, a sprinkling of the dried or minced herbs, and salt and pepper. Repeat to fill the pie.

9. Roll the remaining one third of the dough into a round a little less than ⅛ inch thick and large enough to cover the pie. Lay the round across the top, cut steam vents into it, and crimp the edges.

10. Brush the top of the pie with the egg wash and sprinkle it with salt, pepper, and more dried or minced herbs.

11. Bake the mini pies for 15 to 20 minutes or the larger pie for 35 to 40 minutes. Allow the pies to cool slightly before serving.

make it first
HOMEMADE MEATBALLS

MAKES 10 TO 12 (2-OUNCE) MEATBALLS,
ENOUGH FOR ONE PIE

1. In a large bowl, combine the meats, salt, pepper, Parmesan, thyme, rosemary, paprika, nutmeg, onion, garlic, mozzarella, egg, and 2 tablespoons of the bread crumbs. Using your hands or a wooden spoon, mix thoroughly.

2. Place the remaining bread crumbs in a quart-size plastic container. Lightly form about 2 tablespoons of the meat mixture into a ball and drop it into the bread crumbs. Quickly rotate the container so the meatball becomes coated with bread crumbs.

3. Place the formed meatballs on a parchment-lined baking sheet and refrigerate them for 30 minutes.

4. Preheat the oven to 300°F.

5. Place the oil and butter in a 6-quart saucepan or other high-sided pan over medium to high heat. Once the oil is hot enough to make a tester piece of meat sizzle, transfer the meatballs into the oil with tongs. Put in enough meatballs to fill the pot, but don't crowd them or allow them to touch one another.

6. Fry the meatballs for approximately 4 minutes, or until the cooked side is golden brown. Gently turn them using tongs, reduce the heat, and cook for another 5 minutes.

7. Transfer the fried meatballs to a baking sheet and bake them for 10 to 15 minutes.

Organic ground beef (85% lean)	8 ounces
Organic ground turkey	8 ounces
Sea salt	½ teaspoon
Black pepper, freshly ground	½ teaspoon
Parmesan cheese, freshly grated	¼ cup
Fresh thyme, minced	2 teaspoons
Fresh rosemary, minced	1 tablespoon
Smoked paprika	½ teaspoon
Nutmeg, freshly grated	¼ teaspoon
Yellow onion, small dice	½ cup
Garlic	1 clove, pressed
Mozzarella cheese, freshly shredded	¼ cup
Egg, lightly beaten	1
Bread crumbs	1 cup
Olive oil	1 cup
Unsalted butter	2 tablespoons

make it first
HOMEMADE
TOMATO SAUCE

This is a versatile sauce that will work for dishes well beyond the Meatball Pie. Scratch-made tomato sauce takes just a few minutes to get started, then it's simply a matter of letting it cook down to concentrate the flavors. I made my first batch of tomato sauce way back when I was in high school. It remains one of my favorite sauces to make, and I throw in something different every time. This is a souped-up version that draws its depth of flavors from a blend of herbs and caramelized bits of bacon, onion, and garlic.

Uncured bacon	1 slice, cut into small pieces
Olive oil	2 tablespoons
Unsalted butter	1 tablespoon
Sea salt	½ teaspoon, plus more to taste
Basil, chopped	2 tablespoons
Fresh rosemary, minced (leaves only) or left whole	1 sprig
Fresh thyme, minced	2 tablespoons
Yellow onion	½ large, chopped
Garlic cloves	3, thinly sliced or crushed
Diced tomatoes	1 (12-ounce) can
Crushed tomatoes	1 (28-ounce) can
Tomato paste	4 tablespoons
Chicken stock	1 cup
Red wine	¼ cup
Black pepper, freshly ground	to taste

MAKES ABOUT 1 QUART, ENOUGH FOR ONE PIE

1. Brown the bacon over medium heat in a 6-quart saucepan. Remove the bacon and set aside.

2. Drain off the bacon grease, if desired. Add the oil, butter, and ½ teaspoon salt to the saucepan, followed by half of the basil leaves and the rosemary, thyme, onion, and garlic. Stir, then cook over medium heat until the onion is translucent and the garlic is just golden. Do not let it brown.

3. Add the tomatoes, tomato paste, stock, and wine. Season with salt and pepper to taste, add the cooked bacon, and simmer for 1 hour. Taste and season with more salt and pepper, if needed, and add the remaining basil leaves.

CHICKEN POT PIE

Chicken pot pie really brings out the smiles when presented at the dinner table, especially on cold winter evenings. Don't be intimidated by the separate elements of this recipe. It's really simple and is worth the effort required to play out all the parts. The key to a great pot pie is the sauce, which I feel is best when made separately from the chicken and vegetables. Make the crusts ahead of time and keep them in the freezer to reduce your prep time.

◇◇

MAKES ONE 9-INCH POT PIE

◇◇

Dough for Paprika Butter Crust or British Short-Crust Pastry (page 60 or 42)	1 recipe
Egg	1
Worcestershire sauce	⅛ teaspoon
Milk	3 cups
Chicken and Vegetables (page 178)	1 recipe
Unsalted butter	4 tablespoons (½ stick)
Unbleached all-purpose flour	3 tablespoons
Sea salt	⅛ teaspoon, or to taste
Black pepper, freshly ground	to taste

1. Roll out the dough for the bottom crust and use it to line a 9-inch pie pan; set aside. In a small bowl, lightly beat the egg, Worcestershire, and ¼ teaspoon of the milk, and set aside.

2. Preheat the oven to 375°F and set the rack in the center position.

3. In a mixing bowl, toss together 2 to 3 cups each of the cooked chicken and vegetables in a bowl, then spread the mixture in the unbaked piecrust.

4. Roll the dough for the top crust into a round large enough to cover the dish and set it aside.

5. Make the béchamel sauce: In a medium-size, heavy-bottomed saucepan, melt the butter and add the flour and salt. Stir together until the roux turns light brown.

6. Whisk in the remaining milk. It will bubble vigorously—that's okay. Stir occasionally as the sauce simmers, and cook for 5 to 7 minutes, until it thickens. Taste and add a touch more salt if needed.

7. Pour 2 to 3 cups of this béchamel sauce evenly over the filling in the pie.

8. Lay the top crust over the filling, crimp the edges, and apply the egg wash, using a pastry brush. Sprinkle with salt and pepper if desired.

9. Set the pie pan on a baking sheet and bake for 35 to 45 minutes, until the top crust is golden and the sauce is bubbling lightly.

VARIATION

Individual Chicken Pot Pies—These are great because they help cut down on the squabbles at the dinner table—everyone wants their fair share of crust! To make them, butter eight to ten 1-cup baking dishes or ramekins and lightly sprinkle them with salt. Divide the dough into 2-ounce portions and roll them into rounds about 4 inches across. Brush the rounds lightly with flour, then gently fit them into the prepared dishes. Fill each pie with ¼ cup vegetables, followed by ¼ cup chicken, and a final ¼ cup vegetables. Pour ⅓ cup béchamel sauce on top of each pie and gently fold the edges of the crust to the center. Brush the tops with the egg wash. Bake the pies for 30 minutes.

CHICKEN AND VEGETABLES

Olive oil	3 tablespoons
Chicken, cut up into pieces	1 whole
Onion	1 medium, chopped
Sea salt	1½ teaspoons
Black pepper, freshly ground	1 teaspoon
Garlic	3 cloves, sliced
Fresh rosemary, minced	1 tablespoon
Fresh thyme, minced	1 tablespoon
Chicken stock	1 quart, plus more as needed
Carrots	3, peeled and sliced
Celery	3 stalks, chopped
Peas, fresh or frozen	1½ cups

MAKES ENOUGH FOR ONE CHICKEN POT PIE

1. Heat the oil in a 6-quart saucepan over medium heat. Add the chicken, onion, salt, and pepper. Loosely cover the pan to accelerate the cooking.

2. After 4 to 5 minutes, turn the chicken and add the garlic, rosemary, and thyme. After 2 minutes, add the stock and stir well, scraping the bottom of the pan to release any caramelized bits of chicken or onion. Replace the cover and cook for 15 to 20 minutes, checking to be sure the liquid doesn't evaporate. To prevent scorching, keep a small amount of liquid in the bottom of the pot; add more stock if the liquid evaporates.

3. Remove the chicken from the pan and set it aside to cool. Add the carrots and celery to the liquid and simmer for 3 to 5 minutes. Remove them with a slotted spoon and combine in a bowl with the peas. Any leftover juice remaining in the pot can be mixed with the béchamel sauce (page 175) before you assemble the pie, if desired.

4. Use two forks to pull the chicken meat from the bones and skin, shredding it into bite-size pieces. Set the meat aside in a bowl to cool slightly.

SHEPHERD'S PIE

For a cold, wintry afternoon, I like tinkering in the kitchen to make a hearty beef stew baked with a topping of cheesy mashed potatoes. The crispy taters are what it's all about, and everything gets cooked in one large pot.

ONE CASSEROLE TO SERVE 6 TO 8

Olive oil	2 tablespoons
Sea salt	1 teaspoon
Yellow onions	2, diced
Garlic cloves	3, minced or pressed
Celery stalks	2, diced
Carrots	4, chopped
Fingerling or new red potatoes, chopped	2 cups
Beef, top round or sirloin	2 pounds, cut into ½-inch cubes
Black pepper, freshly ground	1 teaspoon
Paprika	1 teaspoon
Beef stock	4 cups
Red wine	½ cup
Rosemary	2 sprigs
Sage, chopped	2 tablespoons
Garlic powder	1 teaspoon
Onion powder	1 teaspoon
Unsalted butter	4 tablespoons (½ stick)
Unbleached all-purpose flour	2 tablespoons
Decadent Potatoes (page 180)	1 recipe

1. Add the oil to a 6-quart, heavy-bottomed stock pot or Dutch oven and warm it over medium heat.

2. Add the salt to the pan, followed by the onion, garlic, celery, carrots, and potatoes. Stir often while the vegetables brown, 5 to 7 minutes.

3. Add the meat, pepper, and paprika and continue to stir while the meat browns, another 5 minutes.

4. Add 3 cups of the stock, the wine, rosemary, sage, and garlic and onion powders. Stir, and reduce the heat to low.

5. Make a roux: Melt the butter in a small, heavy-bottomed saucepan. Stir in the flour and cook until it turns medium brown in color and gives off a nutty aroma. Whisk in the remaining 1 cup stock—it should bubble vigorously. Stir the mixture into the stew.

6. Continue to cook the stew on low heat until it simmers lightly. Raise the burner temperature as needed to maintain a simmer, but cook as slowly as possible to yield tender meat, up to 1½ hours.

7. Preheat the oven to 400°F. Top the stew with the Decadent Potatoes and bake for 25 to 30 minutes, until the potatoes are golden brown across the top.

make it first
DECADENT POTATOES

Russet potatoes, whole	6 (3 pounds)
Unsalted butter	½ cup (1 stick)
Half-and-half	1 cup
Sea salt	½ teaspoon
Black pepper, freshly ground	½ teaspoon
Dried parsley	2 tablespoons
Smoked paprika	2 teaspoons
Dried oregano	1 tablespoon
Dried basil	1 tablespoon
Blue cheese, crumbled	¼ cup
Parmesan cheese, freshly grated	½ cup
Feta cheese, crumbled	¼ cup

Yes, this recipe really does call for three different kinds of cheese—when I say "decadent," I mean it! These ultra-rich mashed potatoes make an incredible topping for the Shepherd's Pie and an equally impressive side dish for a special dinner.

MAKES ENOUGH FOR ONE LARGE PIE

1. Bring a large stockpot of water to a rolling boil. Add the potatoes and cook until they are thoroughly soft, about 1 hour. Meanwhile, prepare an ice bath.

2. When the potatoes are done, reserve ¼ cup of the cooking water from the pot, then drain and dunk the potatoes in the ice bath to stop the cooking process. Peel the potatoes and place them in a large mixing bowl.

3. Add the reserved potato water, butter, half-and-half, salt, pepper, herbs, and cheeses. Mash or stir to thoroughly combine.

4. Use the potatoes as directed in the recipe of your choice or serve them warm as an accompaniment.

VARIATION

To make individual pies, divide the stew among 6 to 8 ramekins and top with the Decadent Potatoes. Bake as directed on page 179.

moroccan-inspired
EGGPLANT AND CARROT PIE

Eggplants	2
Sea salt	2¾ teaspoons, plus more for sprinkling
Olive oil	½ cup plus 1 tablespoon
Carrots	2 pounds
Yellow onion	1, sliced
Garlic cloves	4, sliced thin
Cumin seeds	1 tablespoon
Coriander seeds	1 teaspoon
Smoked paprika	1 tablespoon
Raisins or dried cranberries	¾ cup
Feta cheese, crumbled	1 cup
Black pepper, freshly ground	2 teaspoons
Mint leaves	3 tablespoons, minced
Lime zest	from 1 lime
Lemon zest	from 1 lemon
Cinnamon	2 teaspoons
Unsalted butter	4 tablespoons (½ stick), melted
continued on next page	

The drama of phyllo dough brings a lot of splendor to the table without a lot of effort. Its light flakiness is wonderful for encasing this medley of flavors inspired by North African cuisine.

MAKES ONE CASSEROLE TO SERVE 8

1. Preheat the oven to 400°F and set a rack in the middle.

2. Cut alternating strips of the skin off the eggplants—cut off a ½-inch strip of skin lengthwise, then skip ½ inch and cut off another ½-inch strip and so on, so the eggplant looks striped. This helps keep the eggplant intact but removes a lot of the bulky skin. Toss with 2 teaspoons of the salt and ½ cup of the oil. Spread the eggplant on a baking sheet and roast for 20 minutes. Set aside to cool.

3. Heat 1 tablespoon of the oil in a large, heavy-bottomed saucepan. Add the carrots, onion, garlic, and ¼ teaspoon of the salt and sauté until tender, but not limp. Add the eggplant to the saucepot after the onion has become translucent.

4. Meanwhile, toast the cumin and coriander in a large skillet on the stovetop over medium heat until aromatic, 3 to 4 minutes. Add the paprika to lightly toast for 30 seconds longer, then transfer the spices to a mill and crush them; set the skillet aside without cleaning it.

5. Toss the spice mix with the raisins, feta cheese, ¼ teaspoon of the salt, the pepper, mint, lime and lemon zests, and 1 teaspoon of the cinnamon.

Sugar	1 tablespoon
Phyllo dough	1 package (12 to 16 sheets)
Mint Syrup (page 152)	½ cup
Pomegranate arils	½ cup (from ½ pomegranate)

6. Preheat the oven to 350°F and position racks in the middle and bottom. Prepare a 9-by-13-inch casserole dish by brushing it liberally with some of the melted butter and lightly sprinkling it with the remaining ¼ teaspoon salt and the sugar. Remove the phyllo sheets from their packaging and cover them with a damp cloth.

7. Remove 2 sheets of phyllo from the stack at a time, keeping the remainder covered. Brush them gently with the Mint Syrup, followed by melted butter. Carefully lay the sheets across the casserole dish. Repeat until you have used all the phyllo.

8. Using a slotted spoon, gently scoop the vegetable mix onto the phyllo sheets.

9. Gently fold the phyllo sheets up and loosely gather them over the filling. Brush any exposed phyllo with butter and Mint Syrup. Lightly sprinkle with salt, pepper, and the remaining cinnamon.

10. Bake the casserole for 35 minutes, until the phyllo is lightly toasted brown. Place a sheet pan on the rack directly above the casserole to prevent excessive browning, if necessary.

11. Sprinkle the casserole with fresh pomegranate arils before serving.

POMEGRANATE ARILS

The seeds of a pomegranate are known as arils. To collect intact arils, cut the top from a pomegranate with a paring knife and pry the fruit apart. Holding the fruit in your palm, over a bowl, tap the skin of the pomegranate with a large, heavy spoon to release the arils.

jamaican BEEF PATTIES

FOR THE CRUST	
Unbleached all-purpose or pastry flour	2½ cups (12 ounces)
Sea salt	¼ teaspoon
Turmeric	1 teaspoon
Light brown sugar	1 tablespoon, packed
Egg	1
Cider vinegar	2 teaspoons
Ice water	½ cup
Lard, shortening, or unsalted butter, very cold	14 tablespoons, cut into small pieces
FOR THE GROUND BEEF FILLING	
Unsalted butter	2 tablespoons
Onion	1, thinly sliced
Garlic cloves	4, minced
Ground beef (90 to 95% lean)	1 pound
Egg	1
Milk	½ cup
Bread crumbs	½ cup
Sea salt	1 teaspoon
continued on next page	

A patty is a classic West Indian handheld savory pie that doesn't have to be limited to a ground beef filling—I prefer pulled chicken in mine. Jamaican patties are known for their unusual crust, which gets its bright yellow color from turmeric.

Like a great burger, no matter how well the filling for a beef patty is made, it needs a sauce. Because spice and heat are the main directions of the filling, I like the mouthfeel of Greek yogurt married with a cooling herb such as dill or cilantro.

◇◇◇◇◇◇◇◇◇◇◇◇◇◇◇◇◇◇◇◇◇◇◇◇◇◇◇◇◇◇◇◇
MAKES 12 PATTIES
◇◇◇◇◇◇◇◇◇◇◇◇◇◇◇◇◇◇◇◇◇◇◇◇◇◇◇◇◇◇◇◇

1. Make the crust: Combine the flour, salt, turmeric, and brown sugar in the work bowl of a food processor or standing mixer and mix well.

2. In another bowl, mix together the egg, vinegar, and ice water.

3. Sprinkle the fat pieces over the surface of the flour and pulse to mix until the texture resembles coarse meal. Add the egg mixture and continue to process until a dough comes together—this will take 20 to 30 seconds.

4. Wrap the dough in plastic and chill it for 30 minutes.

5. Meanwhile, make the ground beef filling: In a large, heavy-bottomed saucepan, melt the butter, add the onion and garlic, and sauté until browned and translucent.

6. In a large bowl, combine the meat with the egg, milk, bread crumbs, salt, pepper, curry, cinnamon, cloves, sage, and allspice. Mix well.

7. Add the meat to the pot, reduce the heat to medium-low, and cook slowly. After 5 minutes, add half of the stock and raise the temperature to bring the mixture to a very light simmer. Add the remaining stock and cook it down slowly, about 20 minutes, until the liquid has almost completely evaporated.

8. Preheat the oven to 400°F. Pull off small (2- to 3-ounce) pieces of dough and roll each into a round about 3 inches across. Place ¼ cup filling in the center, moisten the edges, and fold the dough over to make a half moon shape, crimping to seal the edges. Place the patties on a greased baking sheet and bake for 30 to 40 minutes.

9. Meanwhile, combine all the ingredients for the yogurt sauce in a nonreactive bowl, stir well, and refrigerate. Serve the patties warm with the yogurt sauce alongside.

Black pepper, freshly ground	1 teaspoon
Curry powder	½ teaspoon
Cinnamon	¼ teaspoon
Cloves, ground	⅛ teaspoon
Sage, ground	½ teaspoon
Allspice	¼ teaspoon
Beef stock	½ cup
FOR THE YOGURT SAUCE	
Greek yogurt	1 cup
Fresh dill or cilantro, minced	¼ cup
Olive oil	3 tablespoons
Sea salt	½ teaspoon
Cucumbers, peeled and diced	¼ cup
Red onion, minced	2 tablespoons
Balsamic vinegar	2 teaspoons
Superfine granulated sugar	¼ teaspoon

VARIATION

You can easily substitute braised chicken for the ground beef in the filling. Use 1 whole chicken, cut into pieces. Omit the milk and increase the amount of stock to 4 cups (using chicken stock in place of the beef). Cook all the ingredients except the egg together in a covered pot over medium to low heat for about 1 hour. Keep the chicken submerged in the cooking liquid; it will dry out otherwise. Drain off and reserve the liquid. Using your fingers, pull the chicken away from the bone and skin and add it to the work bowl of a food processor. Add the egg and the reserved cooking liquid a little at a time and process it to a fine paste.

INDEX

page references in italic
refer to illustraions

ACKNOWLEDGMENTS

This book was written during a tumultuous period of my life, when I was in mourning over my father's passing. Loss of a loved one is not something you get over, but with time you gain perspective, which helps. This project helped me pour a side of my mind onto pages in a way that brought back many vivid, loving memories of my dad. For that, I'm forever grateful.

It's not possible to create a written work without the input of many individuals who are committed to their craft. I'm lucky enough to have found a team that exemplifies professionalism and was fun to work with. To everyone who had a hand in shaping the outcome of this book, from the taste testers to the printing team to the logistics crew, thank you for all of your support.

I owe a huge debt of gratitude to my mother, who inspired me to follow my heart and introduced me to pies years ago, when I was much shorter. Thank you to my sister, Lenora, who showed me how delicious blueberries and maple syrup can be together as a pie. Your years of baking going all the way back to high school live on in my memories.

Thank you to Joshua Cogan for great pics, once again. Thank you to Lisa Cherkasky for wonderful food styling. Thank you, Alissa Faden, for your creative and consistent design. Thank you to my editor, Jennifer Levesque, and everyone at Stewart, Tabori & Chang for your commitment to this project. Thank you, Kim LaMore, for your commitment to this project, assistance with the photo shoot, and overall extraordinary work at CakeLove. Thank you to the tireless team at CakeLove, who patiently put up with my intrusions in the cake-baking work space to experiment with pies and the endless taste tests!

There are a lot of people I met over the years who gave me pie and crust recipes, talked to me about their best baking memories, tasted my triumphs and tragedies in the kitchen, and gave me words of encouragement. Thank you—your presence in my life helped me reach this point. Thank you for helping me share some of what I love to do.

A special thank-you goes to my wife, Pam, who gives me much more than I could have ever imagined. I am humbled by how lucky I am to have met you.

And the biggest thanks of all goes to my two wonderful girls, Poplar and Leonie! You two make me very proud. I love you so much.

This Old Farm

A Treasury of
Family Farm Memories

Michael Dregni, Editor
Foreword by Roger Welsch

With stories and photographs from Garrison Keillor,
Roger Welsch, E. B. White, Grant Wood, Bob Artley,
Charles Freitag, Bill Holm, Randy Leffingwell,
Andrew Morland, Francis Lee Jaques, Sara Rath,
Sara De Luca, Jim Heynen, Gordon Green,
Patricia Penton Leimbach,
Walter Haskell Hinton, and more.

Voyageur Press

A TOWN SQUARE BOOK

To Beverly Sommers, for sharing her love of E. B. White

Text copyright © 1999 by Voyageur Press
Photographs copyright © 1999 by the photographers and sources noted

Edited by Michael Dregni
Designed by Andrea Rud
Printed in Hong Kong

99   00   01   02   03   5   4   3   2   1

Library of Congress Cataloging-in-Publication Data
   This old farm : a treasury of family farm memories / Michael Dregni, editor.
      p.   cm.
   ISBN 0-89658-411-9
      1. Farm life—United States. 2. Farm life—Canada. 3. Family farms—United States.
   4. Family farms—Canada. I. Dregni, Michael, 1961–
   S521.5.A2T48   1999
   630'.97—dc21   98-37711
                                CIP

Published by Voyageur Press, Inc.
123 North Second Street, P.O. Box 338, Stillwater, MN 55082 U.S.A.
651-430-2210, fax 651-430-2211

Distributed in Europe by Midland Publishing Ltd.
24 The Hollow, Earl Shilton, Leicester LE9 7NA England
Tel: 01455 233747

Educators, fundraisers, premium and gift buyers, publicists, and marketing managers: Looking for creative products and new sales ideas? Voyageur Press books are available at special discounts when purchased in quantities, and special editions can be created to your specifications. For details contact the marketing department at 800-888-9653.

On the endpapers: *Pioneer farmers in Fairdale, North Dakota, in 1912 work their fields with an eight-bottom plow pulled by a Pioneer brand farm tractor made in Winona, Minnesota. (Fred Hultstrand History in Pictures Collection, NDIRS-NDSU, Fargo)*

On the frontispiece: *A farm woman carries bountiful sheaves of wheat. (Photograph by J. C. Allen & Son)*

On the title pages: *A halo of golden morning sun shines over a classic, gable-roofed barn. (Photograph by Ray Atkeson)*

Inset on the title page: *The happy farm family with their brand new Minneapolis-Moline U Series tractor. (Minnesota Historical Society/Minneapolis-Moline archives)*

Riding old Nellie
Facing page: *Old Nellie was always a patient ride for the farm children, even after she had put in a hard day's work in the harness. (Photograph by J. C. Allen & Son)*

Sunset on shed
Page 6: *The red-painted wood of an old shed ages gracefully in the evening sun alongside an antique gas pump and cattle chute. (Photograph by Willard Clay)*

8-30-99   Unique

Acknowledgments

I would like to thank all of the people who helped make this book come to life: John O. Allen and his family's incredible photographic legacy; Bob Artley, whom I remember from my days at the *Worthington Daily Globe*; Keith Baum; Martha Cloutier, Library Associate at North Dakota State University; Sara DeLuca; Charles Freitag, Tom Benda, and everyone at Apple Creek Publishing; Sonja Hillgren, Editor at *Farm Journal*; Bill Holm; Jerry Irwin; Henry J. Kauffman; Randy Leffingwell; Patricia Penton Leimbach; Don Luce, Curator of Exhibits at the James Ford Bell Museum of Natural History, for his assistance and knowledge concerning artist Francis Lee Jaques; Andrew Morland; Sara Rath; Ann Regan of the Minnesota Historical Society Press; Dwight and Laura Sale of Specialist Publishing Company; Orlan Skare; Mark Stanton of Raincoast Books; Les Stegh, Deere & Company archivist; and last but far from least, Roger Welsch.

Contents

Foreword

By Roger Welsch

Humorist Abe Burrows once said, "How ya gonna keep 'em down on the farm, after they've seen the farm?!" I've often applied that witticism to my own piece a land. I hesitate to call it a farm. It's actually little more than a sixty-acre patch of cactus-infested sand and gravel we've tried for twenty-five years to turn into something resembling its official label of "tree farm." It hasn't been easy. "About all that can be said for that place of yours," one local wag opined, "is that if it wasn't there, there would be a hell of a hole down there by the river." And another: "If sand and cockleburs ever come into demand, Rog, you might just be a rich man."

I'd object, but the thing is all those slanders are true. Every word. Anyone with any sense, with any judgment, with any objectivity would look at this scruffy weed patch and say the same thing—although perhaps with more diplomacy.

But it's mine. And it's mine in more than the sense in which a car is mine, or a book, or a hamburger, or even my name. This small fraction of the earth's surface is more like a good wife, or a good dog, or a good set of boots to me. Some of you might cringe at lumping all those things together—especially the part about a wife, but any good wife will understand what a heartfelt compliment that rubric is for any good man. Most of all, a farm is like a wife—or, I suppose, like a husband. I don't say the name "Linda" the same way I say any other name. My Linda is part of me, and I am part of her. Without each other, we are not whole. When I say "farm," referring to this place of ours, well, it almost brings tears to my eyes every time.

The memories! The hopes! The disappointments! The things this land means to me! Brace yourself for a terrible admission: Only once in my entire sixty-two years of life have I threatened to kill someone. It was someone who was about to make a serious attempt to take this place from me, and what was horrifying was that she might have been able to do it. She didn't really want the place; she just didn't want me to have it. I had to tell her coolly and calmly that if she did, I would kill her. I meant it, and I have the feeling that she must have been able to tell from the look in my eyes that I meant it from the bottom of my heart. That I couldn't bear the thought of losing this farm of mine, of living without it.

That's a terrible confession, and I write it with immense discomfort and embarrassment today. But that's how much I love this place. It is like my wife, my children, and a part of my soul. A large part of my soul.

There are other farms in my life too, although not so cherished. I could to this day walk blindfolded around my Uncle Fred and Aunt Mary's farmyard near Yoder, Wyoming, or Uncle Sam and Aunt Emma's near Lingle, even though I haven't been to either place for decades. I remember clearly, at this very moment, the smell of the barns, warm and heavy, the machine sheds, the water in the irrigation ditches, the dust from the haying sweeps. I remember the differences in the taste of the well water at each place, the fly specks on the windows of the empty hired man's shack, the sound of the player piano at Emma and Sam's, the rattle of the arrowheads in the jar in Uncle Fred's front room cupboard. I can see the cats and dog—seven of them, although they have been gone now for what? Probably more than fifty years. I can feel the sting of the wasps, the stench from the hog lot and the potato silage, the soft feel of a cow's flank

All saddled up and nowhere to go
A youngster sits astride his favorite goat ready to ride the range—or at least romp through the farmyard. (Photograph by J. C. Allen & Son)

against my face as I tried to milk like Uncle Fred.

What is it about farm memories like that? Why are they etched so deeply in my psyche? Why do they bring a catch to my heart, almost every time they come to mind? And why are there so many other Americans with an inventory of the same kind of warm, powerful farm memories?

A few years ago a New York publisher sent me on tour to promote a book I had written about rural life. I was dismayed to find that I would be interviewed by media representatives of, for example, a Chicago radio station aimed at an African-American audience, a late-night talk show in Las Vegas, and a social commentator at a radio station in Beverly Hills. These are not the sort of places I would look for people interested in stories about farming and small-town life in the middle of the Great Plains! I complained to the publicist in charge of the tour, but the schedule was set, and I went, goofy as the notion of selling a farm-life book in the city seemed to be.

It didn't take long for me to realize I was wrong. Race and gender, origins and inclinations, politics and religion, area code or zip code, occupation or inclination—none of such differences makes a wit of difference when it comes to a repository, somewhere in the brain, where memories of a farm are stacked and stored. No matter how expensive a suit the person with whom I was talking wore, no matter how old or young, they each and every one instantly pulled out a story about farm life. Some laughed as they told me their experiences; others were stopped in mid-sentence by the tears that blinded them. For some it was a matter of scant moments resting in the shade of a rural elm while Dad fixed a tire on the family car during a vacation. For others, it was a better part of a lifetime spent getting their mail RFD. Some expressed relief that they would never again have to face the agonies of farming; others—most others—lamented how rarely they managed to regain the joys.

That's what the essays in this collection are about—not any specific farm, or even any specific people. The writers in these pages are sympathetic strings, resonating to a harmony we all have within us. Read and see. Aren't these your stories too? Your memories? Don't they make you feel good or feel bad not because of the writer's reactions but because of your own, pulled back from your own rural experiences?

This attachment we all seem to have for farming leaves us curiously dissatisfied. It's not as if we are all on one side of the fence or the other, that we hate the farm or love it. We all treasure the good, tremble before the bad, laugh and cry, avoid and miss the feel of the farm. I firmly believe that is more a product of the farm being a farm, than we being what we are, however.

Recent studies have shown two clear facts that seem to be utterly contradictory. First, farming is one of the most dangerous occupations in America, right up there with mining and logging. Add to that the further dangers of economics, something the logger and miner don't need to worry quite so much about, and the weather, and the markets, and the railroads, and international politics, and domestic politics, and the price of fuel, and . . . Well, you get the idea.

A second survey, however, just as clearly shows that no occupation is quite so personally satisfying as farming.

That's quite a declaration: As dangerous, risky, hard, dirty, and frustrating as this old farm can be, the peace that it brings me is central to my being. Just like taking a wife, or raising a kid, or training a dog, or breaking in new boots. Am I exaggerating the importance of the farms in my life? Well, let me wipe these tears from my eyes, give me a minute to pull myself together again, and I'll tell you about what it was like to have a water fight at Uncle Fred and Aunt Mary's . . . Or to play in the irrigation ditch with my cousins Kathleen, Charlotte, and Janice . . . Or the winter we went without electricity for almost a week . . . Or about the last time the whole family was here for Christmas . . .

Roger Welsch
Primrose Farm
Dannebrog, Nebraska

Fields of plenty
Sumptuous fields of yellow sweet clover and grasses wave in the wind before a white-painted farmstead glowing in the sun. (Photograph by Willard Clay)

This Old Farm

Memories of the farm I lived on for a time in southeastern Minnesota make me feel rich. I remember the elegant old farmhouse with its large kitchen, coal furnace, and my bedroom looking out through the branches of the gigantic oak trees. I remember the beautiful ancient barn with its hayloft where we played. I remember piloting a John Deere tractor from my father's lap at age eight, sitting high above the cornfields and looking out over the corn stalks as far as I could see. And I remember the chickens, cows, farmyard cats and dogs, and my ornery Shetland pony, Charlie.

Memories are what this book is all about. It is a scrapbook of the good times and the bad down on the farm. There are photos of old days, yesterday, and today. There are stories about harvesting grain crops by hand with the aid of a scythe, and tales of the day the future came to the farm in the form of electricity. There are recollections of farm meals, the smells of a farm kitchen, the grace and beauty of barns, and the necessity of outhouses. There are also stories of leaving the farm and of choosing to stay. The stories are nostalgic, sentimental, and sometimes humorous, all paying homage to life on the farm.

The authors of the pieces collected in this anthology come from a wide range of backgrounds and a variety of farming regions in the United States and Canada—grain farms on the Canadian prairie, salt-water farms on the ocean coast, and Midwestern farms ripe with corn.

Among the authors are E. B. White, Garrison Keillor, Bill Holm, Patricia Penton Leimbach, and Ben Logan. Also included are Sara Rath, Jim Heynen, Gordon Green, Sara De Luca, Majorie Myers Douglas, Jerry L. Twedt, Robert Amerson, A. C. Wood, and Henry J. Kauffman.

There is a colorful piece by tractor "rustoration" expert Roger Welsch of CBS TV *Sunday Morning* fame that will inspire all tractor collectors, and a famous vintage essay by comedian Charles "Chic" Sale on a rural carpenter famous for building privies.

The photographs come from a variety of well-known photographers and archives, including Randy Leffingwell, Jerry Irwin, Keith Baum, Andrew Morland, Willard Clay, G. Alan Nelson, Dick Dietrich, Ray Atkeson, Lynn M. Stone, Rick Schafer, Dennis Frates, and the magnificent record of American farm life found in the archives of J. C. Allen & Son.

In addition, there are paintings and other farm art from Charles Freitag, Grant Wood, Walter Haskell Hinton, Francis Lee Jaques, Raymond L. Crouse, and others. Last but not least, there are a selection of drawings by the famous artist Bob Artley, known for his syndicated *Memories of a Former Kid* series.

This book was designed to be part history of the family farm, part tribute, and part just good fun. Enjoy.

Michael Dregni

Sitting pretty on a Johnny Popper
Artist Walter Haskell Hinton created many of the paintings that graced Deere & Company brochures, calendars, and the cover of the firm's famous magazine, The Furrow. *Hinton was adept at evoking the best days on the farm, as shown here in the smiling face of this youth atop his family's tractor. This image appeared on the cover of one of Deere's many brochures for the famous Model A and B tractors. (Deere & Company)*

Chapter 1

The Farming Life

"We come and go, but the land is always here.
And the people who love it and understand it
are the people who own it—for a little while."
—Willa Cather, O Pioneers!, 1913

Farming is special. It is a unique way of life tied to the land and the seasons and the weather, tied to animals and crops, tractors and machinery, to family and hired hands and neighbors. It includes more than its fair share of trials and tribulations, and probably, if it had to be admitted, more than its fair share of good times and rewards that can not be counted on a ledger sheet.

This story serves as an introduction to the farming life and all that is special about it.

Moonrise
Left: *The moon shines above the silos, red barn, and sheds of a classic farmstead. (Photograph by Dick Dietrich)*

"... This Land of Ours"
Above: *Minneapolis-Moline promised that its lineup of Prairie Gold tractors was just what was needed down on the farm. This 1930s advertisement showcased Minne-Mo's R, Z, and U Series tractors, including its pioneering UDLX Comfortractor and R model with fully enclosed cabs.*

The Land Remembers

By Ben Logan

Novelist and filmmaker Ben Logan lives in New York City, although he remains rooted to the southwestern Wisconsin farm where he grew up. Ben's memoir of his family's farm, *The Land Remembers: The Story of a Farm and its People*, is a rare book. His writing is poetic and evocative of all that is good—and difficult—about life on the farm. Through his colorful anecdotes and well-crafted stories, he draws forth images that create an indelible sense of place—and a sense of belonging.

This piece is from the introductory chapters of Ben's memoir, and it also provides a fine introduction to this book. Within the framework of the four seasons on the farm, Ben paints a moving picture of what the farm life means to farmers everywhere.

Once you have lived on the land, been a partner with its moods, secrets, and seasons, you cannot leave. The living land remembers, touching you in unguarded moments, saying, "I am here. You are part of me."

When this happens to me, I go home again, in mind or in person, back to a hilltop world in southwestern Wisconsin. This is the story of that farm and its people. That land is my genesis. I was born there, cradled by the land, and I am always there even though I have been a wanderer.

I cannot leave the land. How can I when a thousand sounds, sights, and smells tell me I am part of it? Let me hear the murmur of talk in the dusk of a summer night and I am sitting again under the big maple tree in the front yard, hearing the voices of people I have loved. Mother listens to the whippoorwills with that look the sound always brings to her face. Father has just come from the oat field across the dusty road.

He sits with a half dozen stems in his hands, running his fingers along the heads of grain, asking the oats if tomorrow is the day harvest should begin.

Let me hear drying plants rattle somewhere in a cold wind and I am with the corn-shredding crew. Men are talking about the hill country. "Why, my father used to say he dropped a milk pail once. By the time it stop rolling, couple days later, it was all the way down in the valley. Fellow who lived there said he hadn't bought a new milk pail in thirty years. Didn't know where they came from, he said, they just rolled in any time he needed one."

There is laughter. A big man slaps his thigh.

"Never happens to me," says another voice. "I got me some square milk pails."

Let me feel the softness of ground carpeted with pine needles and I am lying on my back in the middle of a great grove of trees, looking up to where the swaying tops touch the blue. Around me are my three brothers, and we argue endlessly about the mystery of the pines. Where did they come from? How old are they? Could a tree that's three feet through and eighty feet tall come from a seed not much bigger

"The Cloud"
Many farm youths found ample reasons to halt their chores for a rest while they explored the world around them. Artist Francis Lee Jaques painted this portrait of himself as a boy of twelve or thirteen contemplating the majesty of the clouds as his plow lay idle and his team of horses lunched on prairie grass. It was this fascination with nature that lead Jaques to become an artist, painting and drawing images of the natural world that graced museum dioramas, magazines covers, bird guides, and his own books. (James Ford Bell Museum of Natural History)

than the head of a pin?

Let the smell of mint touch me. I am kneeling along a little stream, the water numbing my hands as I reach for a trout. I feel the fish arch and struggle. I let go, pulling watercress from the water instead.

Let me see a certain color and I am standing beside the threshing machine, grain cascading through my hands. The seeds we planted when snow was spitting down have multiplied a hundred times, returning in a stream of bright gold, still warm with the sunlight of the fields.

Let me hear an odd whirring. I am deep in the woods, following an elusive sound, looking in vain for a last passenger pigeon, a feathered lightning I have never seen, unwilling to believe no person will ever see one again.

Let me look from a window to see sunlight glitter on a winding stream and I am in the one-room schoolhouse in Halls Branch Valley. A young teacher has asked me to stay after school because of a question I asked. Voice full of emotion as it seldom is during the school day, she reads to me of an Indian speaking to his people. He

Planting bean seeds one by one
Using old tobacco cans to carry their seeds, two farm boys walk the rows planting beans by hand. (Photograph by J. C. Allen & Son)

sweeps his hands in a circle, taking in all lands, seas, creatures, and plants, all suns, stars, and moons. "We are a People, one tiny fragment in the immense mosaic of life. What are we without the corn, the rabbit, the sun, the rain, and the deer? Know this, my people: The *all* does not belong to us. We belong to the *all*."

Let me hear seasons changing in the night. It is any season and I am every age I have ever been. Streams are wakening in the spring, rain wets the dust of summer, fallen apples ferment in an orchard, snow pelts the frozen land and puts stocking caps of white on the fence posts.

I cannot leave the land.

The land remembers. It says, "I am here. You are part of me."

There is no neat and easy way to tell the story of a farm. A farm is a process, where everything is related, everything happening at once. It is a circle of life; and there is no logical place to begin a perfect circle. This is an unsolved paradox for me. Part of the folly of our time is the idea that we can see the whole of something by looking at the pieces, one at a time.

Yet how else tell the story of a farm?

There were two hundred sixty acres of cultivated fields, woods, and pasture land sprawled out along the narrow branching ridgetop. There was the cluster of buildings, dominated by the main barn with its stanchions for dairy cows, stalls for work horses. Attached to the barn was a tall silo, which oozed the strong smell of fermented silage when it was filled

Plowing from sunrise to sunset

Above: *An Amish farmer steers his team of six draft horses to pull plow bottoms through the spring fields. On many days, farm work runs from "can" to "can't": From dawn when you first can see to dusk when you can't. (Photograph by Keith Baum)*

"Farming in Canada"

Right: *Tractor and implement makers often published books chock full of how-to advice for farmers. This promotional guidebook to farming in Canada was given away in the late 1940s by the Cockshutt Plow Company of Brantford, Ontario, "For the purpose of assisting Returned Veterans from World War II in their Settlement on the Land."*

and made a marvelous, echoing place to yell into when it was empty. A second barn, mostly for hay and young cattle, had a machine-shed lean-to. An eight-foot-tall wood windbreak connected the two barns. Across the barnyard, like the other side of the compound in a fort, was the great tobacco shed. It stood on poles rather than foundations and it creaked and groaned in the wind.

There were the bulging granary, with bins for oats; a slatted corncrib with white and yellow ears showing; a hog house with roof ventilators turning restlessly in the wind; a milkhouse next to the tall steel-towered windmill; and a woodshed with sticks of oak for the kitchen range and heating stoves.

There was the house. It had two wings, the walls of the old one very thick because the siding hid what it had once been—a log house. "You can say you grew up in a log cabin, even if it doesn't show," Mother used to tell us.

In the yard around the house were lilacs, elms, box elders, junipers, white pines, and one immense soft maple tree that looked as if it had been there forever. On the east side of the yard was the orchard with its overgrown apple, cherry, and plum trees. On the west was the rich black soil of the garden.

The farmstead stood on a hilltop, like a castle, like the center of the world. A dusty road went straight into the woods to the west and wound over knolls and swales to the east until it disappeared down the big hill that led to Halls Branch Valley. Look in any direction and there were other ridges, with dots of houses and barns, and the blue shadows of other ridges still beyond them, each a full world away from the next narrow ridge. Down below, in the valley, was yet another world. The valleys had different trees and animals. Even the seasons were different—watercress stayed green all winter in the valley springs.

Below our orchard, a ravine led down to a timbered hollow which broadened and joined the crooked valley of the Kickapoo River. That ravine and

Covered bridge

Covered bridges were common through much of farming country. The roof and walls kept the bridge route clear of snow and ice, as the suspended bridge flooring could become dangerously slick. The Smith Rapids covered bridge in Price County, Wisconsin, reflects the warming sun on a bright winter day. (Photograph by G. Alan Nelson)

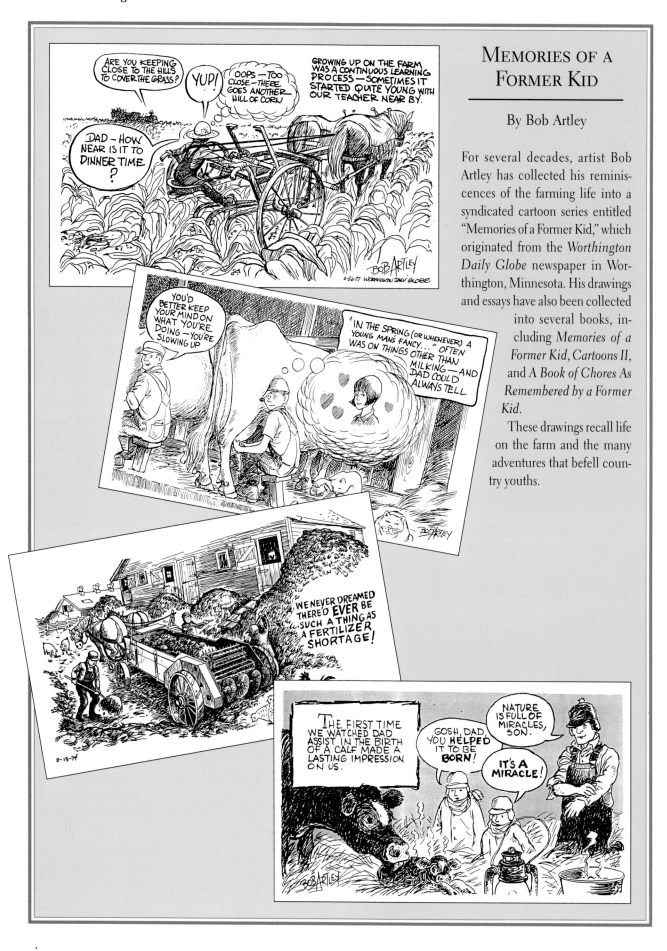

MEMORIES OF A FORMER KID

By Bob Artley

For several decades, artist Bob Artley has collected his reminiscences of the farming life into a syndicated cartoon series entitled "Memories of a Former Kid," which originated from the *Worthington Daily Globe* newspaper in Worthington, Minnesota. His drawings and essays have also been collected into several books, including *Memories of a Former Kid*, *Cartoons II*, and *A Book of Chores As Remembered by a Former Kid*.

These drawings recall life on the farm and the many adventures that befell country youths.

hollow brought to us the whistle of the "Stump Dodgers," the steam locomotives of the Kickapoo Valley and Northern Railroad, so loud on foggy nights the engine seemed to be coming right through the house. That whistle was joined sometimes, when the wind was in the west and the air just right, by the sound of trains along the Mississippi, nine miles to the west.

The nearest neighbors were a half mile away and seemed farther because the buildings were half hidden by a hill and because each farm was its own busy place.

In our own hilltop world there were Father, Mother, and four boys: Laurance, the oldest; then Sam, Junior; then Lee, and me, the youngest. There were two years between each of us. We were as alike as peas in a pod, as different from one another as the four seasons.

There was someone else to make seven of us. Lyle Jackson came as a hired man the year I was born. He stayed on and became such a part of us that even the neighbors sometimes called him the oldest Logan boy.

If the farm had a name before Lyle came, it was soon lost. Lyle, who had grown up near the village of Gays Mills, was used to more people. He took one look out along that isolated ridge, shook his head, and said, "Hell and tooter. We better call it Seldom Seen."

From then on Seldom Seen was the only name ever used for that farm. The seven of us, and the land with all its living things, were like a hive of bees. No matter how fiercely independent any one of us might be, we were each a dependent part of the whole, and we knew that.

Father was the organizer of our partnership with the land. Because he had come from out beyond the hill country, I was always searching for his past, but I could not easily ask him questions, nor could he easily answer. It was as though his earlier years did not belong to us. That part of his life had happened in a foreign language and did not translate into a new place and time.

He came from the Old Country, as he put it. That meant southern Norway and the community of Loga, which was once a little kingdom. "You are descendants of royalty," our Uncle Lou used to tell us.

Born fourth of eight sons and daughters, Father was named Sigvald Hanson Loga. The year was 1880. I know his world included the rising and falling of the tides, storms along a rocky coast, midnight sun and winter snow. I know he fished in open dories, offshore and up into the canyonlike fjords. And always at Christmas there was a sheaf of grain for the birds. What kind of birds in his childhood land? What color? Which ones stayed all winter? I never knew. I didn't ask.

There is a picture in my mind of Father, in the incredibly long summer evenings, running along dark paths close to the cold North Sea. He ran sometimes toward an old mill to surprise whoever, or whatever, made a light shine from the window of that long-deserted place. He would get to the mill and find nothing, no light, no sound except for the rushing water that was no longer harnessed to work for man.

"Yet," Father would say, "my brothers watching me from home said the light never left the window."

"But I was there," he would tell them.

"So was somebody else," they would say.

They pursued that light summer after summer, one running, the others watching, but the end was always the same.

"Maybe it was the reflection of the moon or the Northern Lights," I once suggested.

Father nodded and smiled, "We thought of that. There was no glass in the window."

It was one of the few stories he told me of his boyhood. I loved the mystery of it, though another mystery was even greater—the idea that my father had once been as young as I.

Father ran away from home and went to sea when he was fifteen, on an old schooner sailing with timbers for the coal mines of England. "Windjammers," he called the ships, with a mixture of ridicule and pride. For three years he lived with the windjammers. Then there was a voyage when a great storm took his ship. For eleven days it was carried far out into the open Atlantic. Finally the storm ended. Half starved, the crew rerigged enough sail to get the battered schooner headed back toward Norway. Almost every crewman was from that one little community. They came home to families who thought they were dead.

Father was eighteen then.

Here glimpses of his mother appear, the grandmother I never knew, though she lived to be ninety: a stern-faced woman in a metal picture with mountains in the background, a brass candlestick, a tin box for matches, a letter in a foreign language each Christmas, and a silver spoon inscribed with the words *Sigvald, fra Mudder.*

She gathered her sons after that stormy voyage and told them, "I would rather never see you again than to have you lost, one by one, to the sea."

She brought out the box. To each son went passage money to the New World. To the village silversmith she took a pair of old candlesticks. He melted them down and made for each son a silver serving spoon.

Father and three brothers landed in New York in 1898. At Ellis Island an immigration official suggested they add an "n" to the name Loga to make it "more American." They didn't know if they had a choice or not, so they left Ellis Island with the name Logan.

Father also left that island with "not a word of English, ten dollars in my pocket, and the whole country before me." The ten dollars took him to south central Wisconsin, where his first job was grubbing stumps from newly cleared land. His pay—fifty cents a day. "Young Norwegians were cheaper than blasting powder in those days," he told us.

Father had worked as a hired man on many different farms. He and Lyle talked about their experiences sometimes on summer evenings under the big maple tree. It was endless, adult talk. I could run a mile into the dark woods and come back to find the talk still going on.

They had seen what happens on farms given mostly to tobacco, with the other fields going to ruin. They learned about different combinations of beef, dairy cattle, and hogs. They had worked for men who loved the land, treating it with respect, working with it. Other farmers seemed to hate the land, taking a living from it, giving nothing back.

They found people were different on ridge and valley farms. Some were happier down below where the days were shorter, the wind gentle, storms hidden by steep hillsides. Others were happier on the hilltop, where you could prove yourself by standing against the summer storms and winter blizzards, enduring the stony fields and loneliness, with other ridges beyond yours, like great rollers on the sea.

When he was ready to buy land, Father chose the ridge.

People who came to visit us on our hilltop talked as if they were on an expedition to the end of the world. A cousin of Mother's always drove miles out of the way to avoid the steep hill coming up from Halls Branch Valley. Outsiders just weren't used to the ups and downs of southwestern Wisconsin. It was a small area, missed by the glaciers that had flattened out the country all around it.

Lyle nodded when he first heard about the glaciers. "That figures. Even the ice had sense enough to stay out of these hills. Now wouldn't you think people would be as smart as ice?"

Some of our visitors were from towns. They climbed carefully out of their cars, looking down at the ground with every step, expecting a bear or timber wolf or rattlesnake to get them any minute. They recoiled from every leaf because it might be poison ivy, and they asked questions we couldn't answer. It would have meant educating them about a world they didn't even know existed.

One of the summer-night voices I remember is that of a bachelor neighbor who shaved once a month, whether he needed it or not. He didn't care much for town people. "I got relatives," he said, "that come when the strawberries are ripe and leave before milkingtime. I guess it must be different in town. Don't know. Never lived there. I guess in town a man can be a banker, barber, storekeeper, just be good at one job. A farm needs a man who's some kind of revolving son of a bitch. You got to help calves get born, nursemaid a dozen different crops, be your own blacksmith, cut the testicles out of male pigs, fix machinery, keep the windmill going. . . ."

"Of course, that's just before breakfast," Lyle interrupted with his cat-that-ate-the-canary grin.

The hill country was filled with voices that I remember. Some of them, the older ones mostly, were forever trying to put the past in proper order. I heard them at ice-cream socials, at school picnics, at stores in town, and under our own big maple tree.

"Was it eighteen ninety-five that we didn't get but fourteen inches of rain?"

"I thought it was twelve inches."

"When was it frost came in the middle of August? Never saw so much soft corn in my life."

A small group might come over to Father. "Say, Sam, we been talking about your farm. Wasn't it Banty McPherson who broke the first land?"

"That's what we been told."

"Well, when was that?"

"The deed says eighteen sixty-four."

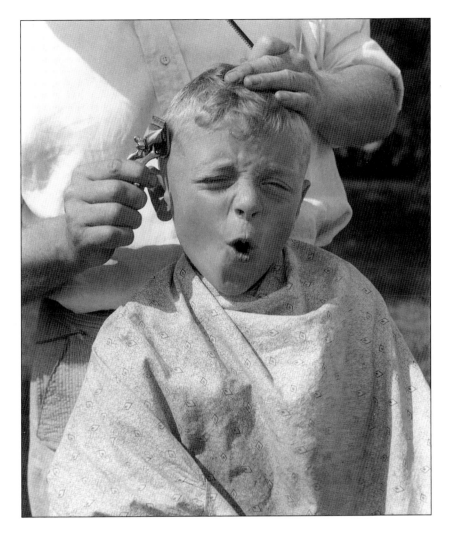

Haircut time
Home haircuts were common down on the farm. With the usual accompanying cries and grimaces, this towheaded youngster gets his locks shaved for the first hot days of summer. (Photograph by J. C. Allen & Son)

"There, I told you! I said the Civil War was still going on."

"Well, I thought Pat Mullaney lived there then. He used to tell about Indians crossing his land just below where the buildings are now. They was carrying lead from some little mines down in Halls Branch. Carried it down to the Kickapoo and took it by canoe clean down to Illinois someplace. Was lead still that scarce after the war was over?"

The voices went on and on, putting events and past years together.

Years were hard to separate on the farm. A year is an arbitrary, calendar thing. Our lives revolved around the seasons. Spring was each year's genesis, the beginning of new life, the awakening of the sleeping land. Summer was heat, sun, harvest, and always work, with muscles aching, shirts covered with dust and sweat and the white rings of salt from earlier sweat.

Fall was the end of harvest, end of the growing season, a glorious burst of color and sun-warmth before killing frost turned the land gray and cold. Fall was a moody time, full of both life and death, a time when we were reminded of the power outside us, reminded that the seasons happen to us. We do not invite the change to come.

Winter was in-between time, the frozen land resting under blowing snow. The farm seemed to shrink in winter, with the farmstead bigger and more important. The animals were inside the barns, the fields were empty. Even the winter birds gathered near the buildings. We were in the house more, and it was a time when we reached out past the frozen fields to explore a bigger world in our books and conversation.

Then, magically, spring again, the rebirth of the rolling seasons, the unfailing promise of the awakening land.

Another perfect bovine day

Above: *Two Guernsey cows share gossip while nestled in a field of dandelions. (Photograph by Lynn M. Stone)*

The Joys of Owning a Massey-Harris Tractor

Facing page: *This 1950s Massey-Harris Buyers' Guide spelled out all of the joys of farming with the pride of Canada, tractors, machinery, and implements from the venerable Massey-Harris. The real message was on the cover, however: Plow your fields with a Massey-Harris 44 tractor, and you'll finish with time left over to nap while Junior wets a line in the old fishing hole.*

"Spring came to the prairie with the suddenness of a meadow lark's song. Overnight the sky traded its winter tang for softness; the snow, already honeycombed with the growing heat of a closer sun, melted—first from the steaming fallow fields, then from the stubble stretches, shrinking finally to uneven patches of white lingering in the barrow pits. Here and there meadow larks were suddenly upon straw stacks, telephone wires, fence posts, their song clear with ineffable exuberance that startled and deepened the prairie silence—each quick and impudent climax of notes leaving behind it a vaster, emptier prairie world. The sky was ideal blue. Crows called; farmers, impatient as though it were the only spring left in the world to them, burning with the hope that this one would not be another dry year, walked out to their implements, looked them over, and planned their seeding—barley here, oats there, wheat there, summer fallow there."

—W. O. Mitchell, *Who Has Seen the Wind*, 1947

MASSEY·HARRIS

Buyers' Guide

A complete line-up of Tractors, Combines, and Implements . . . each better-built, better engineered to make your job of farming easier, faster, more profitable.

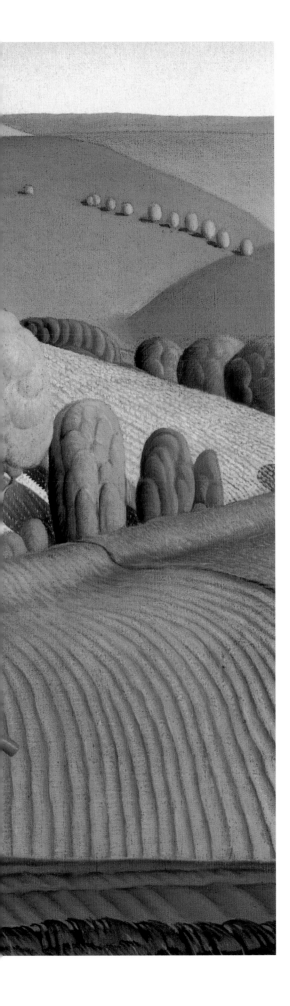

Chapter 2

A Place on Earth

"In this age, art and the farm might seem far apart. Yet words like 'functional,' 'basic,' and 'traditional,' that define modern art, also describe America's farms."
—Eric Sloane, *Our Vanishing Landscape*, 1955

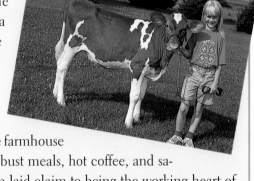

To a farm family, the farmstead was often the center of the universe. It was a small, simple place around which the family's world revolved.

The center of the farmstead was the farmhouse kitchen, source of robust meals, hot coffee, and savory smells. The barn laid claim to being the working heart of a farm, whereas the outhouse privy, also known as the "necessary house," was just that, a necessity. These stories celebrate the place on earth that was the farmstead.

"Fall Plowing"
Left: *Grant Wood was the quintessential artist of the farmlands. His select palette of colors bring life to his images of the Iowa farms and small towns where he was raised. With a technique of full, rounded dimensions and heavy shading, his trees, haystacks, and plants appear ripe and bountiful while his depiction of the rolling hills gives the fields all the glory of the open sea. This painting of a plow at rest before a farm vista was created in 1931. (Deere & Company)*

A girl and her calf
Above: *A proud 4-H contestant shows off her Guernsey calf. (Photograph by Lynn M. Stone)*

The Kitchen

By Jerry L. Twedt

Jerry L. Twedt was born and bred on a farm in rural Roland, Iowa. In his remembrance of things past, *Growing Up In The 40s*, he writes in evocative and colorful prose of his childhood days down on the farm. His reminiscence resurrects the aura of a time when farmers had one foot firmly planted in ages-old traditional values while the other foot was poised to step into the atomic age. It was a time when family farms and family values seemed as permanent as a great red barn—a time that sometimes now seems sadly to be gone with the wind.

The world has moved from the Industrial Age to the dawn of the Computer Age, and much has changed in agriculture during the intervening years. Still, as Jerry writes, the golden days on the farm will forever be bred in a farm family's bones.

The farm kitchen was a combination cook house, meeting hall, communications' center, dining room, bathhouse, first-aid station, study hall, dressing room, play area, and, when necessary, juvenile court. It was truly a family room. The reasons for the kitchen's omnibus character were basic: no indoor bathroom, no central heating, and the farm wife's desire to keep the dining room and parlor clean, in case company dropped by. Odd as it may seem, the kitchen served all of these different functions with a minimum of confusion.

Any discussion of a farm kitchen has to begin with the distinctive aroma. I say distinctive because each one smelled slightly different. They all smelled great. Just different.

The foundation of this difference was the fuel burned in the cook range. Corn cobs gave off a rather acrid odor. Coal was pungent and musty. Wood, which was by far the most pleasant, produced an aromatic, sweet scent. Since these fuels were often used in various combinations, the smells from the firebox was in a constant state of flux, as were the cooking odors, which came from the top of the stove and the oven.

Food preparation took hours, so the indescribable aroma of freshly baked bread would blend with the tangy scent of rhubarb pie. And these, in turn, would mingle with the smells of a simmering pot roast, boiling potatoes, and cooking vegetables picked fresh from the garden. To this bouquet were added flower, spices, molasses, honey, soap, and floor wax. All of these aromas, combined with the perspiration and musk of the women who produced and conducted them, created each kitchen's atmosphere. It was in this atmosphere that the family lived.

The kitchen was generally a light and cheerful room, and almost without exception, the middle area was dominated by a sturdy table covered with a brightly colored oil cloth. It was here the family ate ninety percent of its meals.

When not in use for meals, the table served almost any function ranging from workbench to writ-

Cornerstone of the kitchen

The cast-iron, wood-fired stove was the cornerstone of all farm kitchens. Just as the farm's tractor ruled the fields, the stove was the center of activity within the house. It provided an oven to roast holiday turkeys and a stovetop to prepare everyday meals. It was the source of wondrous cooking smells and the bane of a child's chores, as it needed to be fed with a never-ending supply of wood or corn cobs. And on a cold winter day, the stove also served as a source of heat, making the kitchen glow with warmth. (Photograph by J. C. Allen & Son)

ing desk. And, just as in the movies, it even at times became an operating table. However, instead of a hero with a bullet wound, the patient was usually a newly born pig having trouble breathing.

The cupboards and refrigerator were similar to those found in any town or city kitchen of the period, but the sink was something else, again. Due to no indoor plumbing, there were no faucets. Instead there was a small pump connected to a cistern. The water from this pump was soft rainwater and good only for washing clothes, dishes, and dirty little boys. The drinking water had to be carried in by pail from the deep well outside. Most drinking pails had a porcelain finish and sat on a stand beside the sink or on the sink board. If it were a classy kitchen, the dipper matched the pail.

Another interesting aspect about sinks was their drains. Some drains connected to pipes and emptied themselves into the ground, while others drained into five gallon pails directly below the sink. The problem with the latter system is obvious. Before the farm wife could pour anything down the drain, she had to make sure there was room in the pail. And, when the pail was full, some poor soul had to dump it. I say poor soul because emptying the pail was one of my jobs.

Getting the pail out from beneath the sink was no easy job . . . especially for an uncoordinated boy like myself. Dad had enclosed the sink with a wooden cabinet, so as to hide the pail. In doing so, he put a one-by-two brace beneath the door. This brace did help keep the cabinet solid, but it was a real obstacle in removing the pail. Instead of being able to slide the pail, I had to lift it over that miserable brace. And since the pail was almost always near overflowing, lifting it out of the cabinet without spilling was nearly impossible. My greatest fear was that I would spill all that dirty water over Mother's clean floor. I never did, but there were few times I did not have puddles to mop up.

The heart of any kitchen was the cook range. It was here that all food was prepared, and all canning and baking done. Standing on its squat iron legs, the old cook range looked indestructible. And to a large extent, it really was. With the exception of the heating gauge on the oven, which never seemed to work anyway, there was hardly anything that could go wrong. My mother's range was used until the day it was sold for junk.

All ranges looked pretty much alike. They measured approximately fifty by twenty-five inches, and stood about thirty inches high. On the back of some ranges, raised above the surface about twenty-four inches, were small compartments used to keep food warm. The front of the stove was often decorated. Our range had a white and tan porcelain finish on the oven door.

As you faced the range, the left hand section was the fire box. Above the fire box were "burners" on which the frying and cooking were done. These burners were circular pieces, which could be removed from the range's surface. By doing so, a farm wife could put a skillet or a pot directly over the flame. Below the fire box was a compartment for ashes.

The center of the range was devoted to the oven. It was large and spacious, and with the exception of a heating element, looked much the same as any modern-day oven. The surface above the oven was not nearly as hot as that above the firebox, so it was here the pots were put to simmer and some special baking was done.

To the right of the oven was the reservoir. It held approximately ten gallons of water and was the only source of hot water in any quantity. However, it was not a very dependable source. When the range was not in use, the water quickly cooled.

Between the ages of seven and twelve, I was responsible for the care and fueling of the range. I took over from my brother, Pete, and served until my younger brother, Paul, relieved me. During those years, I was more or less in charge of keeping the cob basket and coal bucket filled, carrying water for the reservoir, and helping Mother clean out the ashes. I say more or less, because Mother had to catch me before I did anything!

What I liked best about the range was the oven door. Not the oven . . . the oven door. After being out on a cold, wintry day, there was no better place to thaw out than sitting on the oven door. The heat would penetrate my back and spread through the rest of my freezing body like hot syrup saturating a pancake. If my brothers and sisters also had been out, we fought over who would get to sit on the door first. Since Pete was the biggest, he usually won. This brought great cries of anguish from the rest of us, and such statements as, "You always get to sit on the door

Sunrise

Work typically starts on the farm—in the kitchen as well as in the farmyard and fields—at the first sight of the sun. (Photograph by Willard Clay)

first!" and "Just wait 'til I get bigger!" Naturally, Mother was none too thrilled with us sitting on the oven door at all, to say nothing of fighting over who was to sit first. There was always the very real possibility that the door would break. But, she didn't dare yell at us too much because she loved to sit there herself. In fact, Mother was sitting on the oven door the first time she and I had a serious discussion.

It was December of 1941, and I was anxiously awaiting Christmas. Much to my distress, I was told by a fellow first grade classmate that there was no Santa Claus. And, what was worse, only babies believed Santa was real. I certainly didn't want to be considered a baby, so I pretended that I already knew old St. Nick was make-believe. However, the idea of there being no Santa Claus deeply disturbed me, so I asked

Mother about it as soon as I got home from school.

"Mom," I blurted out, "is there really a Santa Claus?"

Mother smiled at me from her seat on the oven door and said, "Of course, there is!"

"Are you sure? Gary told me that Santa Claus was pretend."

Perhaps it was the way I asked the question, but for whatever reason, Mother knew it was time to lay to rest a child's most beautiful illusion. She put me on her lap and, as gently as she could, explained to me that Santa was not a real person, but that he represented the joy and spirit of Christmas.

I solemnly listened to her and then asked the question that was really bothering me. "If Santa Claus doesn't bring the presents, who does?"

Wringing out the wash
The kitchen was the center of the house, and it was headquarters for many tasks, from cooking and baking to the less glamorous chores such as washing clothes. Even the advent of the self-powered washing machine failed to make washing day fun, as the job still required sweat, tears, and muscle to wring the wash through the mangle. (Photograph by J. C. Allen & Son)

"Daddy and I do." Mother replied.

"Oh," I said, jumping up. "OK!"

After all, to a six-year-old, it is not who gives the presents that is important, only that they are given!

During the days leading up to Christmas, the cook range performed a very special task in our home. It baked the lefse.

Lefse, a flat, circular, unleavened bread, was a Christmas delicacy at our home. Probably the best way to describe lefse is to compare it to a potato pancake. They look much alike, only lefse is thinner and larger. To my Norwegian ancestors, lefse was a staple food; but in the years following the emigration to the United States, it became holiday fare.

When the time came to make the lefse, usually in early December, Mother prepared the dough and rolled it out into individual lefses, each a circle measuring about sixteen inches in diameter. Then, Dad baked them on top of the oven portion of the range. Getting the lefse from the table to the stove, and flipping them over so they could bake on both sides, was a delicate operation. To accomplish the task Dad used the small piece of wood that fits in the bottom of a window shade. He carefully eased the stick under the lefse until it was in the center. Then, he gingerly lifted up the stick and carried the lefse to the stove. With a slight flipping motion he laid one half of the lefse on the range. Next, he slowly twisted the stick causing the top half to roll flat onto the stove top. When it

was time to turn the lefse, he repeated the process. Watching Dad bake the lefse was great fun for me. There was drama to it. Would the lefse break or wouldn't it? Would Dad be able to turn it over without tearing it, or wouldn't he? Dad was very good. He seldom ruined one.

Lefse is still made around Roland, but, since there are no more cook ranges, it is now baked on large circular electric lefse grills. The lefse is baked mostly by older women, and then sold to people who love to eat it but do not have the grill or the "know how" to make their own. Unless some of the younger women learn to make lefse, the traditional Christmas dinner of lutefisk and lefse will become only a delicious memory.

Another gastronomic delight which seems to be fading from the scene is homemade bread. There was no smell more pleasant than the aroma of baking bread. It seemed to permeate the air. Just walking into the kitchen made one's mouth water.

When I was small, Friday was Mother's day for baking bread. It was the one day of the week she didn't have to yell at me to get the coal and cobs. While the oven heated, Mother formed the loaves and buns. What I loved most about this was punching the dough back down after it rose.

How Mother knew when the oven was heated to the proper temperature is still a mystery to me. Since the gauge never worked, Mother put her arm into

Canning time

Store-bought vegetables and fruit in tin cans were non-existent way back when—and probably wouldn't have been trusted even if they were available. Home canning required hours of work—and it was dangerous as well, considering the care needed in watching the steam pressure gauge. If a family wanted to eat through the winter months, however, home canning was an essential part of farm life. (Photograph by J. C. Allen & Son)

the oven, paused a moment, then either put more fuel into the fire box or popped in the bread. However she did it, the results were delectable!

One of the depressing aspects of farm life during the nineteenth and early twentieth centuries, was the family's isolation from other people. This situation was dramatically altered when telephone poles and miles of line became a common sight along the country roads. Not only did the telephone connect surrounding farms, it also enabled the rural family to communicate easily with the outside world.

The kitchen was the natural place for the telephone to be installed because it was the central gathering place. Installation there made it convenient to answer one's own calls and handy to listen in on the calls of one's neighbors. The fine art of "rubber necking" was born and nurtured on the rural lines of Ma Bell.

A rural party line often included up to fourteen phones. It will come as no shock to learn that the line was generally busy. Having so many on one line was annoying, but sometimes it proved interesting and even hilarious.

We had the old wooden, wall crank-telephone, the type which has become so dear to antique enthusiasts. Phoning someone on an old crank-telephone was not as simple as just dialing a number. If you wanted to call a person who was not on your line, you had to crank one long ring. This would connect you with

"Central," to whom you would give the number you wished to call. If you did not know the number, you could always just ask for the person by name. The operator knew everybody in the community.

However, if you wanted to call one of those who shared your party line, it was not necessary to go through Central. All you did was crank the ring that was designated in the phone book for that party. For example, our ring was three long and three short. Another farmer might have one long and two short. A third family might have one long and three short. The reason it was necessary to have individual rings was because when you rang one party on a line, the phones of all who shared that line would ring also. It is no wonder then that it was common for two or three parties to answer the same call.

It also was common for four and five way conversations to develop. Two women would be talking. One would ask a question that the second party could not answer. A third woman, who had been rubber necking, would chime in with the answer. Then, someone else would join, and, before you knew it, half the women on the line were talking to each other. These conversations were fun for the women involved, but pity the person who wished to make a call! Those party line group therapy sessions could last for an hour.

"Rubber necking" was considered bad form, but most everyone did it to some extent. Even during short conversations, it was rare not to hear two or three tell-

Mom's homemade pie

Pies were often one of mom's prides. Whether they were filled with freshly gathered fruit or mincemeat, as shown here, homemade pie made life worth living. (Photograph by J. C. Allen & Son)

"Yes," Mother said icily, after a long pause, then hung up.

All the way home from school I was informed that I was rude, inconsiderate, had a big mouth, and had embarrassed Mother terribly. All of which I am sure was true, but I still chuckle when I think about it.

Although Mother was embarrassed by what I did, the situation was far from being as embarrassing as a party line call that took place when she and Dad were first married. The story was told to me as follows.

The owner of the farm my parents rented was going away for the summer and asked if Mother and Dad would care for his dog. They agreed to take the animal, not knowing she was a huge St. Bernard. Another surprise was her name, Myrtle, which also happened to be my mother's name. My crazy uncles enjoyed this coincidence immensely.

Myrtle, the dog, was friendly enough, but had a habit of running away every time she was left untied. So, Dad spent more time than he would have liked, chasing around the countryside after Myrtle, Myrtle the dog that is.

tale clicks of the receivers being lifted. This used to annoy me. . . no, in truth, it made me damn mad! But I never did anything about it until one day I was calling from high school for Mother to come pick me up. She must have been outside the house, because I had to ask Central to ring several times. As I waited, I heard half-a-dozen clicks. By the time Mother answered, I was seething.

"Hello?" Mother said.

"Hello, this is Jerry," I replied. "Wait a minute!"

"What's the matter?"

"I want to make sure everybody is on. Is everyone on?" I asked sarcastically. "I don't want anybody to miss anything!"

There was dead silence on the line.

"Can you come pick me up?" I continued.

One day at noon, when Dad was in eating dinner, he received a call from my Uncle Leonard Twedt, who, at the time, lived about a mile down the road. The conversation went something like this.

"Hello, Harris? This is Leonard."

"Hello, Leonard. How are you?"

"I'm fine. Say, did you know that Myrtle has run away again?"

"No!"

(At this point, there were audible titters from the rubber neckers.)

"I told you to tie her up with a heavier rope," Leonard continued.

"I did. But she's as strong as a ox!"

(The titters became chuckles.)

"Where is she, Leonard?" Dad added.

"She's down here at my place chasing the chickens!"

(The chuckles became open laughter.)

"Chasing chickens, you say." Dad said.

"Yah, what should I do with her?"

"Well, tie her to a tree, and I'll come down and pick her up."

(The rubber neckers were roaring!)

According to Dad, Mother's face was beet-red with anger and embarrassment. I doubt, very much, if any of us five children were conceived that night.

Once a week, on Saturday night, the kitchen was transformed into a bathhouse. A galvanized tub was placed in the middle of the floor. The bath water was heated on the cook range in a large fifteen gallon wash-boiler. The boiler was put on the stove and filled in the late afternoon, so that the water would be hot by seven-thirty. Following supper, the kitchen was closed off from the rest of the house, and by bath time, it was almost like a sauna.

The baths began with the youngest member of the family, Linda, and progressed by age, ending with Dad. For the little children, the tub was fine, but the bigger one grew, the more cramped the tub became. Poor Dad couldn't fit in it at all, and was forced to sit on the edge. Being last, Dad faced another problem, a shortage of hot water. Add this situation to the fact that he was forced to wash himself in water already used by six other people, and it is easy to realize why he desired a modern bathroom as much as Mother.

It all seems quite archaic when compared to present standards. Today, a house with only one bathroom is thought to be primitive. But, it was all we knew, and no one thought much about it. Considering the time, mess, and work involved, however, I think it is understandable why farm families took full baths only once a week.

Odd as it may seem, I look back on the Saturday night bath with fond memories. This is probably because I remember them from a child's perspective. Whatever the reason, the baths were fun. There was the cozy atmosphere of the kitchen itself, which created a sort of drowsy, warm feeling that gave one a sense of well-being. There also was a great deal of laughter and horseplay as one child got out of the tub

and another in. And, when I was older, I had the added thrill of charging through the kitchen when my older sister, Herma, was in the tub. I never saw anything, though. She had the fastest towel in the state!

What I remember best about bath night was listening to the radio. As we had our baths, we would listen to "Truth or Consequences," "Lux Radio Theatre," and the "Iowa Barn Dance Frolic!" The next best thing to going to town and seeing a movie, was listening to "Lux Radio Theatre." I would get so caught up in the story that I would forget to wash. Those were the days when Hollywood was a magical name. When the announcer began the program by saying, "Lux presents Hollywood," I got goose bumps of anticipation. Of all the plays, I still remember, "A Farewell to Arms." At the end, when Henry walked out into the rain, I sat in the tub and cried.

Following "Lux Radio Theatre" was the "Iowa Barn Dance Frolic." It was never as good as the "Grand Ole Opry" from Nashville, but the participants had a lot of fun. The show was broadcast from the KRNT Theatre, Des Moines, and featured the performers from radio station WHO. There was Slim Hayes, Zelda Scott, The Song Fellows, and the program's host, Cliff Carl. For a while, one of the featured acts was the Williams Brothers. Mother remembers Cliff Carl always had to lift the youngest brother, Andy, up on a stool so he could sing into the microphone. It was a warm, happy show, which seemed to be right at home in the steamy kitchen.

The farm kitchen of the 1940's was the most important room in the house, as is its modern day counterpart. Even though the modern farm kitchen is indistinguishable from a suburban kitchen in appearance, it still continues many of the old functions. In it, a farmer and his wife still discuss everything from the price of hogs to which children need what clothing. Ninety percent of their meals are still eaten there. And if a neighbor, relative, or friend drops by, he is still seated at the kitchen table and served a cup of black coffee. In spite of all the rapid, technological changes that have overcome the rest of the farm, the kitchen still maintains its basic character and purpose. It remains much more than just another room . . . it is home.

And God Said: "Let There Be Red"

By Bill Holm

Bill Holm is an uncrowned poet laureate of small towns everywhere. He is part prairie radical, part village agnostic, part town crier, and his writings may remind readers of Sinclair Lewis and Walt Whitman. Ultimately, he has a voice that is all his own.

Bill lives in the small Minnesota prairie town of Minneota, where he was born in 1943. Along with teaching at Southwest State University in Marshall, Minnesota, he has taught American literature at the University of Iceland in Reykjavik and at Xi'an Jiaotong University in central China. He is the author of several books of poems, including *The Dead Get By With Everything* and *Boxelder Bug Variations*, as well as a number of books of essays and prose, such as *The Heart Can Be Filled Anywhere on Earth: Minneota, Minnesota*.

This elegy to the barn comes from Bill's book of essays, *Landscape of Ghosts*, published by Voyageur Press. As he says half in jest in the book's introduction, it is a volume "full of pictures of stuff nobody wants to look at and of essays on subjects no one wants to read about." To too many folk, a barn is just that. To others who grew up on a farm and can call to mind the special smells of a barn, who can remember the joy of playing in a hayloft as sunlight filtered through the roof, and who can still feel in their muscles the myriad barnyard chores they once did, a barn means much more.

"Were you born in a barn?" asked your mother in a sardonic voice after discovering one of your messes, or after having to close a door you had left open in your childhood forgetfulness and sloth. "Just like Jesus," a smart comeback, earned you either the back of a hand or a stern command to bring your chaos into civilized order.

Actually, if your mother thought about that question, and if you were born on a normal farm, she would have realized that it was not an insult at all. The barn, most frequently, was larger, cleaner, better appointed, sometimes warmer, and in its architecture, more elegant than your house. It was all right for human beings to be cramped, uncomfortable, and cold, but cattle, horses, and pigs deserved better, and hay needed to stay drier than children.

The famous old story by Mary E. Wilkins Freeman, "The Revolt of Mother," set in New England, is a sort of prefeminist fable. It could as well have been set in the Midwest. Mother's behavior, rather than making a political statement, is a touchstone of

Hex signs

An old-timer feeds his chickens as he sits in the sun reflected off his red barn. Painted with Pennsylvania Dutch hex signs to ward off evil influences and bring good luck, this classic barn with its stone foundation and walls stands as a timeless monument to farming. (Photograph by Jerry Irwin)

simple rationality. Maybe that's the function of true political gestures: to restore fellow citizens to the light of reason. Father, after promising for too many years to build a new house to replace the cramped wreck in which mother has raised their children almost to adulthood, cannot resist the temptation to build a new barn instead in order to expand his livestock herd. He builds a fine new barn, goes off to dicker for more cattle, and brings home his new stock, only to find that Mother moved into the new barn, stove, four-poster bed, crystal punchbowl, oak rocker, and all—the whole catastrophe. She has no intention of moving back, so the poor livestock have to make do with the old house.

It's a fine comic reversal, so long as you are of Mother's party. Most of my boyhood neighbors in Swede Prairie township would have tried to figure out how to get Mother up to the Cities for a few days to calm her down, so that they could discreetly move her back where she belonged. Then they could proceed to run that silage auger into the east side and buy ten more head.

In the Cities, Father puts on his necktie, snaps shut his briefcase, and goes off in his Volvo every morning to battle the dragon of freeway traffic before doing his daily hunting and gathering at a desk under fluorescent lights in a glass and iron box. He surfaces again into the domestic world after dark, if golf or late meetings have not distracted him on the way home. So goes the old cliché of the American salary man. Like all clichés, it's about half true.

In the other part of this cliché, Mother stays at home in a fine suburban house, vacuuming carpets, dusting bric-a-brac, ferrying daughter to dance class, son to Little League, then stopping at the mall to price new sofas, sideboards, and decorator prints of charming rural scenes before station wagoning back down the cul-de-sac to make ginger cookies and pot roast. The metaphor behind this imaginary family, of course, is that the urban domestic world and the world of business and affairs are invisible to each other, separated by sharp demarcations of space and habit. This

Red barn

Barns don't get any redder than this. With white trim and the ranch's brand painted on the end, a barn and its outbuildings bask in the autumn sun below the Wallowa Mountains of Oregon. (Photograph by Rick Schafer)

"Let there be red . . ."
A well-aged red barn and the fall foliage glow in the autumn sun. (Photograph by Jerry Irwin)

cliché, mostly true, is a primary distinction between urban and rural life.

On a farm, business and domesticity face each other across a narrow yard with iron and intractable faces. They deal with each other, mix, negotiate, interpenetrate, not always gladly, but always necessarily. One sees what the other does at every moment of every day in every season. What is taken from one world is received by the other. These two worlds are a balance scale with manure and a yard light between them. If a new truckload of feeder cattle weights one end, the other rises until a new washing machine or living room suite brings back the balance. The idea of a farm as a happy unity painted by Norman Rockwell is the purest nonsense. The house and the barn are a pair of contraries, often in silent war with one another, at their best in a state of creative tension. The barn is the world of business and affairs. Historically and practically, it wins.

If you drive by almost any deserted farmstead, notice that the barn has outlasted the house. It was better built and better maintained through most of its history. Often a barn went on giving useful service, storing hay, livestock, machinery, long after the house turned into a rest home for mice and pigeons, or a practice target for marauding teenage boys. By the time the barn developed its elegant lean, a harbinger of its end, the house usually suffered a terminal illness and was either cremated or bulldozed into the rock pile.

The only inflexible rule of barn architecture was red—no other color would do. A barn was something like Henry Ford's description of customer options on the Model T. He would make one for you in any color you wanted so long as it was black. Beyond red, barn design provided more avenues for the expression of whimsy, creativity, and newfangled fashion than a house. The gaiety of cupolas; the imaginative trim

SOD HOUSES

"He was building a sod house. The walls had now risen breast-high; in its half-finished condition, the structure resembled more a bulwark against some enemy than anything intended to be a human habitation. And the great heaps of cut sod, piled up in each corner, might well have been the stores of ammunition for defense of the stronghold."
—O. E. Rölvaag, *Giants in the Earth*, 1927

Sod house style
The interior of a North Dakota sod house in 1923 shows much about the life of the prairie pioneers. This large sod home was whitewashed on the inside and featured wood-plank flooring, which was a rarity, as many sod houses merely had stamped dirt floors. The family's patchwork quilt covers the bed, and a mail-order catalog waits on the table. (Fred Hultstrand History in Pictures Collection, NDIRS-NDSU, Fargo)

"Choice lands . . ."
One million acres of choice land awaited adventurous pioneers, as this 1883 advertisement proclaimed. Like other railroads in Canada and the United States, the Chicago & Northwestern sold its land to farmsteaders, who would in turn give the railroads business and a destination. This ad promised that the "Great Wheat Belt" boasted a "climate unsurpassed for healthfulness."

Home sweet home
Many a farmstead in Canada and the United States began with a sod house. Pioneers coming west dug up the earth and stacked the "bricks" of sod to create the walls of a home that often housed the family for years, if not decades. This proud North Dakota farmer poses in front of his sod house in the 1920s. (Fred Hultstrand History in Pictures Collection, NDIRS-NDSU, Fargo)

on a hay barn door; the haughtiness of weather vanes and lightning rods; the sense of height and soaring in a steeply pitched roof; the shape of the barn itself: rectangle, hexagon, circle; the grand size that proclaimed wealth and power; the meticulous stone masonry of the foundation; the ingenious trapdoors and feeding chutes; the narrow medieval stairs into the hay mow; the vaulted cathedral ceilings to keep the alfalfa safe and dry; the nooks and crannies where cats slept between their shifts savaging barn rats and giving apoplexy to pigeons; the imperial rows of orderly stanchions for milk cows; the grand canal of the gutter . . . There was poetry in most barns, but only expository prose in the house. Mrs. Wilkins' revolting mother probably meant to make her children into artists by moving them into the new barn. It's an odd paradox (but then what paradox isn't?) that the world of practical business fed the soul while the house fed the body its everyday hot dish and watery coffee.

Some of the grandest lines of American literature were born in a barn. Long Island was still rural when Walt Whitman grew up there in the 1820s, and he remembered the barns of his own childhood with delight in "Song of Myself."

The big doors of the country barn stand open and ready,
The dried grass of the harvest-time loads the slow-drawn
 wagon,
The clear light plays on the brown gray and green
 intertinged,
The armfuls are pack'd to the sagging mow.

I am there, I help, I came stretch'd atop of the load,
I felt its soft jolts, one leg reclined on the other.
I jump from the cross-beams and seize the clover and
 timothy,
And roll head over heels and tangle my hair full of
 wisps.

If you read those last two lines aloud, you might be tempted to do somersaults all over your living room.

Star barn

Not all beautiful barns are red, as this white barn attests. This stylish barn and accompanying outbuildings in Middletown, Pennsylvania, feature matching cupolas, gothic-arched windows, and a star motif. (Photograph by Keith Baum)

BARN RAISING

By Randy Leffingwell

"Architecturally speaking, the pioneer builder showed his ignorance gracefully. His implements were a square, a compass, a straight-edge, and little else but good sound logic. What resulted was a severe and simple beauty without embellishment."
—Eric Sloane, **American Barns and Covered Bridges**, 1954

Built the old-fashioned way

In Amish farming communities, barns are still built the old-fashioned way: Friends and neighbors gather together to erect the edifice—often in one day's time. Under the leadership of master Amish barn builder Josie Miller, some one hundred volunteer carpenters arrived at this central Ohio farmstead early on a Saturday morning to build a new barn to replace a 150-year-old one that had recently been lost to a fire. "I don't make blueprints," Miller said. "Oh, sure, I make drawings sometimes. To figure the beam lengths. But how it goes up? I know all that." (Photograph by Randy Leffingwell)

Watching the work

Left: *Wives, friends, and daughters of the barn raisers gather to watch the work. At noon, the women serve a large lunch that will give the carpenters sustenance to work into the evening. (Photograph by Randy Leffingwell)*

Raising the roof beams

Below: *At the time of this barn raising, seventy-five-year-old barn builder Josie Miller had been constructing nearly a dozen barns annually since 1940. By 5 P.M. on this Saturday, the walls and roof had been assembled on the prelaid foundation and the roof was shingled. All that was left to do was paint the barn, work that was saved for another day. (Photograph by Randy Leffingwell)*

Does it surprise you that children love hay barns more than churches, school rooms or their own cramped houses?

As a grown man Whitman thought not of the excitement of barns, but of their calm and loveliness, and what could be seen looking out from them.

A Farm Picture

Through the ample open door of the peaceful country barn,
A sunlit pasture field with cattle and horses feeding,
And haze and vista, and the far horizon fading away.

The little scene he paints has been photographed on farm co-op calendars for a long time now, and though a visual cliché, has not lost its power to charm and take us away for a few seconds from the frenzy of our noisy century.

The most famous barn around Minneota when I was a boy belonged to my eccentric cousins, Victor and Elvira Josephson, twins, university educated, the last living children of their wealthy father. They read books, raised an army of cats, never married, and built round buildings. The barn went up around 1910, an experimental design from the University of Minnesota Agriculture Extension, a pre–World War I state-of-the-art cow, horse, and hay house. It sat surrounded by a fine grove next to the Yellow Medicine River, almost invisible from the county road, only the top of the shingled dome and a gleaming cupola peeking above the trees.

Victor and Elvira died a month apart in the mid-sixties. The house burned the night after the sale. The new farmers who bought the land plowed straight up to the river, leaving the round barn for the first time in its history fully exposed to marauding photographers. They rose to the bait with their cameras, and for about fifteen years Kodak made a fortune, developing all-season photographs of that splendid barn.

But no livestock lived there any more: The round barn, since it served no practical purpose, was left to the mercy of weather and decay. The shingles on the vast, steeply curved roof slid off as they rotted randomly, leaving maybe a hundred holes of light forty feet above your head. The effect, like a low sky full of star points, was more romantic and lovely in its dying

than it had ever been while still in good repair. The round roof was an acoustical marvel, too. I practiced opera arias there on sunny afternoons. Even a church choir duffer sounded like Caruso after a passionate Italian phrase reverberated around that roof and bounced back onto the bare wood floor, hayless for the first time in its history. A plainsong would have sounded well, too, but somehow seemed culturally misplaced in the barn of Icelandic agnostics.

Not only eyes and ears were charmed by that barn; the nose loved it best of all. Once cattle and horses have eaten and shat and slept, been born and died in a room, the boards smell of them. The smells of old hay, leather, sour milk, dust, cats, petrified manure, cheap pipe tobacco, haunt you forever in old barns. Oddly, almost no one thinks of those smells as decay, sadness, or failure. There are a kind old quilt pulled over your nose on a blizzardy night. Whoever bottled that smell would earn the gratitude of the human race. One sniff might calm an army or almost make a politician truthful.

It was a sensual old barn too. I once fell in love with an Icelandic woman from the old country, and took her there on a fine summer afternoon. This is what happened.

Round Barn

She and I go to an old round barn by the river.
The barn is full of the smell of old hay.
Wind whistles through missing shingles in the high dome.
Iron stalls are empty now.
We see hoof prints on black dirt, made by cattle long since dead and eaten. From a nail she takes down a horse harness, leather dried and cracked.
"From Iceland," she says, and caresses it.
We walk into the empty hayloft, fifty feet high, shaped like a cathedral dome. The last sunlight blown into the holes in the dome by prairie winds shines the floor like a polished ballroom.
I walk under the dome, open my mouth, and sing — an old Italian song about the lips of Lola the color of cherries.
The sound rolls around the dome and grows.
It comes back to me transformed into horse's neighing.

The barn is gone now, its lumber recycled and its old

Rainbow over machinery shed
The old machinery shed never looks so good as when the rain clears, and a rainbow creates a halo above it. (Photograph by Willard Clay)

cattle yard growing rich soybeans. But the country-side wherever you are will still provide a curious old barn or two for you to visit when your life presents you with the need. Old barns are fine places for singing, for contemplation, for love. If, in old age, you grow crotchety and awkward, and some snarly young attendant snaps at you, "Were you born in a barn?" smile sweetly and answer, "Yes, me and all the other gods . . ."

Privies

By Henry J. Kauffman

Henry J. Kauffman practices what he preaches. Born on a farm in York County, Pennsylvania, he has become proficient at many of the once-widespread crafts associated with farming life. He has taught courses and written books on blacksmithing, pewter spinning, and copper-, tin-, and silversmithing. He is also the author of more than a dozen titles on art associated with the farm, including his studies of *American Axes*, *Architecture of the Pennsylvania Dutch Country*, *Pennsylvania Dutch American Folk Art*, and many more.

In his architectural and social history, *The American Farmhouse*, from which this section is taken, Henry finally gives the lowly outhouse its due. He writes about privies with a tone that is at once technical and at the same time, fun. Finally, the "necessary house" has been raised on a pedestal!

After discussing most of the outbuildings connected with farmhouses, one finally comes to privies. They obviously cannot be bypassed, and one writer about farm buildings maintains that they are the most important of all. At certain times one would happily accept such a statement as the truth.

Perhaps the first problem, particularly for the uninitiated, is to define the word *privy*. After looking in dictionaries, it is found that they are very evasive about the matter. The first dictionary solved the problem in its own way by not including the word. Another dictionary defined privy as "a latrine." The next logical step was to look up the word *latrine*, only to discover that "a latrine is a privy." Another dictionary was very informative by saying that a privy "was a necessary," however, there was no definition for "necessary." Finally, another dictionary solved the problem by not-

ing that a privy was "an outdoor toilet." That statement obviously settles the matter.

One of the first problems in building a privy is to determine its location. In New England some are known to be an appendage to the house, but in Pennsylvania they were usually built in the backyard. Then the distance is a matter between odor versus convenience. The solution varies with each farm site.

After the location is selected, the next problem is to select the material of which it should be built. Most of them are built of wood, either vertical boarding with wide cracks for ventilation, or clapboards, which are virtually airtight. One must decide whether they want snow in the winter or the prospect of great heat in the summer. A few are built of brick or stone, and these are elegant types, usually found with dwellings of either of the two materials. Wooden ones are usually painted to match the color of the house, the color of the trim is also a repeat of the house treatment.

After deciding upon the material, one is confronted with the shape the building should be. These are tough architectural problems. Not having found any

Victorian outhouse

Privy construction has ranged from the classic-yet-simple necessary-house box to flights of whimsy such as this Victorian-style his-and-hers outhouse crowned by a cupola. While barn and farmhouse architecture has been studied, photographed, and analyzed, little due has been given to the biffy. Yet, whether purposeful or fanciful in construction, all have served the same purpose with a grace of their own. (Photograph by Keith Baum)

octagonal or round ones, the only choices left seem to be either square or rectangular. The final decision must be based on the need, namely, will it be a one- or two-seater. If a two-seater is needed, the obvious answer is a rectangular shape, otherwise it should be square.

In any case, the problem of the height of the seats must be reckoned with. In case there are many heights to be accommodated, an average must be struck; however, with growing children the average will constantly change. Perhaps the solution is a three-, four-, or five-seater. One was found in Ohio with two seats the same height. The use of such a facility poses a difficult social problem. No inquiry was made about the solution.

Provision must also be made to fasten the door on both the inside and the outside. Care must be taken so that the fastening facilities do not function at unwanted times. Cases have been known where the outside functioned while the occupant was on the inside, and a more alarming emergency is for the inside retainer to function while the person is on the outside.

There is also a serious matter in ventilating the building. Traditionally there are cut-outs in the door such as hearts, half-moons, diamonds, etcetera. These seem to be very inadequate, since they might only indicate in which wall the door is located. That fact is important to know. Of course many have windows, and presumably they can be opened or closed as the occupant wishes. A few have elaborate windows which seem to be installed permanently.

Then there are matters of interior decor. For example, the floor might be covered with linoleum. This material is very satisfactory for it can be scrubbed each Friday when general housecleaning is done. Maybe the color should be coordinated with that of the exterior. However, none have been found that were painted in the interior. A more elegant treatment might be the use of a braided rug, discarded from household use. This might also be color-coordinated. Rugs are not as satisfactory as linoleum, since occupants often have muddy shoes. One floor visited was made of cement, along with the stools which had "bought" seats. It is obvious that all kinds of variations are found.

In the old days the privy was a depository for obsolete mail-order catalogues. They have been replaced with a modern holder for a roll of toilet tissue.

The scarcity of privies causes one to believe that they are slowly going out of style. After all, a modern bathroom is more convenient and comfortable.

Frosty morning
The dash to the outhouse was never made as quickly as on cold mornings when a new snow had fallen during the night.
(Photograph by G. Alan Nelson)

"When memory keeps me company and moves to smiles or tears,
A weather-beaten object looms through the mist of years.
Behind the house and barn it stood, a hundred years or more,
And hurrying feet a path had made, straight to its swinging door...."
—James Whitcomb Riley, "The Old Backhouse"

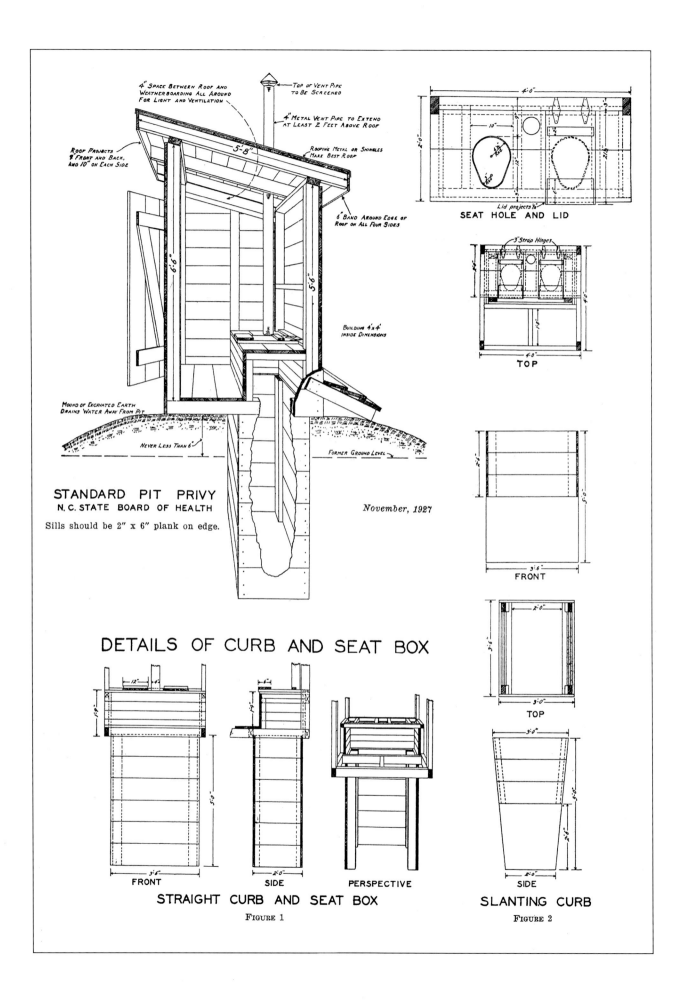

4" SPACE BETWEEN ROOF AND
WEATHERBOARDING ALL AROUND
FOR LIGHT AND VENTILATION

TOP OF VENT PIPE
TO BE SCREENED

4" METAL VENT PIPE TO EXTEND
AT LEAST 2 FEET ABOVE ROOF

ROOF PROJECTS
9" FRONT AND BACK,
AND 10" ON EACH SIDE

ROOFING METAL OR SHINGLES
MAKE BEST ROOF

5'-8"

6'-6"

5'-6"

6" BAND AROUND EDGE OF
ROOF ON ALL FOUR SIDES

BUILDING 4'x 4'
INSIDE DIMENSIONS

MOUND OF EXCAVATED EARTH
DRAINS WATER AWAY FROM PIT

NEVER LESS THAN 6'

FORMER GROUND LEVEL

STANDARD PIT PRIVY
N. C. STATE BOARD OF HEALTH

Sills should be 2" x 6" plank on edge.

November, 1927

SEAT HOLE AND LID

4'-0"

10"

Lid projects ½"

3" Strap Hinges

TOP

4'-0"

2'-6"

FRONT

3'-6"

5'-0"

2'-0"

TOP

3'-6"

3'-0"

3'-0"

SIDE

5'-0"

2'-6"

2'-0"

SLANTING CURB

FIGURE 2

DETAILS OF CURB AND SEAT BOX

12"

FRONT

SIDE

PERSPECTIVE

3'-6"

2'-0"

5'-0"

STRAIGHT CURB AND SEAT BOX

FIGURE 1

The Specialist

By Charles Sale

In 1929, stage actor and comedian Charles "Chic" Sale of Urbana, Illinois, self-published a small book based on one of his vaudville routines concerning a rural carpenter by the name of Lem Putt. The slim volume, titled *The Specialist*, detailed Lem Putt's specialty: He was a champion architect, engineer, and constructor of outhouses. As Sale introduced his character, "Lem Putt—that wasn't his real name—really lived. He was just as sincere in his work as a great painter whose heart is in his canvas; and in this little sketch I have simply tried to bring to you recollections of a man I once knew, who was so rich in odd and likeable traits of character as to make a most lasting impression on my memory."

The little book tickled people's funny bones and found a big market. Published in the midst of the Great Depression, it is still in print to this day and has sold more than two million copies worldwide. In fact, the book struck such a chord with people that it worked its way into popular jargon. Some folk began calling an outhouse not a "Lem Putt" but a "Chic Sale"—to the author's everlasting consternation.

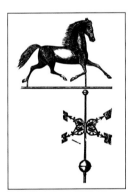

You've heerd a lot of pratin' and prattlin' about this bein' the age of specialization. I'm a carpenter by trade. At one time I could of built a house, barn, church or chicken coop. But I seen the need of a specialist in my line, so I studied her. I got her; she's mine. Gentlemen, you are face to face with the champion privy builder of Sangamon County.

Luke Harkins was my first customer. He heerd about me specializin' and decided to take a chance. I built fer him just the average eight family three holer. With that job my reputation was made, and since then I have devoted all my time and thought to that special line. Of course, when business is slack, I do do a bit paper-hangin' on the side. But my heart is just in privy buildin'. And when I finish a job, I ain't through. I give all my customers six months privy service free gratis. I explained this to Luke, and one day he calls me up and sez: "Lem, I wish you'd come out here; I'm havin' privy trouble."

So I gits in the car and drives out to Luke's place, and hid behind them Baldwins, where I could get a good view of the situation.

It was right in the middle of hayin' time, and them hired hands was goin' in there and stayin' anywheres from forty minutes to an hour. Think of that!

I sez: "Luke, you sure have got privy trouble." So I takes out my kit of tools and goes in to examine the structure.

First I looks at the catalogue hangin' there, thinkin' it might be that; but it wasn't even from a reckonized house. Then I looks at the seats proper and I see what the trouble was. I had made them holes too durn comfortable. So I gets out a scroll saw and cuts 'em square

Biffy blueprint
The North Carolina State Board of Health issued this blueprint advising homebuilders on how to construct the perfect two-hole necessary house. All the details were here for the do-it-yourselfer—except advice on whether to cut a moon or star into the door.

with hard edges. Then I go back and takes up my position as before—me here, the Baldwins here, and the privy there. And I watched them hired hands goin' in and out for nearly two hours; and not one of them was stayin' more than four minutes.

"Luke," I sez, "I've solved her." That's what comes of bein' a specialist, gentlemen.

'Twarn't long after I built that twin job for the school house, and then after that the biggest plant up to date—a eight holer. Elmer Ridgway was down and looked it over. And he come to me one day and sez: "Lem, I seen that eight hole job you done down there at the Corners, and it sure is a dandy; and figgerin' as how I'm goin' to build on the old Robinson property, I thought I'd ask you to kind of estimate on a job for me."

"You come to the right man, Elmer," I sez. "I'll be out as soon as I get the roof on the two-seater I'm puttin' up for the Sheriff."

Couple of days later I drives out to Elmer's place, gettin' there about dinner time. I knocks a couple of times on the door and I see they got a lot of folks to dinner, so not wishin' to disturb 'em, I just sneaks around to the side door and yells, "Hey, Elmer, here I am; where do you want that privy put?"

Elmer comes out and we get to talkin' about a good location. He was all fer puttin' her right alongside a jagged path runnin' by a big Northern Spy.

"I wouldn't do it, Elmer," I sez; "and I'll tell you why. In the first place, her bein' near a tree is bad. There ain't no sound in nature so disconcertin' as the sound of apples droppin' on th' roof. Then another thing, there's a crooked path runnin' by that tree and the soil there ain't adapted to absorbin' moisture. Durin' the rainy season she's likely to be slippery. Take your grandpappy—goin' out there is about the only recreation he gets. He'll go out some rainy night with his nighties flappin' around his legs, and like as not when you come out in the mornin' you'll find him prone in the mud, or maybe skidded off one of them curves and wound up in the corn crib. No, sir," I sez, "put her in a straight line with the house and, if it's all the same to you, have her go past the wood-pile. I'll tell you why.

"Take a woman, fer instance—out she goes. On the way back she'll gather five sticks of wood, and the average woman will make four or five trips a day. There's twenty sticks in the wood box without any

Saturday night bathtime

As the saying went, you took a bath once a week whether you needed it or not—and a dive into the old fishing hole or a dip in the cow's watering trough didn't count for much. Saturday night was traditionally bathtime, and the metal bathtub was brought from its storage place to serve its weekly duty for the whole family. The kitchen was usually the site for bathing, as hot water was available directly from where it had been heated on the wood stove.

trouble. On the other hand, take a timid woman, if she sees any men folks around, she's too bashful to go direct out, so she'll go to the wood-pile, pick up the wood, go back to the house and watch her chance. The average timid woman—especially a new hired girl—I've knowed to make as many as ten trips to the wood-pile before she goes in, regardless. On a good day you'll have your wood box filled by noon, and right there is a savin' of time.

"Now, about the diggin' of her. You can't be too careful about that," I sez; "dig her deep and dig her wide. It's a mighty sight better to have a little privy over a big hole than a big privy over a little hole. Another thing; when you dig her deep you've got her dug; and you ain't got that disconcertin' thought stealin' over you that sooner or later you'll have to dig again.

"And when it comes to construction," I sez, "I can give you joists or beams. Joists make a good job. Beams cost a bit more, but they're worth it. Beams, you might say, will last forever. 'Course, I could give you joists, but take your Aunt Emmy, she ain't gettin' a mite lighter. Some day she might be out there when them joists give way and there she'd be—catched. Another thing you've got to figger on, Elmer," I sez, "is that Odd Fellows picnic in the fall. Them boys is goin' to get in there in fours and sixes, singin' and drinkin', and the like, and I want to tell you there's nothin' breaks up an Odd Fellows picnic quicker than a diggin' party. Beams, I say, every time, and rest secure.

"And about her roof," I sez. "I can give you a lean-to type or a pitch roof. Pitch roofs cost a little more, but some of our best people has lean-tos. If it was fer myself, I'd have a lean-to, and I'll tell you why.

"A lean-to has two less corners fer the wasps to build their nests in; and on a hot August afternoon there ain't nothin so disconcertin' as a lot of wasps buzzin' 'round while you're settin' there doin' a little readin', figgerin', or thinkin'. Another thing," I sez, "a lean-to gives you a high door. Take that son of yours, shootin' up like a weed; don't any of him seem to be turnin' under. If he was tryin' to get under a pitch roof door he'd crack his head everytime. Take a lean-to, Elmer; they ain't stylish, but they're practical.

"Now, about her furnishin's. I can give you a nail or hook for the catalogue, and besides, a box for cobs. You take your pa, for instance; he's of the old school and naturally he'd prefer the box; so put 'em both in, Elmer. Won't cost you a bit more for the box and keeps peace in the family. You can't teach an old dog new tricks," I sez.

"And as long as we're on furnishin's, I'll tell you about a technical point that was put to me the other day. The question was this: 'What is the life, or how long will the average mail order catalogue last, in just the plain, ordinary eight family three holer?' It stumped me for a spell; but this bein' a reasonable question I checked up, and found that by placin' the catalogue in there, say in January— when you get your new one—you should be into the harness section by June; but, of course, that ain't through apple time, and not countin' on too many city visitors, either.

"An' another thing—they've been puttin' so many of those stiff-coloured sheets in the catalogue here lately that it makes it hard to figger. Somethin' really ought to be done about this, and I've thought about takin' it up with Mr. Sears Roebuck hisself.

"As to the latch fer her, I can give you a spool and string, or a hook and eye. The cost of a spool and string is practically nothin', but they ain't positive in action. If somebody comes out and starts rattlin' the door, either the spool or the string is apt to give way, and there you are. But, with a hook and eye she's yours, you might say, for the whole afternoon, if you're so minded. Put on the hook and eye of the best quality 'cause there ain't nothin' that'll rack a man's nerves more than to be sittin' there ponderin', without a good, strong, substantial latch on the door." And he agreed with me.

"Now," I sez, "what about windows; some want 'em, some don't. They ain't so popular as they used to be. If it was me, Elmer, I'd say no windows; and I'll tell you why. Take, fer instance, somebody comin' out— maybe they're just in a hurry or maybe they waited too long. If the door don't open right away and you won't answer 'em, nine times out of ten they'll go 'round and 'round and look in the window, and you don't get the privacy you ought to.

"Now, about ventilators, or the designs I cut in the doors. I can give you stars, diamonds, or crescents— there ain't much choice—all give good service. A lot of people like stars, because they throw a ragged shadder. Others like crescents 'cause they're graceful and simple. Last year we was cuttin' a lot of stars; but this year people are kinda quietin' down and runnin' more to crescents. I do cut twinin' hearts now and then for young married couples; and bunches of grapes for the newly rich. These last two designs come under the head of novelties and I don't very often suggest 'em, because it takes time and runs into money.

"I wouldn't take any snap judgment on her ventilators, Elmer," I sez, "because they've got a lot to do with the beauty of the structure. And don't over-do it, like Doc Turner did. He wanted stars and crescents both, against my better judgment, and now he's sorry. But it's too late; 'cause when I cut 'em, they're cut." And, gentlemen, you can get mighty tired, sittin' day after day lookin' at a ventilator that ain't to your likin'.

"I never use knotty timber. All clean white pine— and I'll tell you why: You take a knot hole; if it doesn't fall out it will get pushed out; and if it comes in the door, nine times out of ten it will be too high to sit there and look out, and just the right height for some snooper to sneak around, peak in—and there you are—catched.

"Now," I sez, "how do you want that door to swing? Openin' in or out?" He said he didn't know. So I sez it should open in. This is the way it works out: "Place yourself in there. The door openin' in, say about forty-five degree. This gives you air and lets the sun beat in. Now, if you hear anybody comin', you can give it a quick shove with your foot and there you are. But if she swings out, where are you? You can't run the risk of havin' her open for air or sun, because if anyone comes, you can't get up off that seat, reach way around and grab 'er without gettin' caught, now can you?" He could see I was right.

So I built his door like all my doors, swingin' in, and, of course, facing east, to get the full benefit of th' sun. And I tell you, gentlemen, there ain't nothin' more restful than to get out there in the mornin', comfortably seated, with th' door about three-fourths open. The old sun, beatin' in on you, sort of relaxes a body—makes you feel m-i-g-h-t-y, m-i-g-h-t-y r-e-s-t-f-u-l.

"Now." I sez, "about the paintin' of her. What color do you want 'er, Elmer?" He said red. "Elmer," I sez, "I can paint her red, and red makes a beautiful job; or I can paint her a bright green, or any one of a half-dozen other colors, and they're all mighty pretty; but it ain't practical to use a single solid color, and I'll tell you why. She's too durn hard to see at night. You need contrast—just like they use on them railroad crossin' bars—so you can see 'em in the dark.

"If I was you, I'd paint her a bright red, with white trimmin's—just like your barn. Then she'll match up nice in the daytime, and you can spot 'er easy at night, when you ain't got much time to go scoutin' around.

"There's a lot of fine points to puttin' up a first-class privy that the average man don't think about. It's no job for an amachoor, take my word on it. There's a whole lot more to it than you can see by just takin' a few squints at your nabor's. Why, one of the worst tragedies around heer in years was because old man Clark's boys thought they knew somethin' about this kind of work, and they didn't.

"Old man Clark—if he's a day he's ninety-seven—lives over there across the holler with his boys. Asked me to come over and estimate on their job. My price

"The Specialist"

The cover of "The Specialist," which has been continuously in print since its publication in 1929. As the book's hero, biffy builder extraordinaire Lem Putt, modestly said, "I seen the need of a specialist in my line. . . ."

was too high; so they decided to do it themselves. And that's where the trouble begun.

"I was doin' a little paper hangin' at the time for that widder that lives down past the old creamery. As I'd drive by I could see the boys a-workin'. Of course, I didn't want to butt in, so used to just holler at 'em on the way by and say, naborly like: 'Hey, boys, see you're doin a little buildin'.' You see, I didn't want to act like I was buttin' in on their work; but I knowed all the time they was going to have trouble with that privy. And they did. From all outside appearance it was a regulation job, but not being experienced along this line, they didn't anchor her.

"You see, I put a 4 by 4 that runs from the top right

straight on down five foot into the ground. That's why you never see any of my jobs upset Hallowe'en night. They might *pull* 'em out, but they'll never upset 'em.

"Here's what happened: They didn' anchor theirs, and they painted it solid red—two bad mistakes.

"Hallowe'en night came along, darker than pitch. Old man Clark was out in there. Some of them devilish nabor boys was out for no good, and they upset 'er with the old man in it.

"Of course, the old man got to callin' and his boys heard the noise. One of 'em sez: 'What's the racket? Somebody must be at the chickens.' So they took the lantern, started out to the chicken shed. They didn't find anything wrong

Dancing around the biffy
A new necessary house was always ample reason to celebrate.

there, and they started back to the house. Then they heerd the dog bark, and one of his boys sez: 'Sounds like that barkin' is over towards the privy.' It bein' painted red, they couldn't see she was upset, so they started over there.

"In the meantime the old man had gotten so confused that he started to crawl out through the hole, yellin' for help all the time. The boys reckonized his voice and come runnin', but just as they got there he lost his holt and fell. After that they just *called*—didn't go near him. So you see what a tragedy that was; and they tell me he has been practically ostercized from society ever since."

Well, time passed, and I finally got Elmer's job done; and, gentlemen, everybody says that, next to my eight holer, it's the finest piece of construction work in the county.

Sometimes, when I get to feelin' blue and thinkin' I hitched my wagon to the wrong star, and may be I should have took up chiropracty or veterany, I just pack the little woman and the kids in the back of my car and start out, aimin' to fetch up at Elmer's place along about dusk.

When we gets to the top of the hill overlookin' his place, we stops. I slips the gear in mutual, and we jest sit there lookin' at that beautiful sight. There sits that privy on that knoll near the wood-pile, painted red and white, mornin' glories growin' up over her and Mr. Sun bathin' her in a burst of yeller color as he drops back of them hills. You can hear the dog barkin' in the distance, bringin' the cows up fer milkin', and the slow squeak of Elmer's windmill pumpin' away day after day the same as me.

As I look at that beautiful picture of my work, I'm proud. I heaves a sigh of satisfaction, my eyes fill up and I sez to myself, "Folks are right when they say that next to my eight holer that's the finest piece of construction work I ever done. I know I done right in Specializin'; I'm sittin' on top of the world; and I hope that boy of mine who is growin' up like a weed keeps up the good work when I'm gone."

With one last look as we pulls away, I slips my arm around the Missus and I sez: "Nora, Elmer don't have to worry, he's a boy that's got hisself a privy, a m-i-g-h-t-y, m-i-g-h-t-y, p-r-e-t-t-y p-r-i-v-y."

Chapter 3

Working the Land

"The sod, which had been slumbering there undisturbed for count-less ages, was tough of fibre and would not give up its hold on the earth without a struggle. It almost had to be turned by main strength, piece by piece; it was a dark brownish colour on the under side—a rich, black mould that gave promise of wonder- ful fertility; it actually gleamed and glistened under the rays of the morning sun, where the plow had carved and polished its upturned face...."
—O. E. Rölvaag, *Giants in the Earth*, 1927

In the early 1800s, the land was tilled with a team of horses pull-ing perhaps one of blacksmith John Deere's pioneering plows. By the dawn of the 1900s, steam power had made inroads onto the largest

farms, whereas small farmers had more horses and sometimes hired men to help them do their work. By the 1920s, the gas-powered farm tractor was becoming a staple of farms through-out North America. In one hundred years, farming had changed forever.

These recollections talk about the changes in working the land and what they meant to the farmer.

Threshing day

Left: *Threshing day in the 1890s brought the whole neighborhood to-gether to help each other with chores that would have been insurmount-able for one farm family alone. With the arrival of the self-powered combine in the 1930s, this sharing of work became a thing of the past. (Fred Hultstrand History in Pictures Collection, NDIRS-NDSU, Fargo)*

"Power"

Above: *The horse's power was replaced by mechanical horsepower on farms starting with the arrival of the great steam tractors in the 1870s. By the 1910s and 1920s, the debut of the Fordson, International Har-vester Farmall, and John Deere's Model D 15/27 tractor meant that work horses were often put out to pasture.*

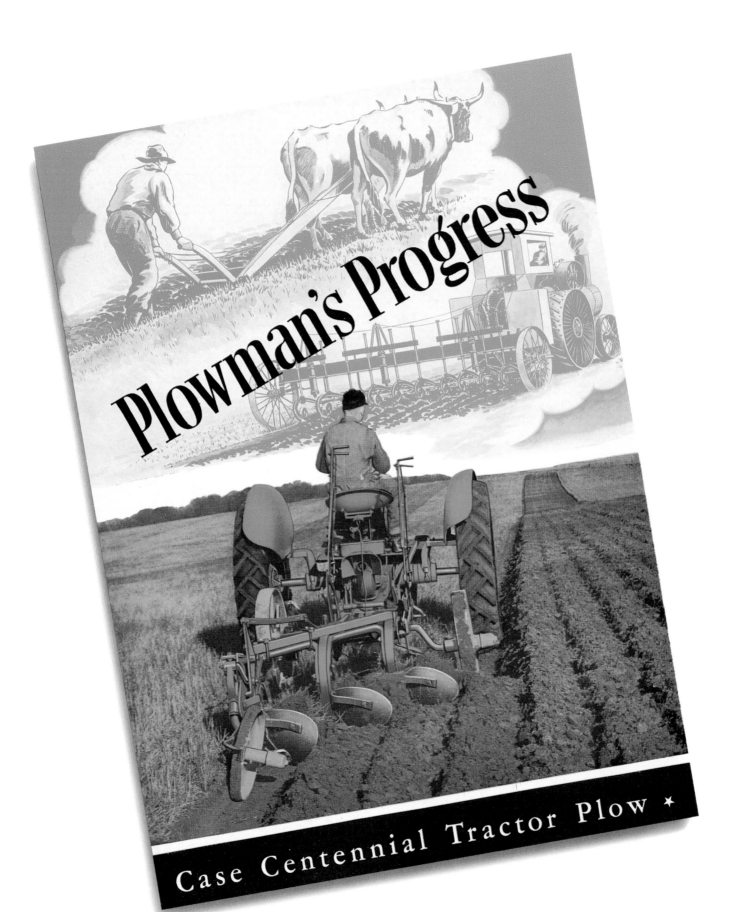

Plowman's Progress

Case Centennial Tractor Plow ★

The Old-Time Harvest Field

By A. C. Wood

Ontario farmer and folk philosopher A. C. Wood wrote eloquently of rural life on the Canadian prairies in his colorful tome, *Old Days on the Farm*, from 1918. He tells of great farming events in those pioneering years, from old-timers's homesteading yarns to the day when the circus came to the nearby town. His book is a rare collection of history and insights into farming lore of another era, written by someone who lived through the years in which agriculture underwent the dramatic change of mechanization.

In this excerpt, he recalls the hard work and great joys in the old-time harvest field, remembering the different eras of harvesting—from cutting grain with scythes to the early self-binding reapers.

And there's the harvest field of other days—another poetical spot, surely. To have seen several lusty men laying low the golden grain with their swinging cradles was a sight to be remembered. I've made sheaves behind a cradler and I once cut two acres of grain with that old-fashioned reaping tool—perhaps I'm qualified to write about the old-time harvest field. It required a man who was a direct descendant of Anak—a strong man mentioned in the Good Book, you know—to cut five acres of grain in a day, and he wouldn't feel like going to a moving picture show when the sun went down.

What a picture that ten-acre wheat-field makes in the August sunshine, gently undulating in golden billows, set in motion by summer zephyrs. Farmer Brown is proud of it, and, with reason. It represents honest toil and the staff of life—the world's bread—and no defence is needed before the court of posterity or any other court for any wealth acquired from it.

It's honest money gotten thataway.

To-morrow the farmer and his two stalwart sons will harvest that field of wheat. The blades of their "grapevines," "turkey wings" or "muleys,"—these were some of the names applied to the different makes of grain cradles of other days,—have been ground to razor keenness on the old grindstone in the shed.

They have to wait an hour or two in the morning for the dew to clear away. They whet their shining blades, those brawny three, and with breasts bared and shirt-sleeves rolled up to shoulders, advance to the charge.

The swish, swish, swish of severing scythes resounds; this, and the rhythmical tinkling of the shorn stems against the cradle blades, is the deathsong of the wheat.

"Plowman's Progress"

The evolution in plowing was aptly illustrated on the cover of this J. I. Case Centennial Plow brochure. The J. I. Case Company of Racine, Wisconsin, was established in 1842 and was one of the pioneers in many aspects of farm machinery.

Those three mighty reapers sway from side to side with steady swing across the field leaving three ribbons of yellow—three well-butted swaths behind.

A few years ago that field was a forest and there are still some stumps as evidence of the mightier growth that fell before the woodman's axe. The ground is uneven, full of "cradle knolls," as the pioneer termed the hillocks left by overturned tree-stumps. It is rough going, but, that dauntless three, in slant array, like wild geese or ducks a-flying, swing and sweep through cereal glades until the long day's task is done and that ten acres of wheat is laid low.

The binding and shocking is a task for the morrow.

Warm work, that cradle swinging—well, I guess yes. Many visits were made that day to the cool grey jug in the hollow stump. A man didn't have to go "east of Suez," as Kipling says, to raise a thirst in cradling days. Let him swing a big, heavy cradle all day long, over uneven ground, and with snags, and snakes, and stones, and stumps, hidden in the grain and he'd have a thirst that would need a whole lot of liquid to quench. In shilling-a-gallon whiskey days they say it was not considered improper for cradlers to take a stone jug to the field, which jug did not contain water. And I've heard stories that cradlers had to be steadied by a man holding them from behind until they'd get the proper swing on. When they'd get rightly under way they could maintain a balance and win through with their swaths.

I well remember our first machine reaper—a big clumsy contraption with a reel to throw the grain onto a platform. It took two men and a team to work it. One man drove and another swept the grain off the shelf or platform when enough had accumulated to make a sheaf. I recall that there was a projection or shelf at the rear of the platform, and on this, as a small boy, I used to ride and let my bare feet trail among and be tickled by the stubbles. Despite the weight of that reaper and that the ground was rough and grain crops heavy, I was permitted to ride by my indulgent father.

Horse power

Happily, even today horse farming is not dead. A team of workhorses pulls a New Holland implement as an Amish boy in Lancaster County, Pennsylvania, works his family's fields. (Photograph by Keith Baum)

Thirsty crew
After a day working the harvest fields in the 1920s, nothing hit the spot like a cup of cool water. (Photograph by J. C. Allen & Son)

Then came the self-raking reaper and it was thought that the acme of perfection had been reached in harvesting machinery. The binding had still to be done by hand. It could never be that any mechanical contrivance might be invented that would make bands of straw and tie sheaves. We never thought of twine being used for such a purpose and, if we had, it's likely we'd have felt that there was not enough string in the wide world for such uses. In those days twine for fishing lines was, on occasion, difficult to get. But inventive ingenuity and the march of progress solved the problem. Now the self-binding reaper holds sway.

"The origin of the word 'tractor' was originally credited to the Hart-Parr Co., in 1906 to replace the longer expression 'gasoline traction engine,' which W.H. Williams, the company's sales manager, who wrote the advertisements, considered too cumbersome. The word actually was coined previously and was used in 1890 in patent 425,000, issued on a tractor invented by George H. Edwards, of Chicago."
—**U.S. Department of Agriculture,**
***Power to Produce,* 1960**

Threshing gang

Above: *A threshing crew poses in the 1910s with the machine that made it all possible, a gigantic steam-powered tractor of the type built by the firms of J. I. Case, Huber, Frick, and many others in Canada and the United States. Such steamers were expensive to purchase and required a full crew of workers to operate, so only large farmers or custom threshing crews could afford one. The machines were also dangerous: If the engineer failed to keep an eye on the pressure gauge, the boiler could—and too often did—explode. (Fred Hultstrand History in Pictures Collection, NDIRS-NDSU, Fargo)*

"Stands Supreme"

Left: *Jerome Increase Case's firm was a pioneer in designing, engineering, and producing farm machinery from steam-powered tractors to threshers to some of the first internal-combustion-engined, lightweight farm tractors. The firm's symbol was the eagle known as "Old Abe," which had been the mascot of a Civil War regiment from Wisconsin.*

Big Load

By Robert Amerson

In his fictionalized memoir, *From the Hidewood: Memories of a Dakota Neighborhood*, Robert Amerson recounts life on his family's farm in the remote Hidewood Hills of eastern South Dakota in the 1930s and 1940s. His stories tell of real events, but they are told in the voice of a novelist. He fills gaps in his memory with details from his imagination. While the stories include chapters on members of his family, they really focus on his own character.

This selection describes a day in the life of the young Bob Amerson, who is caught on the threshold of a new, modern era in farming and events pulling him to another world away from the farm. Yet, this young man still needs to prove himself to the old-timers. In the end, this memoir of a farm is also a coming-of-age story.

Below treeless hills leading to the Hidewood Creek, behind the dark-red barn on Elmer Krause's bottomland place, the threshing rig all morning long had roared and groaned and bellowed, proclaiming its unquestioned primacy in the order of neighborhood life. From the extended nozzle of the pipelike blower a pale yellow plume streamed upward, tufts of straw and chaff first rushing into view against the sky, then seeming to think better of it, quickly losing momentum, wafting wide in gentle arcs onto the conical pile being carefully constructed. Thresherman George Roecker knew how to build a straw pile that would last, would shed inevitable rains and snow melt-off. He had learned his craft from his pioneer father forty years before, running the old steam-engine rigs.

Still, the shape of the straw pile could be only incidental to a thresherman's central responsibilities—to separate out the grain itself, to obtain the most from a farm's harvest. His stubby figure moved about rest-lessly, now stopping in the thin dust at the rear of the big machine to twist the blower gearwheel and direct the flowing puff a few feet farther to one side; now lifting the galvanized metal door of his blower fan, increasing still more this sound of final harvest action, and inspecting a handful of straw for any signs of escaping precious kernels. He clambered up the metal ladder. Standing high atop the vibrating machine, he checked the half-bushel dump counter, caught grain in his palm, hefted it twice, and looked approvingly down at Elmer in the grain wagon attending the spout: "Good, heavy oats," his gestures meant, and the man who had planted it reciprocated with a grin of satisfaction that replied, "Yes, a farmer hopes all year for this."

The thresherman moved in short steps along the vibrating platform between rotating pulleys and chain gears, then paused, feet apart now, chubby hands splayed over his pot belly, bleary eyes squinting in the dust—taking a moment to survey, to monitor, to assess the tone of his noisy monster at work. Out at the far end of the wide power belt, his faithful old Minneapolis-Moline tractor, its yellow paint almost

Farmall workhorse
International Harvester's great Farmall heralded a true revolution on the farm. This gas-powered, lightweight, general-purpose machine could literally "farm all." As one farmer swore after using an experimental Farmall in 1923, "It's homely as the devil, but if you don't want to buy one you'd better stay off the seat." The styled Farmall Model H, like this one, was a tried-and-true workhorse that won praise on many farms. (Photograph by Andrew Morland)

all faded away now, still had the stuff to handle eight bundle teams, two men at a time pitching steadily, one on either side of the feeder. He watched the feeder's relentless crossbars force the side-by-side sheaves below him into the chopping knives that cut the binding twine and pushed headed grain into the roaring teeth of the twenty-eight-inch cylinder. He listened again to the separation process itself: the pounding, shaking, sifting, blowing, the steady grind of gears and chains, the whine of belts and pulleys— sounds of a beautiful, well-oiled machine running smoothly under plenty of power. The sounds of threshing time.

One of the two pitchers at the feeder, Bob—just past his sixteenth birthday and running his own bundle team for the first time this year—kept half an eye on the thresherman. He should have felt good about finally being a real part of threshing. Not today. This was one of those crummy days when everything goes wrong. He knew they must be wondering if he could really handle a man's job.

It had started early that morning at home, after the milking. With the sun already up—Pa had said to hurry because with no dew, threshing could get an early start—Bob, moving fast, had been carrying the cream into the house. Maybe he had been rushing too much; all right, maybe he was a little careless and clumsy, too. Anyway, he had tripped on the porch step, and the whole damned can of cream had gone sloshing all over the cement steps and into Ma's hollyhocks. Great feast for the cats and dogs, but a lot less cream to sell this week. Coming in behind him, Pa had exploded in rare exasperation: "I don't see why the hell you can't be more careful!"

But worse had been the tip-over. Working on his second load of the morning, out where Krauses' oats field started running up the side-hill, he'd made the mistake of tossing too many bundles on one side of the wide rack before switching across the windrow to load from the other side. He had noticed the front corner of the rack sloping and teetering, and he worried as he turned the team up the incline. Then, sure as hell, there she went, the whole rack tipping off the bed and on its side, angled against the stubble ground. Nothing broke, but the few bundles that didn't spill out had to be pitched out anyway; bad enough to have the empty rack to lift back on. Worst

of all was the humiliation. His partner, Vernon—and James Koppman, who was loading in a nearby windrow—had to come to his rescue, hoisting the rack up and over. With the time lost, he'd then had to hurry in with half a load in order not to miss his turn at the feeder. And it really hadn't helped much that Little Henry, in his second year at running a bundle team, had tipped, too, later that morning. Somehow, the men sort of expected Henry occasionally to get careless. The fact remained that good bundle haulers did not tip their racks.

Now, across the feeder, Bob saw that Vernon had nearly finished unloading. And he noticed that the thresherman, still atop his machine like a king of the mountaintop, took a quick squint at the sun, reached above where his striped overalls stretched tight over his belly, and pulled at a whang-leather thong anchored there. He briefly considered the heavy watch that slid from the bib pocket, then flipped up his greasy hand. Both pitchers immediately gave him full attention: the first rule of threshing demanded alertness at the dangerous work of pitching into the feeder. He looked straight at Vernon and held up his tethered watch. The man nodded responsively, gravely, and looked across the feeder at his partner.

"Robert!" Vernon's lusty voice, rising above the machine's noise level, had no equal among the other threshers. "Dinnertime. We'll need to clean up around the feeder."

The object of these instructions flicked one more glance toward the thresherman, who had now turned away to start back down the ladder. Bob simply gave a brusque nod across the feeder without looking up, and tried to repress the resentment that surged within him. He formulated words silently. This guy Vernon, just because he's ten years older, always thinks he has to explain everything to me: "Clean up around the feeder"—of course! Did he suppose I was going to drive away and leave him clean up by himself? Bob jabbed his long, three-tine fork into the last pile of bundles, swung them successively up onto the moving crossbars, and tossed up remnants of loose straw raked from the wide board floor of his rack. He unwound and jiggled the black leather lines, signaling the horses to move away from the machine; a slight pull was enough to stop them again. This team of Pa's, came the thought, he had trained them to be like he is himself, unexcitable and steady—most of

A farmer's best friend

Above: *The arrival of small, gas-powered "stationary engines" on farms lent a much-appreciated helping hand to many chores. Stationary engines, powering everything from corn shellers to washing machines, from saws to water pumps, soon became a farmer's best friend. (Photograph by J. C. Allen & Son)*

Famous Fordson

Left: *Henry Ford grew up on a farm and knew firsthand the toil of tilling the earth. After building his Model T automobile, he turned his skills to creating a farm tractor based on the same philosophy of being inexpensive, reliable, and built in massive quantities. After its debut in 1916, the Fordson became the farmer's favorite mechanical mule. By the end of World War I, half the motor cars on earth were Ford Model T; by 1925, 75 percent of the world's tractors were Fordsons.*

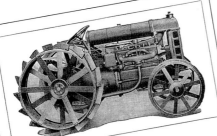

the time. He recalled that first occasion, years ago, when Pa had Tim and Diamond, still colts, approach the noisy movement of the machine, and they had not become jumpy at all, like some horses might. James even had had a runaway two years ago.

Vernon was already working at the spilled bundles and loose stuff under the feeder. Bob found several forksful, then ran his tines perpendicular along the ground to rake in scattered spears with good heads still on them. Vernon's bellowed instructions again penetrated above the clacking of the feeder chain: "Some stones down here, Robert, be careful." Right, Vernon, without your guidance I might just toss one of these rocks up there into the cylinder, and bango, you'd really have something to talk about. But Bob only nodded at him again and continued skimming. The ground crawled and snapped with black crickets that had ridden in from the oats shocks. It made him feel like laughing out loud, remembering the time last year that Vernon, cleaning under the feeder just like right now, had a cricket crawl up his pantleg—just when the women were over by the tractor to pick up lunch pans, so he couldn't even take his overalls down to get at the invading cricket, and the thing must have been taking nips out of his hide in tender places, the way Vernon had grabbed and whooped as he hobbled out of sight behind the straw pile. Bob spoke silently now to his black insect brothers: "Come on, boys, let's do it again!" But in vain. Not even the damn crickets could do things right today.

He unhitched the team, let them drink from the tank, hooked their bridles over the hames, and tied halter ropes to the end of his rack. He found a half-bushel of Elmer's new oats so Tim and Diamond could enjoy their own threshing dinner, then turned toward where the small white house nestled against the barren foothill, the picture framed by distant thunderclouds on the southwest horizon. Only a few straggling threshers were still in view: Vernon, just up ahead, and the grain haulers, Pa and Julius Schleuter, in the shade of the house getting ready to wash up. Far out in the oats field, James Koppman and Clarence Roecker were just coming in with their loads from across the creek. Over near the silenced tractor

Fields of gold
The golden autumn sun shines on a field of corn surrounding a classic farmstead. (Photograph by G. Alan Nelson)

and separator, the rotund thresherman finished writing in his notebook, slipped it into his overall bib's wide pocket, and in quick steps also started toward the house. Bob waited up. Funny, he thought, how the old farmers wear bib overalls and us young guys bibless; he glanced down to admire the side buckle of his field boots, so distinguishable from typical farmer work shoes. Drawing nearer, George untied the red kerchief from around his thick neck, snapped dust from it once, and shoved his denim engineer's cap to the back of his balding head. His friendly look made a gold tooth glint in the sun. "Well, Bob, how's she goin'?" At least old George knew what name to use these days; Vernon kept calling him "Robert." At least he didn't hear "Sonny" much anymore.

"Oh, pretty fair, I guess." Not much point in bringing up the business about racks tipping, unless you have to.

"I guess you'll be goin' back to school next month. Your last year, ain't it?"

"Yup, finally made it to the senior class."

"Well, that's good. I allus wished I'da gone to high school. Tried to get Clarence to go, but he didn't want to. Little Henry, he's quit now too, ain't he." The last was a stated fact; Henry, a year ahead of Bob in high school, had dropped out and was talking about joining the army after he'd finished helping his grandpa with the threshing; Big Henry was getting too old to shovel grain.

"Yeah, quite a few of the farm boys who start don't seem to finish."

"Sure, allus work to do at home. But lots to learn, too. Ever'thing is gettin' more complicated. What you goin' to do after—help your dad farm?" Old George and son Clarence had farmed together for years— two quarters and an eighty, with that powerful old MM tractor.

"Oh, I don't know yet." Bob shot a glance at his walking companion, and felt a sudden revelation: I am taller now than George Roecker. After a lifetime as the peewee of the Hidewood, Bob Amerson is no longer the shortest guy around. The notion emboldened him. "Don't know," he repeated. "Maybe farmin', if I could learn how to run a threshin' machine like you do."

"Heh!" George's gold tooth shone again. "'Fraid you're a little too late for that."

"Too late?"

"Yeah, hell, threshing machines, they're on the way out. It's all gonna be combines from now on; lots of farmers over by town use 'em already. So, no future anymore for threshers; this might be the last year we run this rig, you know."

He had stated it matter-of-factly, but Bob, scrutinizing, detected a kind of hardening in those watery eyes, and the corners of George's mouth seemed to crease down into his ruddy jowls.

They had reached the wash-up area at the north side of the house. The other men had already gone in. George rolled up the sleeves of his stained blue shirt, poured soft water from a pail into the basin set out on an old table, and leaned his face into what he dipped up in both hands. His arms and forehead glowed white, where the sun never got at him. His sudden exhaling into his hands sputtered in the water, and his stubby fingers extended the wet around his closed eyes and into his ears. Then he used soap briefly on his arms and greasy hands. "Well, that takes some of it off anyway," he said, using one of the already-damp towels.

"I'll get the basin," Bob offered, and splashed George's soapy gray water into the weeds.

"Fine," the thresherman nodded, and stepped briskly around the corner of the house. Bob took his time washing up. He had not considered before that this might be the last year of threshing. Not only for him, but for anybody.

On his way through the kitchen, he paused to talk with his mother, who was assisting Bessie Krause with the big meal. The two women every year exchanged help on thresher-dinner days. His three younger sisters and the two Krause girls scooted about like water bugs between kitchen and dining room to serve and clean the table—and get in on the event. In the dining room the lengthened table was set to accommodate the eleven threshers, including the two bundle haulers still coming in. Most of those at the table hunched over their plates in various stages of their meal. Large bowls and platters steamed with constantly replenished food: roast beef and fried chicken with mashed potatoes and gravy; corn, string beans, and asparagus; baking-powder biscuits and thick slices of bread; a variety of jams and jellies and relish and pickles; chocolate cake and apple pie. Bob found a place next to Little Henry and greeted his former schoolmate. "Howya comin', Henry? Looks like more

Big load

Amish boys in Lancaster County, Pennsylvania, load a hay wagon the tried-and-true, old-fashioned way—with pitchforks and muscle. (Photograph by Keith Baum)

grub than we used to get stayin' in town, eh?" Henry looked up, breaking concentration on his plate long enough to crowd an affirmative grin onto his bulging cheeks, and he took another drumstick from the platter that Bob handed him. Conversation around the table was subdued, maybe, Bob thought, waiting to hear from George, the leader—the leader who won't have anybody to lead, after the combines take over threshing.

"By golly, Elmer," the thresherman spoke up now, "these are some good oats we're thrashin' for you today, hey?"

"Yeah, looks like it," the farmer-of-the-day agreed. "This first forty-acre field went pert-near fifty bushel, and the piece across the crick looks even better."

"Ohg, gyeah . . ." The thresherman responded through a mouthful of beef, lifting his fork like a bandmaster's baton to hold attention while he chewed and swallowed. "I been lookin' over at that field all mornin'. Pretty as a picture, those shocks out there so close together, somebody shoulda brought a Kodak. I bet that field will run sixty, seventy bushel."

"Goddam, Elmer," came Julius Schleuter's nasal assertion, "you boys're makin' us grain haulers work too hard, ain't that so, Clarence?" Julius cackled at his own effrontery; easygoing Pa only grinned, going along with the joke. But Vernon picked it up.

"Yeah, seems t'me any farmer with oats yieldin' like this oughta stand for the beer, shouldn't he?"

Through the good-natured laughter Elmer spoke up again. "Okay, you guys, I was goin' t'save this for a surprise, but I might as well tell you now—so neither the grain haulers or the beer guzzlers won't have nothin' t'complain about. I got Fred Wiswall comin' out from town this afternoon with his truck, and he's bringin' along some cold beer."

Hearty laughs and cheerful murmuring greeted this, but the news meant little to Bob. Last week Schleuters had had a tubful of iced beer out in the shade of the tractor to celebrate an exceptional wheat yield, but when Julius had queried Pa about whether Bob should be offered a bottle, Pa had hesitated—probably remembering how Ma felt about drinking—and mumbled back something about "pretty young

Combining

All too often the sun sets as the combine is still at work. (Photograph by Lynn M. Stone)

yet." That was all right; learning how to drink beer or smoke cigarettes was not high on Bob's agenda. While shooting pool or fooling around in town, he had occasionally lit cigarettes experimentally, but he never inhaled, and he shared his mother's disdain for those who let themselves become influenced by alcohol. It could even be dangerous, as they'd seen with James Koppman over at Schleuters' last week. James was not much more experienced than Bob about beer, and the one bottle had made him so silly and wobbly up there on his load above the feeder that George had ordered him to come down and had taken over unloading James's bundles himself. Bob recalled George's story to them later about a guy years ago falling into the feeder, getting chopped to pieces by those knives, ending up as little bits of blood and guts inside the separator. The point about safety had been a somber one, but everybody had to laugh at the end of George's story when Vernon popped out with, "and I bet the worst of it was, George, that the fella plugged up the cylinder on yuh!"

Now, halfway through his meal, Bob became aware of a kind of conspiratorial silence around the table. Several of the threshers had finished eating and leaned back in their chairs, working toothpicks; as Bob watched, Vernon surreptitiously poked an elbow at his neighbor's ribs, and with a suppressed grin shot a glance in Bob's direction. But it was his school pal, alongside him, who was attracting their attention. Apparently when Henry finished with meat and potatoes, without bothering to look around the table and ask for cake or pie, he had reached out to grab what he took to be the nearest dessert, and he was now spooning up the last of a dish of strawberry jam—while everybody watched.

"Henry. Henny, Henny, Henny," Vernon finally intoned. "Bessie Krause's goin' t'charge you extra today for eatin' up all her best preserves."

Little Henry awoke to the reality and looked predictably sheepish. Guffaws around the table.

"I don't know about these high school boys," Vernon continued, loud and deliberate. "What do they teach 'em in that town school, anyway? First, how to tip bundle wagons, by the looks of things. And then to eat strawberry jam for dessert!"

Bob made a show of joining in their chuckling, but inside the familiar resentment rose again. So it happens that the two bundle haulers who tipped racks are also the only two who've been to high school, so what? And Vernon didn't have to lump him in with Henry about the jam.

The entrance of the two late bundle haulers now drew the group's notice. "Where you guys been?" George wanted to know. "I thought maybe you fell in the crick or somethin'."

Clarence Roecker, a taller version of his beefy father, raised an eyebrow and grimaced. "That ain't too far off, at that," he said, and looked half-accusingly at Elmer. "That's a pretty rough and rocky bottom, crossin' the crick."

"Yeh," James Koppman added, rolling a shirtsleeve still higher over his tanned Charles Atlas biceps. "When my steel wheels hit the rocks, the team got all nervous at the noise and the jolt. Couldn't hardly hold 'em."

"What happened?" Elmer asked in some alarm.

"Well, bounced the load too much comin' across, and I lost a whole back corner."

"Lost? How. . . ?"

"Oh, just a few bundles fell in the water," Clarence quickly put in, chagrined. "We fished 'em out, should be okay after they dry."

The thresherman pushed his chair back. "Yeh, well, pretty hard to build a good load that won't drop bundles in rough spots." He stood. "I got a little more greasin' to do. Machine time in about ten minutes." The threshers followed him out.

Standing at the front of his empty rack, Bob trotted his team behind Vernon's toward the waiting shocks of oats that thickly dotted the field, just visible over low willows lining the creek. Henry and Elmer had already hurried out there and were loading; beyond them, the gray and white billows in the southwest sky had become more pronounced. "Dark clouds on the horizon," he said aloud. "Miss Torgerson, in English 4 terms, would you say there's some kind of literary symbolism here?" He had to laugh, seeing himself weighing and sorting out his own feelings about his two worlds—farming and everything that had opened to him after three years of high school life.

So much of farming seemed just plain drudgery—

dull, repetitive physical labor of routine chores, of obligatory work during hot, sweaty summers and bitter cold winters. Sure, pleasant weather came in the spring after the meadowlarks and mayflowers, but then a farmer had to be out there in the field twelve, fourteen hours a day, worrying about getting the crop in on time, eating dust behind machinery—horsepower or tractor power. Fall is maybe the best time of year, he thought, and not only because school starts in September and hunting season soon afterward. Something about the harvest really does satisfy; he was farmer enough to appreciate that. Living off the land, watching things grow, accepting the bounty of nature—they write poems and songs about such celebrations. "We gather together to ask the Lord's blessing . . ."

Tenor harmonies from the Thanksgiving music sung in school chorus last year ran through his mind, but it soon became crowded out by visions of harvest scenes: out in the stubble behind Pa's four-horse binder, acres of dropped bundles, all vulnerable to rain until set into drying shocks, heads up, one by one. Dawn to dusk, you had to be out there at those endless windrows of fallen sheaves, bending over all day long to set butts firmly on the ground, hoping the first two will balance until the next two can be added for support. The tall and slippery ones—oats sometimes and rye always were nearly impossible to make stand. Barley and wheat beards penetrated gloves and shirtsleeves—and you'd better look out for your eyes. You had to take the heat and exhaustion and tedium of it all, with only occasional relief from the brown jug wrapped in wet burlap and left under a bundle out of the sun. You could tip the jug up on one elbow to take on needed water, by now tepid but at least wet, and then you might flop against a shock for five minutes of rest. Why would anybody choose to work like this if they didn't have to? he wondered. Drudgery was the only word for getting the harvest ready to thresh.

But threshing itself saved farm work from total tedium. He recalled early mornings, hearing exciting clanks and rattles over the steady exhaust of George Roecker's Minneapolis-Moline as he eased the big rig down the road and into the driveway, the thresherman standing to steer, waving as he passed by, wedge lugs on his tractor's heavy wheels leaving unaccustomed trails of power and glory across the yard, the monster machine following in its imperial metallic majesty. All the neighbors coming on the place, working together this one time of the year, talking and joking, glad to be freed from normal solitary work, enjoying each other's company and the big dinners, too.

For a kid, just watching all this was enough of a marvel, and gradually you could become a part of it, first tending the machine's grain spout at the wagons. There would always be plenty of sandwiches and cake in the covered dishpans the womenfolk set out in the shade of the tractor; you could kneel there and share lunchtime with the bundle haulers just in with a load. And when you were big enough to handle a fork, you could go out and spike-pitch, helping men load their racks, learning how to set the bundles butts-out above the sideboards, building the load until it got too high for you to reach. Some of the bundle haulers consistently made high, beautiful loads as a matter of pride. In this sense threshing seemed, in isolation, just the opposite of drudgery. It was, in fact, a kind of art that required skills and intelligence, working responsively as part of a team, achieving objectives shared by all.

And the whole thing was soon to disappear. George Roecker's words came back: "No future anymore for threshers; this might be the last year." One of those two-edged blades that they talk about in books, cutting both ways. You can't stand in the way of progress, including tractors and combines and all the other technology coming on. But no more threshing time? No George Roeckers running a threshing ring?

He became aware that Tim and Diamond had slowed. Ahead of them, Vernon had started his team into the creek crossing—a clearing about twenty feet wide, the murky water a foot or so deep. On this side of the cut, several new shocks of still-damp bundles testified to James's accident. Bob eased his horses down the incline and had them follow after Vernon. The hidden rock bottom jarred the rack, pinging against the metal wheels, but it didn't seem so bad if you took it easy.

He had tossed into his rack only a few shocks when he saw Henry, at the end of the next windrow, throw his fork atop a jag that sloped in on all sides—half a load, at best. Henry had to pull by him on the way in and obviously felt a little self-conscious about this pitiful appearance. "Runnin' outa time," he called out to Bob, "afraid I might be late at the feeder." It was a point, Bob had to concede; Henry and partner

Elmer did have to hurry because they were first out after the dinner break, and Elmer as well had already started in. Bob only wished Henry's load looked as decent as Elmer's.

George Roecker had it right, this was a beautiful oats field—the shocks close together, the clean bundles tightly bound and well balanced between weighted heads and neat, flat-cut butts. Bob lost himself in the sheer esthetic pleasure of building his load above the rack boards—keeping the center level of bundles low enough so those he placed, butts-out, at the outside edge would incline heads downward. He had learned this technique early on, from George Roecker's homeless, unmarried brother Jack, who used to work as a spike-pitcher sometimes in George's threshing ring. He could hear the old hunchback's wheezy instructions: "See, you set each bundle in there hard, like this—ah!—an' then it's gonna stay put."

Remembering, Bob wielded his fork. Set the bundles into square corners and straight walls a foot wider than the rack—up, up, throw a few into the center, and up some more. The load was beginning to look good, and he did not feel like stopping as long as he could still make them stay up there. He peered past the corner of his load to check on his partner, and just as he watched, with a long swooping swing, Vernon tossed his fork high into the air, and it curved gracefully, tines down, to stick proudly atop his load, like the courthouse flagpole. Vernon's load was . . . well, respectable maybe, but not much more. Over at the next two windrows now, James and Clarence were back, starting new loads. Time was getting short.

Bob again appraised his own load. The outside edges of trim butts were built nearly straight up, just about as high as he could set them firmly. Vernon's noontime wisecrack came back to taunt him: "I don't know about these high school boys." He decided to lay in one more level row of bundles, shoving at the very end of the fork handle with the palm of his leather-gloved hand as he lifted and stretched; then he tossed up a few more into the center, to round it out. He stepped back to survey his work of art. If it wasn't a masterpiece, it was as close as he would ever come to it. Bigger than anyone else's load he'd seen all during threshing. He crouched for the fork swoop; it flew high, but the tines did not turn downward, and he had to jump out of the way when the fork tumbled down off the high load. On the third try it at

SHARING THE GOOD TIMES AND THE BAD

By Robert J. C. Stead

Robert J. C. Stead's 1916 novel, *The Homesteaders: A Novel of the Canadian West*, is a classic of Canadian literature, telling the tale of a group of pioneers who set out to build a life on the prairies. In this selection, the author describes how the homesteaders shared their farm machinery, their household tools, and their lives with each other. After a bountiful harvest, the pioneers looked to the future without fear—little knowing what winter had in store for them.

None of these pioneers was possessed of a complete farming equipment, but each had something which his neighbour lacked, and they made common cause together in their struggle with Nature. Thus Harris had no mower, but when haying season came he was able to borrow Morrison's, at the same time lending his plough to Riles, who simultaneously accommodated Morrison with his hayrack. Among the women exchanging became something of an exact science. Mrs. Grant was the proud possessor of a very modern labour-saver in the shape of a clothes-wringer, as a consequence of which wash-day was rotated throughout the community, and it was well known that Mrs. Riles and Mrs. Harris had to do their churning alternately. But it was Mrs. Morrison's sewing-machine that was the great boon to the community, and to it, perhaps, as much as the open-hearted hospitality of honest Tom and his wife, was due the fact that their house became the social centre of the district.

And so the first summer wore away and the first harvest was at hand. Any disappointment which had been occasioned by backward conditions earlier in the season was effaced by the wonderful crop which now crowned the efforts of the pioneers. On their finest Eastern farms they had seen nothing to equal the great stand of wheat and oats which now enveloped them, neck-high, whenever they invaded it. The great problem before the settlers was the harvesting of this crop. It was a mighty task to attempt with their scythes, but there was no self-binder, or even reaper, within many miles.

Finally Morrison solved the problem for the whole community by placing an order, at a fabulous figure, for a self-binder from the United States. It was a cumbrous, woodenframe contrivance, guiltless of the roller bearings, floating aprons, open elevators, and sheaf carriers of a later day, but it served the purpose, and with its aid the harvest of the little settlement was safely placed in sheaf. The farmers then stacked their grain in the fields, taking care to plough double fire-guards, with a burnt space between, as a precaution against the terrifying fires which broke over the prairie as soon as the September frosts had dried the grass. A community some twenty miles to the eastward boasted a threshing mill, and arrangements were made for its use after it had discharged the duties of its own locality. The machine was driven by horse-power, and in the dawn of the crisp November mornings the crescendo of its metallic groan could be heard for miles across the brown prairie. It, too, with its hand feed, its open straw-carriers, its lowdown delivery, which necessitated digging a hole in the frozen earth to accommodate the bags, and its possible capacity of six hundred bushels a day, bears mean comparison with its modern successor; but it threshed grain at a lower cost per bushel, and threw less into the straw than has ever been accomplished by the mighty steam and gasoline inventions which have displaced it. . . .

So, in high spirits, they planned for their winter. There were long hours, and little diversion, and the desolation of bleak, snowbound prairies on every side, but through it all they kept up their courage and their hopefulness. Mary spent much time with her needle, from which John, when he felt she was applying herself too closely, beguiled her to a game of checkers or an hour with one of their few but valued books. To supplement their reading matter Mrs. Morrison sent over her little library, which consisted of "The Life of David Livingstone" and a bound number of "The Gospel Tribune." And there were frequent visits and long evenings spent about a cosy fire, when the Morrisons or the Grants, or the Rileses, dropped in to while away the time. The little sod house was warm and snug, and as the men played checkers while the women sewed, what cared the pioneers for the snow and the cold and the wind whistling across the plains?

Country roads

Overleaf: *A classic farmstead lays nestled among rolling hills along a gravel country road.* (*Photograph by Dick Dietrich*)

least stayed up there, never mind the flagpole.

He laid a hand on Diamond's round rump, stepped upon the evener, and reached up to where the lines were tied on the standard, climbing the boards to rest a foot on the topmost crossboard. The load level still loomed well above him. For the first time a small voice inside intimated alarm: Did I overdo it? Can I even make it to the top? He leaned heavily against the front wall of bundle butts, grasping tied twines to pull himself up and make a kind of eagle's nest from which he might drive the team. He found his uncooperative pitchfork and used it to rearrange the top of the load. It was his highest ever—might even be dangerous, standing up this high to pitch into the feeder; George would worry about balance and control, with or without the influence of any beer.

He clucked at the team, and the tugs tightened. James, his boxer's torso again bared to the sun, paused as the big load pulled by. "You're crazy, Bob!" he called out.

"Crazy? Nah, I just don't know my own strength."

"Anyhow, what don't fall off into the crick is gonna get just as wet in the rain."

Bob looked around to the southwest. He hadn't noticed how fast the thunderstorm was coming up. And—the crick. The crossing. Maybe he had put it out of mind too much, letting other thoughts take over as he was building this load, bundle by bundle. James is probably right. Nobody in his right mind would try to cross with a load this high. What makes me do these things—foolish pride? Misplaced enthusiasm of inexperience? Just plain careless, Pa might call it. Well, what the hell. What was that Latin phrase he'd learned from his teacher? *Quod erat faciendum*— we have done what we had to do. Do it right while we've still got the chance. Behind him, the blue cloud covered the sun and aimed gray streaks at the earth, maybe a mile away. When it rains it pours, just one of those days when things happen.

Up ahead, Vernon had long since crossed the creek, apparently without mishap, and was approaching the rig. Now: down the incline to the creek bed; he kept the lines tight, and the neck yoke pulled away from the horses as they tried to hold the weight back; hooves splashed. "Hoo-o-o— easy now," he called to them. The first submerged rocks clanged against his wheels, and the high load jiggled all around him. The horses seemed to understand that the next moments would

not be easy, and they began to surge forward, building momentum to help carry the heavy load up the opposite incline. The entire rack wobbled and swayed but remained intact. Then, abruptly—clonk! Everything stopped. Tim and Diamond, uncertain, alternated in trying to move ahead, then backing against the rack front; panic was imminent. He held the lines steady and spoke to them, and they calmed. All became eerily quiet except for the babble of the flowing water. Now what?

He must have chosen a path this time to the left of where he had crossed behind Vernon before. He could see that just below the surface, a larger, solid rock blocked the left front wheel. Even if he could pull over it, the danger was that the high load would be shaken fatally, could even tip over right into the water. Only one maneuver seemed worth the risk. Softly talking to his team, he pulled them gently to the right, hoping that the blocked front wheel would somehow skid around the big rock; the risk included the possibility of breaking the long, wooden wagon tongue—and then they'd really have to send out a rescue mission. The horses strained to the right, the tongue bent . . . but did not snap, and with a grinding crunch the left wheel came up and over the blocking stone's slant, rocking the load dizzily this time, but the horses felt the motion now and leaned into their tugs. Then the front wheels were on dry land and the team, digging in, only had to pull up and safely over the incline. Bob looked back at the crossing. He had learned his early lessons well. Not a single bundle had fallen. "The Roecker Method comes through again!" he shouted, waving his fist at the creek.

Now he could turn his attention to the rig, still a quarter-mile distant. With everything in shadow, the details were hard to make out, but Vernon had parked his load alongside the faded yellow hump of tractor where he now stood with the thresherman. Henry and Elmer, at the feeder, had not yet finished unloading: he was on time for his turn, in spite of the extra minutes taken to build a load, in spite of the trouble at the crossing. Under the grain spout, Fred Wiswall's wide blue truck had replaced the wagons.

Small popping sounds on his straw hat reminded him of the weather, and a backward glance confirmed that the vertical gray shower was gaining on him. Occasional thunder began to growl. By the time he got close enough to hear the roar of the tractor and separator, splotching drops slanting down visibly had darkened his shirt. At the truck, Pa and Julius scrambled to help Fred spread a tarp over the box. Henry finished unloading before Elmer did—one of the advantages of a small rackful was less work at unloading, too—and then pulled up to start cleaning up under his side of the feeder. Some of the bundles there, already getting wet, produced loud groans of complaint from the whirring cylinder teeth deep inside. The machine seemed to know when it was time to stop.

George, standing on his tractor now, signaled with both arms and the bundle pitchers quit pitching in. The thresherman waited until after the bundles under the knives had passed through the angry grunts of the cylinder, and when nothing more wafted from the blower, he pulled back the hand-clutch lever, letting the separator coast to stillness. His short legs took him around in the rain to the front of his tractor to remove the big jack that had been braced against the wheel lug for belt tension. Then he bounced up again to inch the tractor ahead. Vernon was there to lift the heavy belt from the power pulley, roll it expertly, and stow the coil within the machine, safe from a soaking. Then George and Vernon together hurried—odd, seeing older men run like that—toward the nearby barn, where everyone else by now looked out from the shelter of its broad doorway. Bob tied the lines, climbed down from his load, and raced past the tractor, behind them.

"Dang," Elmer was saying in the huddled group, "And I was hopin' we could finish up today, too."

"Ah, hell," George said, watching the rain from the doorway and drying his round face with the red kerchief. "There's another day a-comin'. And if there ain't, we won't need t'thrash."

Some of the men standing around exchanged glances, letting traces of grins acknowledge the wisdom of their leader's words. But the thresherman remained silhouetted at the doorway, his back to the others, looking out into the slackening rain. Finally he turned to them, motioning with a stubby thumb back at the scene outside.

"Now there's a load of bundles," he said, and even in the obscure light that gold tooth gleamed. "Been a long time since I seen a load built like that, just so square and high, like a picture. That's pitchin' bundles."

Bob felt attention focus upon him, but his quick surreptitious glances revealed no one looking his way. Nor did anyone else speak. In the silence he imagined what some of them must be thinking: smart-ass kid, showing off, making the rest of us look bad. Even Henry might be sore, he thought, but I don't care. A guy has to do something right, for once.

"Say," Elmer's voice interrupted his uncomfortable quiet. "That case of Grain Belt's in ice water, in the tub over there. If we're just gonna stand around, might as well get at it now." He nudged the truck driver. "C'mon, gimme a hand." Fred and Elmer hurried through the wet to where the shade of the tractor should have been, and they returned with the heavy washtub between them, brown bottles sloshing and clinking against ice chunks. They set it well inside on the barn floor. The threshers began to gather around it, picking out dripping bottles, prying caps off, and then passing the metal opener along.

Outside, past George's silhouette again at the doorway, the rain had almost stopped; the rumbling thunder each time became more distant. To the southwest Bob could see some blue sky showing through. But rainwater glistened shiny on the flat top of the threshing machine, and the slanting feeder dripped like . . . what? Like something out of a science textbook, the proboscis of some undiscovered metal dinosaur with a very bad cold. Threshing was over for today, all right—the sun would have to shine for hours before those darkened bundles on the two loads out there would be ready. He took another moment to appraise from this distance his square corners and high walls, rounded just right on top. Yessir. "Now there's a load of bundles."

A big hand grasping a wet bottle suddenly appeared before his eyes. "Here," Vernon was saying to him quietly. "Fella does a man's work should have a man's drink." Bob hesitated, then accepted the offer without further ceremony, without even looking around at Pa first; no need to worry today about anybody falling off a high load into the feeder. The opener worked the same as on pop bottles. Over at the doorway, George raised his beer briefly toward the others. "Well, boys, here's how." They tipped up; there were gurgles and scattered *ahs* of satisfaction. Light showed amber through his own bottle's neck above the diamond-shaped label. The froth tasted bitter at first, but he figured he could get used to it.

Roger's Rules for Restoring a Tractor for Fun and Profit

By Roger Welsch

Roger Welsch needs little introduction, especially to vintage tractor fans. As a television personality on CBS TV's *Sunday Morning* program, Roger has spread the word about vintage tractors wherever the airwaves travel. His writings on tractors appear regularly in *Successful Farming* magazine's "Ageless Iron" section, as well as in *Esquire*, *Smithsonian*, and *Nebraska Farmer*. In addition, he is the author of more than twenty books, including *Old Tractors and the Men Who Love Them* and *Busted Tractors and Rusty Knuckles*. As John Carter of the Nebraska State Historical Society noted, "We all knew sooner or later that Roger would write a book about religion."

In this essay, Roger details all of the important parts of tractor repair and restoration that are left out of the official shop manuals.

I've been in this business of restoring old tractors for, oh, almost a whole year now, so I pretty much know everything there is to know. And I am fully prepared to share all that information. No sense in us both making the same mistakes.

The most important, most frequent question about restoration is, "Why?" (Or, in the case of my wife Lovely Linda, "Why?!!!") My own reasons range from cosmetic (I find that after a day lying under a tractor, putting on an oil pan maybe, my hair takes on new body and luster) to philosophical (uh . . .).

I got started on Allis-Chalmers WCs last summer.

I had just come off a week with my CBS News crew, after a week on book tour for Random House, after spending one hour alone with my daughter Antonia — all stresses that had pushed my blood pressure to something like 489-over-366.

At that moment, I decided I would spend the next day away from the telephone and my office, away from the mail basket, away from anyone from New York City, away from everything that means anything.

I'll . . . I'll . . . I got it! I'll repair the broken brake on my Allis WC!

Now, you have to understand that to this point in my life I had never so much as changed the oil in a vehicle. My 1937 Allis WC was simply a utility tractor to me.

Like father, like son
Love for farm tractors can begin at a dangerously young age, as this painting by artist Walter Haskell Hinton suggests. Dad takes time out from spring plowing with his brand-spanking-new Model D to oil the axle bearings on junior's own homemade Deere tractor. (Deere & Company)

But I spent the next day in a gentle, warm sun, taking the brake lever and shoe out of a junked tractor and putting them on my Allis.

That evening my blood pressure was 4.5-over-2. My pulse was about two a minute. I decided that anything that had that sort of calming influence over my much-abused body deserves further exploration. And I became a dedicated tractor tinkerer.

Why tractors? Because you can work on them standing up, and for a guy of my age and build, that's really important.

Why *old* tractors? Because there's none of that foreign metric nonsense. Just good ol' American inches, pounds, hairs, and smidgins.

In fact, with old tractors there are not even problems with all that electrical stuff like amps and volts that nobody understands anyway. On an Allis WC there are exactly four wires, one leading to each spark plug. Even that can be confusing, but usually four wires are within my grasp.

With old tractors, you don't hook up a computer to figure out what's going on inside. One of my ancient manuals shows how to brace up a tree limb so you can pull the engine on your 19-horsepower beast. The manufacturer understood that these machines were going to be worked on out under a cottonwood tree by a guy who owns three wrenches, a claw hammer, and a bent screwdriver—which is to say, me.

While you don't need a lot of tools, a big part of restoring old tractors is buying tools. There's not a man alive, and only a few women, who wouldn't be perfectly happy buying a NAPA store or Snap-On Tools truck, closing its doors to the public, and spending a lifetime admiring all those neat, shiny tools. Having a "shop" for restoring tractors is a lot like owning a NAPA franchise except without all the trouble of customers.

In fact, tractor restoration is a great economic alternative for those times when your $500,000 in certificates of deposit or gold bullion are not paying off the way you think they should.

Say you buy a junked John Deere B for $500, haul it into your $5,000 shop, and use your $2,000 worth of tools to take it apart. You put about $2,500 worth of parts into it and a few hundred dollars of gooey things. You invest a couple thousand hours of labor and a few thousand dollars for medical treatment (burns, busted knuckles, stomach pumping for the time you

poured the Mountain Dew on a stuck tappet and drank the Liquid Wrench). Before you know it, you have transformed a $500 piece of green junk into a $1,200 show piece, more than doubling your initial investment.

Where else can you get such a return on a buck? Isn't America great?!

A remarkable proportion of the time spent on restoration consists of sitting or standing around and staring. Take auction sales, for example.

That's where you get old tractors. Well, not exactly. It's not where you get them, it's where other people get them. Go to all the sales you want, but you'll never buy a tractor. They always go too high. Always.

If you take $300 to Fleischblum's sale, the tractor there will go for $310. If you take $350 to Kosmolinski's sale, their tractor will go for $360.

On the other hand, when you talk with your buddy Lunchbox, he'll say, "Kosmolinski's? You shoulda been over at Grembeck's. His WC, never spent a night out of the shed, went for $35, with a spare set of wheels."

What you do is tell Lunchbox that the next time he sees a WC going for less than $300, he should pick it up for you. He will, but the funny thing, it will always cost you exactly $300.

When you're not at sales, you'll be standing and staring at parts stores ("Now, was that a 9/32-inch bolt tree 3/8 inches long, or a 3/9-inch bolt 32 inches long?"). Or at tractor manuals ("insufficient clearance shims in the crush shell will result in spontaneous destruction of the engine within the first minute of operation, so torque all castellated nuts to 22.2 square-footpounds on ¼-inch lugs, 47.3 inch-ounces on 37/64-inch lugs, or else"). And finally you'll be staring at your wife ("What do you mean, what will I do with it if I ever get it running?").

Old tractors are good tractors because they have only 46 parts. Okay, some have a few more, some a few less, but 46 parts is a good working number.

This past winter I completely dismantled an Allis WC, touching all 46 parts in it. And I put it back together. No, it doesn't run, but at this point in my restoration career, "running" is not the most important thing in the world.

By the way, I have made a general announcement that should that WC ever decide to go ahead and run, I am going to drive it to town and park it outside Eric's

"A Step Ahead"

Above: *The 1930s were a time of dramatic innovation in the farm tractor field. The Oliver Farm Equipment Corporation of Chicago promoted the styling and mechanical improvements of its Model 70 Row Crop with this evocative painting by artist M. E. Swenson. The image compared the new streamlining of the tractor with the latest railroad locomotive while still tying the tractor to its roots with the father waving to his son.*

"Tom Brent and his Tractor"

Right: *Many 4-H youths learned the lessons of maintaining the family's farm tractor from this famous book that explained everything from engineering theory to hands-on repair.*

Tavern. I'm going to pull a big table over close to the door and prop the door open so I can hear it run. Then I'm going to invite everyone in town to join me in a glass of cheap champagne. Eric thinks it's a great idea, but he isn't going to order the champagne yet—the stuff he carries only has a shelf life of three years.

Everyone's a comedian—but not everyone is a restoration expert.

Tractor humor

Above: *Nothing was more outrageous to a farmer than the idea of actually being able to pay cash for new machinery. This cartoon appeared in the* Country Gentleman *magazine in the 1910s.*

"Forever Red"

Left: *Restoring old iron has become a hobby of farmers everywhere. Iowa artist Charles Freitag captures the appeal of tractor restoration in his painting of a father at work on his Farmall M while his sons juggle the wrenches and polish their International Harvester pedal tractor. (Apple Creek Publishing)*

Ghost Tractors

"At Stromp's Dump there is a double row of ancient, sheet-metal combines flanking the entrance to the place, stretching off to the east and west almost as far as you can see. It reminds me of a Maya monument. I'll bet that on the vernal and autumnal equinoxes, if you stand in just the right place, maybe over there by that rusting steam traction engine, the sun rises right between that double row of combines, and some day archeologists will write about it."
—Roger L. Welsch, "What, Me Quarry?"

Scrap metal drive

During World Wars I and II, scrap metal drives melted down many a classic farm tractor, turning plowshares into swords for the patriotic war effort. This 1940s ad from Minneapolis-Moline threatened farmers that liberty—in the form of the Statue of Liberty—was in danger if they didn't harvest their old tractors for the war. Unstated, naturally, was also the fact that farmers would then need a new tractor, preferably a Prairie Gold Minne-Mo.

Haunted tractor

Right: *The radiator of a forgotten Fordson pokes through the weeds of a farm backlot. (Photograph by Andrew Morland)*

Out to pasture

Far right: *The ghosts of tractors past are evoked by artist Charles Freitag's painting of an old Johnny Popper. (Apple Creek Publishing)*

Charles Freitag

Chapter 4

All Creatures Great and Small

"All the good ideas I ever had came to me while I was milking a cow."
—**Grant Wood, American artist**

Farmers often came to feel a kinship with the animals they raised or worked. The horses that pulled the plow, the hens that laid eggs, or the dairy cows that gave milk for the breakfast table—all of them became more than mere beasts of burden or producers of bacon. As evidence, consider the affectionate names that were donned on farm animals, names such as Bossy the cow and Dobbin the horse.

These essays tell of the farmer's devotion to all creatures great and small on the farm.

Milking
Left: *In his 1930 poem titled simply "The Cow," Ogden Nash wrote, "The cow is of the bovine ilk; One end is moo, the other milk." (Photograph by J. C. Allen & Son)*

Milkmaid
Above: *A winsome milkmaid calls in the cows for milking.*

About Cows

By Sara Rath

Sara Rath has become an expert on things bovine. She is the author of *The Complete Cow*, published by Voyageur Press and Raincoast Books, a scholarly, yet light-hearted look at beef and dairy cows, from bovine mythology to the evolution of worldwide cow breeds to cows in pop culture. She also authored the book *About Cows* and is currently at work on a book about pigs.

Sara was born and raised in the rural Wisconsin town of Manawa, where her grandfather was World Champion Cheesemaker for many years. It's thus no surprise that the rural world plays a central role in all of her writing, including her six other books of poetry, fiction, and nonfiction.

This piece offers a warm homage to the cow and all things bovine.

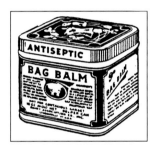

The Cow. She has been a part of our lives since we turned away from Mother's breast. And before.

When we learned to talk, we chanted nursery rhymes about the cow that jumped over the moon or the cows in the corn. And is there a child alive who has not sung of Old MacDonald's cow, "With a moo-moo here, and a moo-moo there . . ."?

Cows are a part of the countryside idyll, painted by artists, pictured in our minds, and taken for granted when we drive along rural roads. The cluster of black and white Holsteins lying in the shade chewing their cud has become a symbol of placid contentment.

The more practical among us might scoff at such a romantic point of view. They are the sort that cleverly create doggerel like this:

Though eulogies are penned perforce
In honor of the dog and horse,
The cow excels them definitely
In matters of fidelity.
In winter wind or summer breeze
She labors for our milk and cheese,
And scientific tests have shown
She puts the ice cream in the cone.
When in Elysian fields she rests,
She leaves us numerous bequests—
Wallets, gelatins, and shoes,
Soaps and pocketbooks and glues;
Bequeaths her very bones, indeed,
To pulverize for poultry feed.
The briefcases she leaves behind
Protect the plans of humankind,
And belts—her halo and her crown—
She keeps our pants from falling down.

—Nat Curran
The Chicago Tribune
1945

Truthful as that may be, the influence of cows in our lives goes much deeper than mere measurement of material goods. Once cattle were wild animals. They were hunted, just as all wild animals were hunted. Then they became domesticated. No one really knows how that happened, but one hypothesis is that in that transitional period of prehistory, when man was changing from hunter to pastoralist, from time to time the hunter brought home the offspring

Children and their calf
Two youngsters pet their pet Guernsey calf. (Photograph by J. C. Allen & Son)

of the species he slew. He might have thought a calf was too small and useless for meat and hide, or he might have had pity on the poor trusting creature and brought it back to the cave for his own family to play with and raise.

Whatever the case, in the early days of our existence, we became a cattle culture. As proof, much of our vocabulary has been derived from words that once related to cattle. The word "daughter," which corresponds to the Greek "thaughter" and the Sanskrit "duhitar," means the *milker*. In Sanskrit, "soldier" meant *one who fights about cows*. The "morning" was *the calling of the cattle*; the "evening" was *the milking-time*. The Latin word for money, "pecunia" (from which "pecuniary" and "impecunious" derive), and the word "fee" both come from the old word *pecus*, meaning *cattle*. "Stock" (as in "stocks and bonds") refers to the use of cattle as currency. In old Anglo-Saxon, movable property is called "cwichfeoh," or *living cattle*, whereas immovable property, such as buildings and land, has a name that translates as *dead cattle*. *Chattel*, meaning non living personal property, comes from the word "cater," which was used in the sense of "wealth." And the words for prince, king, lord, and the like, all meant *herdsman*, or *head of pastoral family*.

Thus, virtually from the beginning, livestock became man's chief interest, his main source of wealth, and his principal means of exchange. Cows led men from a state of savagery to higher planes of existence, pulling plows, drawing carts, assuaging hunger and thirst. The influence of cattle upon the mental development and material advancement of humanity is immeasurable. This was recorded in Biblical times

Milking time
Above: *A diary farmer leads his herd of Holstein cows down the road to home for milking. (Photograph by Jerry Irwin)*

Inquisitive cows
Facing page: *A herd of curious Jersey cows stands before a stylish round barn. (Photograph by Jerry Irwin)*

(Abraham was "very rich in cattle, in silver, and in gold"), exemplified in mythology (where cattle were fleecy clouds pasturing "in the infinite meadows of heaven," whose full udders dropped down "rain and fatness" upon the land), and stamped into the coinage of ancient Greece, where the image of an ox was imprinted on new money.

So, what it comes down to is this. Your grandparents may have had a farm and raised cows. You may have been born on a farm. You may have milked twenty-five cows a day for thirty years, and that's how you learned to love these gentle animals. But even if you've never had any "hands-on" experience, cows have had an important role in your life . . . even before you eagerly reached for your bottle of baby formula.

Helping hand

Above: *A farm youth lends a hand to pull another boy onto a patient old Dobbin. (Photograph by J. C. Allen & Son)*

Mare and colt

Facing page, top: *A Belgian draft horse mare stands tall alongside her colt. (Photograph by Keith Baum)*

Watering time

Facing page, bottom: *A farm girl leads her horses to water and offers them a drink. (Photograph by J. C. Allen & Son)*

Sheep shearing

Above: *Shearing the sheep is always a big job accompanied by lots of protests from the sheep community. Early shears worked like scissors; these later shears were powered by the assistant who turned the cranking apparatus that ran through the bevel-driven arms. Electric-powered shears were a welcome invention when they finally hit the farm. (Photograph by J. C. Allen & Son)*

Ewe and lambs

Left: *A group of three lambs stands close by a ewe. (Photograph by Keith Baum)*

"A cow is a completely automated milk manufacturing machine. It is encased in untanned leather and mounted on four vertical movable supports, one in each corner. At the rear, the machines carries the milk-dispensing apparatus as well as an automatic fly swatter and insect repeller."
—Anonymous, "The Miraculous Cow"

Death of a Pig

By E. B. White

Celebrated poet, storyteller, and essayist E. B. White is forever linked with the *New Yorker* magazine, for which he wrote for many years, and with his delightful children's books, *Stuart Little*, *Charlotte's Web*, and *The Trumpet of the Swan*. In addition, he wrote for the *Atlantic Monthly* and *Harper's Magazine*, and authored numerous other books of essays, including *One Man's Meat*, *The Second Tree from the Corner*, and *The Points of My Compass*. Finally, he was the co-author with William Strunk Jr. of *The Elements of Style*, probably the best-known and most respected book on writing and English language usage.

White was also a farmer. He lived, worked, and wrote at his saltwater farm at Allen Cove, Maine for many years, and it was during the autumn of 1947 that the events detailed in this selection from the *Essays of E. B. White* took place. Simple and touching, it is an elegaic, philosophical look at farming, the raising of animals, and the affinity one man can feel for his pig.

I spent several days and nights in mid-September with an ailing pig and I feel driven to account for this stretch of time, more particularly since the pig died at last, and I lived, and things might easily have gone the other way round and none left to do the accounting. Even now, so close to the event, I cannot recall the hours sharply and am not ready to say whether death came on the third night or the fourth night. This uncertainty afflicts me with a sense of personal deterioration; if I were in decent health I would know how many nights I had sat up with a pig.

The scheme of buying a spring pig in blossomtime, feeding it through summer and fall, and butchering it when the solid cold weather arrives, is a familiar scheme to me and follows an antique pattern. It is a tragedy enacted on most farms with perfect fidelity to the original script. The murder, being premeditated, is in the first degree but is quick and skillful, and the smoked bacon and ham provide a ceremonial ending whose fitness is seldom questioned.

Once in a while something slips—one of the actors goes up in his lines and the whole performance stumbles and halts. My pig simply failed to show up for a meal. The alarm spread rapidly. The classic outline of the tragedy was lost. I found myself cast suddenly in the role of pig's friend and physician—a farcical character with an enema bag for a prop. I had a presentiment, the very first afternoon, that the play would never regain its balance and that my sympathies were now wholly with the pig. This was slapstick—the sort of dramatic treatment that instantly appealed to my old dachshund, Fred, who joined the vigil, held the bag, and, when all was over, presided at the interment. When we slid the body into the grave, we both were shaken to the core. The loss we felt was not the loss of ham but the loss of pig. He had evidently become precious to me, not that he represented a distant nourishment in a hungry time, but

A girl and her piglet
A young girl cradles a piglet to scratch the nape of its neck. (Photograph by Lynn M. Stone)

that he had suffered in a suffering world. But I'm running ahead of my story and shall have to go back.

My pigpen is at the bottom of an old orchard below the house. The pigs I have raised have lived in a faded building that once was an ice house. There is a pleasant yard to move about in, shaded by an apple tree that overhangs the low rail fence. A pig couldn't ask for anything better—or none has, at any rate. The sawdust in the icehouse makes a comfortable bottom in which to root, and a warm bed. This sawdust, however, came under suspicion when the pig took sick. One of my neighbors said he thought the pig would have done better on new ground—the same principle that applies in planting potatoes. He said there might be something unhealthy about that sawdust, that he never thought well of sawdust.

It was about four o'clock in the afternoon when I first noticed that there was something wrong with the pig. He failed to appear at the trough for his supper, and when a pig (or a child) refuses supper a chill wave of fear runs through any household, or ice-household. After examining my pig, who was stretched out in the sawdust inside the building, I went to the phone and cranked it four times. Mr. Dameron answered. "What's good for a sick pig?" I asked. (There is never any identification needed on a country phone; the person on the other end knows who is talking by the sound of the voice and by the character of the question.)

"I don't know, I never had a sick pig," said Mr. Dameron, "but I can find out quick enough. You hang up and I'll call Henry."

Mr. Dameron was back on the line again in five minutes. "Henry says roll him over on his back and give him two ounces of castor oil or sweet oil, and if that doesn't do the trick give him an injection of soapy water. He says he's almost sure the pig's plugged up, and even if he's wrong, it can't do any harm."

I thanked Mr. Dameron. I didn't go right down to the pig, though. I sank into a chair and sat still for a few minutes to think about my troubles, and then I got up and went to the barn, catching up on some odds and ends that needed tending to. Unconsciously I held off, for an hour, the deed by which I would officially recognize the collapse of the performance of raising a pig; I wanted no interruption in the regularity of feeding, the steadiness of growth, the even succession of days. I wanted no interruption, wanted

no oil, no deviation. I just wanted to keep on raising a pig, full meal after full meal, spring into summer into fall. I didn't even know whether there were two ounces of castor oil on the place.

Shortly after five o'clock I remembered that we had been invited out to dinner that night and realized that if I were to dose a pig there was no time to lose. The dinner date seemed a familiar conflict: I move in a desultory society and often a week or two will roll by without my going to anybody's house to dinner or anyone's coming to mine, but when an occasion does arise, and I am summoned, something usually turns up (an hour or two in advance) to make all human intercourse seem vastly inappropriate. I have come to believe that there is in hostesses a special power of divination, and that they deliberately arrange dinners to coincide with pig failure or some other sort of failure. At any rate, it was after five o'clock and I knew I could put off no longer the evil hour.

When my son and I arrived at the pigyard, armed with a small bottle of castor oil and a length of clothesline, the pig had emerged from his house and was standing in the middle of his yard, listlessly. He gave us a slim greeting. I could see that he felt uncomfortable and uncertain. I had brought the clothesline thinking I'd have to tie him (the pig weighed more than a hundred pounds) but we never used it. My son reached down, grabbed both front legs, upset him quickly, and when he opened his mouth to scream I turned the oil into his throat—a pink, corrugated area I had never seen before. I had just time to read the label while the neck of the bottle was in his mouth. It said Puretest. The screams, slightly muffled by oil, were pitched in the hysterically high range of pig-sound, as though torture were being carried out, but they didn't last long: it was all over rather suddenly, and his legs released, the pig righted himself.

In the upset position the corners of his mouth had been turned down, giving him a frowning expression. Back on his feet again, he regained the set smile that a pig wears even in sickness. He stood his ground, sucking slightly at the residue of oil, a few drops leaked out of his lips while his wicked eyes, shaded by their coy little lashes, turned on me in disgust and hatred. I scratched him gently with oily fingers and he remained quiet, as though trying to recall the satisfaction of being scratched when in health, and seeming to rehearse in his mind the indignity to which he had

Pig chase
There's nothing as fast and slippery as a greased pig that doesn't want to be caught during a county fair event. (Photograph by Keith Baum)

just been subjected. I noticed, as I stood there, four or five small dark spots on his back near the tail end, reddish brown in color, each about the size of a house-fly. I could not make out what they were. They did not look troublesome but at the same time they did not look like mere surface bruises or chafe marks. Rather they seemed blemishes of internal origin. His stiff white bristles almost completely hid them and I had to part the bristles with my fingers to get a good look.

Several hours later, a few minutes before midnight, having dined well and at someone else's expense, I returned to the pighouse with a flashlight. The patient was asleep. Kneeling, I felt his ears (as you might put your hand on the forehead of a child) and they seemed cool, and then with the light made a careful examination of the yard and the house for sign that the oil had worked. I found none and went to bed.

We had been having an unseasonable spell of weather—hot, close days, with the fog shutting in every night, scaling for a few hours in midday, then creeping back again at dark, drifting in first over the trees on the point, then suddenly blowing across the fields, blotting out the world and taking possession of houses, men, and animals. Everyone kept hoping for a break, but the break failed to come. Next day was another hot one. I visited the pig before breakfast and tried to tempt him with a little milk in his trough. He just stared at it, while I made a sucking sound through my teeth to remind him of past pleasures of the feast. With very small, timid pigs, weanlings, this ruse is often quite successful and will encourage them to eat; but with a large, sick pig the ruse is senseless and the sound I made must have made him feel, if anything, more miserable. He not only did not crave food, he felt a positive revulsion to it. I found a place under the apple tree where he had vomited in the night.

At this point, although a depression had settled over me, I didn't suppose that I was going to lose my pig. From the lustiness of a healthy pig a man derives a feeling of personal lustiness; the stuff that goes into the trough and is received with such enthusiasm is an earnest of some later feast of his own, and when this suddenly comes to an end and the food lies stale and untouched, souring in the sun, the pig's imbalance becomes the man's, vicariously, and life seems insecure, displaced, transitory.

As my own spirits declined, along with the pig's, the spirits of my vile old dachshund rose. The frequency of our trips down the footpath through the orchard to the pigyard delighted him, although he suffers greatly from arthritis, moves with difficulty, and would be bedridden if he could find anyone willing to serve him meals on a tray.

He never missed a chance to visit the pig with me, and he made many professional calls on his own. You could see him down there all hours, his white face parting the grass along the fence as he wobbled and stumbled about, his stethoscope dangling—a happy quack, writing his villainous prescriptions and grinning his corrosive grin. When the enema bag appeared, and the bucket of warm suds, his happiness was complete, and he managed to squeeze his enormous body between the two lowest rails of the yard and then assumed full charge of the irrigation. Once, when I lowered the bag to check the flow, he reached in and hurriedly drank a few mouthfuls of the suds to test their potency. I have noticed that Fred will feverishly consume any substance that is associated with trouble—the bitter flavor is to his liking. When the bag was above reach, he concentrated on the pig and was everywhere at once, a tower of strength and inconvenience. The pig, curiously enough, stood rather quietly through this colonic carnival, and the enema, though ineffective was not as difficult as I had anticipated.

I discovered, though, that once having given a pig an enema there is no turning back, no chance of resuming one of life's more stereotyped roles. The pig's lot and mine were inextricably bound now, as though the rubber tube were the silver cord. From then until the time of his death I held the pig steadily in the bowl of my mind; the task of trying to deliver him from his misery became a strong obsession. His suffering soon became the embodiment of all earthly wretchedness. Along toward the end of the afternoon, defeated in physicking, I phoned the veterinary twenty

miles away and placed the case formally in his hands. He was full of questions, and when I casually mentioned the dark spots on the pig's back, his voice changed its tone.

"I don't want to scare you," he said, "but when there are spots, erysipelas has to be considered."

Together we considered erysipelas, with frequent interruptions from the telephone operator, who wasn't sure the connection had been established.

"If a pig has erysipelas can he give it to a person?" I asked.

"Yes, he can," replied the vet.

"Have they answered?" asked the operator.

"Yes, they have," I said. Then I addressed the vet again. "You better come over here and examine this pig right away."

"I can't come myself," said the vet, "but McFarland can come this evening if that's all right. Mac knows more about pigs than I do anyway. You needn't worry too much about the spots. To indicate erysipelas they would have to be deep hemorrhagic infarcts."

"Deep hemorrhagic what?" I asked.

"Infarcts," said the vet.

"Have they answered?" asked the operator.

"Well," I said, "I don't know what you'd call these spots, except they're about the size of a housefly. If the pig has erysipelas I guess I have it, too, by this time, because we've been very close lately."

"McFarland will be over," said the vet.

I hung up. My throat felt dry and I went to the cupboard and got a bottle of whiskey. Deep hemorrhagic infarcts—the phrase began fastening its hooks in my head. I had assumed that there could be nothing much wrong with a pig during the months it was being groomed for murder; my confidence in the essential health and endurance of pigs had been strong and deep, particularly in the health of pigs that belonged to me and that were part of my proud scheme. The awakening had been violent and I minded it all the more because I knew that what could be true of my pig could be true also of the rest of my tidy world. I tried to put this distasteful idea from me, but it kept recurring. I took a short drink of the whiskey and then, although I wanted to go down to the yard and look for fresh signs, I was scared to. I was certain I had erysipelas.

It was long after dark and the supper dishes had been put away when a car drove in and McFarland

Farm cats

Above: *Farm cats and kittens are always a special, indeterminate breed. These feline characters often subsist on their own, catching mice in the barns and always waiting for a squirt of fresh milk at milking time. (Photograph by Keith Baum)*

Egg-laying contest

Right: *Farmers were challenged to spur their hens to win this international egg-laying contest with its $285 in prize purses. (Minnesota Historical Society)*

got out. He had a girl with him. I could just make her out in the darkness—she seemed young and pretty. "This is Miss Owen," he said. "We've been having a picnic supper on the shore, that's why I'm late."

McFarland stood in the driveway and stripped off his jacket, then his shirt. His stocky arms and capable hands showed up in my flashlight's gleam as I helped him find his coverall and get zipped up. The rear seat of his car contained an astonishing amount of paraphernalia, which he soon overhauled, selecting a chain, a syringe, a bottle of oil, a rubber tube, and some other things I couldn't identify. Miss Owen said she'd go along with us and see the pig. I led the way down the warm slope of the orchard, my light picking out the path for them, and we all three climbed the fence, entered the pighouse, and squatted by the pig while McFarland took a rectal reading. My flashlight picked up the glitter of an engagement ring on the girl's hand.

"No elevation," said McFarland, twisting the thermometer in the light. "You needn't worry about erysipelas." He ran his hand slowly over the pig's stomach and at one point the pig cried out in pain.

"Poor piggledy-wiggledy!" said Miss Owen.

The treatment I had been giving the pig for two days was then repeated, somewhat more expertly, by the doctor, Miss Owen and I handing him things as he needed them—holding the chain that he had looped around the pig's upper jaw, holding the syringe, holding the bottle stopper, the end of the tube, all of us working in darkness and in comfort, working with the instinctive teamwork induced by emergency conditions, the pig unprotesting, the house shadowy, protecting, intimate. I went to bed tired but with a feeling of relief that I had turned over part of the responsibility of the case to a licensed doctor. I was beginning to think, though, that the pig was not going to live.

He died twenty-four hours later, or it might have been forty-eight—there is a blur in time here, and I may have lost or picked up a day in the telling and the pig one in the dying. At intervals during the last day I took cool fresh water down to him and at such times as he found the strength to get to his feet he would stand with head in the pail and snuffle his snout around. He drank a few sips but no more; yet it seemed to comfort him to dip his nose in water and bobble it

about, sucking in and blowing out through his teeth. Much of the time, now, he lay indoors half buried in sawdust. Once, near the last, while I was attending him I saw him try to make a bed for himself but he lacked the strength, and when he set his snout into the dust he was unable to plow even the little furrow he needed to lie down in.

He came out of the house to die. When I went down, before going to bed, he lay stretched in the yard a few feet from the door. I knelt, saw that he was dead, and left him there: his face had a mild look, expressive neither of deep peace nor of deep suffering, although I think he had suffered a good deal. I went back up to the house and to bed, and cried internally—deep hemorrhagic intears. I didn't wake till nearly eight the next morning, and when I looked out the open window the grave was already being dug, down beyond the dump under a wild apple. I could hear the spade strike against the small rocks that blocked the way. Never send to know for whom the grave is dug, I said to myself, it's dug for thee. Fred, I well knew, was supervising the work of digging, so I ate breakfast slowly.

It was a Saturday morning. The thicket in which I found the gravediggers at work was dark and warm, the sky overcast. Here, among alders and young hackmatacks, at the foot of the apple tree, Lennie had dug a beautiful hole, five feet long, three feet wide, three feet deep. He was standing in it, removing the last spadefuls of earth while Fred patrolled the brink in simple but impressive circles, disturbing the loose earth of the mound so that it trickled back in. There had been no rain in weeks and the soil, even three feet down, was dry and powdery. As I stood and stared, an enormous earthworm which had been partially exposed by the spade at the bottom dug itself deeper and made a slow withdrawal, seeking even remoter moistures at even lonelier depths. And just as Lennie stepped out and rested his spade against the tree and lit a cigarette, a small green apple separated itself from a branch overhead and fell into the hole. Everything about this last scene seemed overwritten—the dismal sky, the shabby woods, the imminence of rain, the worm (legendary bedfellow of the dead), the apple (conventional garnish of a pig).

But even so, there was a directness and dispatch about animal burial, I thought, that made it a more decent affair than human burial: there was no stop-

Fresh chicks

New baby chicks were often mail-ordered from the distant city via retailers such as the gigantic Sears Roebuck & Co. of Chicago. Here, a farm mother and her son let fresh chicks loose in the hen house. (Photograph by J. C. Allen & Son)

over in the undertaker's foul parlor, no wreath nor spray; and when we hitched a line to the pig's hind legs and dragged him swiftly from his yard, throwing our weight into the harness and leaving a wake of crushed grass and smoothed rubble over the dump, ours was a businesslike procession, with Fred, the dishonorable pallbearer, staggering along in the rear, his perverse bereavement showing in every seam in his face; and the post-mortem performed handily and swiftly right at the edge of the grave, so that the inwards that had caused the pig's death preceded him into the ground and he lay at last resting squarely on the cause of his own undoing.

I threw in the first shovelful, and then we worked rapidly and without talk, until the job was complete. I picked up the rope, made it fast to Fred's collar (he is a notorious ghoul), and we all three filed back up the path to the house, Fred bringing up the rear and holding back every inch of the way, feigning unusual stiffness. I noticed that although he weighed far less than the pig, he was harder to drag, being possessed of the vital spark.

The news of the death of my pig traveled fast and far, and I received many expressions of sympathy from friends and neighbors, for no one took the event lightly and the premature expiration of a pig is, I soon discovered, a departure which the community marks solemnly on its calendar, a sorrow in which it feels fully involved. I have written this account in penitence and in grief, as a man who failed to raise his pig, and to explain my deviation from the classic course of so many raised pigs. The grave in the woods is unmarked, but Fred can direct the mourner to it unerringly and with immense good will, and I know he and I shall often revisit it, singly and together, in seasons of reflection and despair, on flagless memorial days of our own choosing.

THE MULE: "VERY KORRUPT AT HARTE"

By Josh Billings

"Josh Billings" was the pseudonym of Henry Wheeler Shaw. Under the "Uncle Josh" pen name, Shaw made people laugh with his down-home writing and rural philosophy. This piece, written in the late 1800s, was an introduction to—and warning to stay away from—mules.

The mule is haf hoss, and haf Jackass, and then kums to a full stop, natur diskovering her mistake. Tha weigh more, akordin tu their heft, than enny other kreetur, except a crowbar. Tha kant hear enny quicker, nor further than the hoss, yet their ears are big enuff for snow shoes. You kan trust them with enny one whoose life aint worth enny more than the mules. The only wa tu keep them in a paster, is tu turn them into a medder jineing, and let them jump out. Tha are ready for use, just as soon as they will du tu abuse. Tha haint got enny friends, and will live on huckel berry brush, with an ocksasional chanse at Kanada thissels. Tha are a modern invenshun, i dont think the Bible deludes tu them at all. Tha sel for more money than enny other domestik animile. Yu kant tell their age by looking into their mouth, enny more than you kould a Mexican cannons. They never hav no dissease that a good club wont heal. If tha ever die tha must kum rite to life agin, for i never herd nobody sa "ded mule." Tha are like sum men, very korrupt at harte; ive known them tu be good mules for 6 months, just tu git a good chanse to kick sumbody. I never owned one, nor never mean to, unless there is a United Staits law passed, requiring it. The only reason why tha are pashunt, is bekause that are ashamed ov themselfs. I have seen eddikated mules in a sirkus. Tha kould kick, and bit tremenjis. I would not sa what I am forced to sa again the mule, if his birth want an outrage, and man want tu blame for it. Enny man who is willing tu drive a mule, ought to be exempt by law from running for the legislatur. Tha are the strongest creeturs on earth, and heaviest, ackording tu their sise; I herd tell ov one who fell oph from the tow path, on the Eri kanawl, and sunk as soon as he touched bottom, but he kept rite on towing the boat tu the nex stashun, breathing thru his ears, which stuck out ov the water about 2 feet 6 inches; i didn't see this did, but an auctioneer told me ov it, and i never knew an autcioneer tu lie unless it was absolutely convenient.

Talkin' about mules and other things that kick . . . I undertook to break a kicking heifer once. I read a treatise on the subject and followed the directions close and got knocked endwise in about 5 minutes. I then sot down and thought the thing over. I made up my mind that the fellow who wrote the treatise was more in the treatise business than he was in the kicking-heifer trade.

Farm dogs

Farm dogs have many jobs, from watchdog to herding work to family pet. Whatever their resumé, they all start out as puppies, as with this golden retriever pup. (Photograph by Lynn M. Stone)

*"Whoever has really looked into the eye of a shrewd old sow should feel humility.
It is a bright clear eye, more like the eye of a human than the eye of any other animal. It looks at
you quite directly, even with what might be described as a piercing gaze. The look sizes you up,
appraises you and leaves you presently with the impression that
the old sow has indeed a very low opinion of you. . . ."*
—Louis Bromfield, "A Hymn to Hawgs," 1955

Chapter 5

A Patchwork Quilt of Farm Living

*"Farming is healthy and moral and respectable and in the
long run may become profitable."*
—**Chase County (Kansas)** *Leader* **newspaper, 1871**

Life on the farm comprises many elements. There are the obvious pieces, such as the chores and the fieldwork, family and friends. But there are many other elements that hold the social fabric of rural communities together, from the country church to the county fair, the one-room schoolhouse to holiday picnics. Together, these pieces form a patchwork quilt of farm living.

These reminiscences chronicle many of the different facets of the farm life.

Dinner bell

Left: Everyone came when the dinner bell rang. Whether you called it "supper" or "dinner," artist Walter Haskell Hinton's painting captures the farmwife's call to the table in an image that appeared in a classic John Deere calendar. John Deere's early two-cylinder tractors were known variously as "Poppin' Johnnies" or "Johnny Poppers" because the engine's sound was so distinctive, and farm wives could tell from the note of the engine when their husbands had idled down the tractor to come in for supper. (Deere & Company)

Helping hand

Above: The arrival of the power clothes washer and other similar powered household tools signaled nothing less than a revolution on farms everywhere. While these tools were often billed as "labor savers," in truth they merely saved farm families time from one chore that they could then devote to another.

Food and Those Who Ate It

By Majorie Myers Douglas

Majorie Myers Douglas grew up in the city "abysmally ignorant of farming," as she writes in her memoir, *Eggs in the Coffee, Sheep in the Corn*. She soon gained a full, hands-on knowledge of farming when she and her husband moved to his family's stock farm near Appleton, Minnesota. Over the next seventeen years, from 1943 to 1960, Marjorie became a "farmwife," as she proudly calls herself.

At first, she was "curious" about farm living, but that was soon remedied: "With a year-old daughter in diapers and no running water in the farmhouse, I soon found my curiosity satisfied." From that starting point, Marjorie soon became completely involved in all aspects of her newfound farm home.

This selection pays homage not only to the famous farm food, but also to the farmhouse kitchen, the family and hired hands who gave the food the respect it deserved, and last but hardly least, to the farmwife who could work miracles.

Food is the magnet around which so many of my farm memories cluster. Small wonder. Hearty food in vast quantities was needed three times a day. I remembered the obstetrician who had looked at Anne—newborn, long and slender—and said, "Babies are like empty stockings. Just fill her up." I hadn't appreciated the remark at the time, but I had been at the job of filling people up ever since.

You've heard of a "generous hand" in cooking? Well, Mother Douglas certainly had one. Her largess extended even to the pets, and items like leftover pork chops and dressing were broken up for the dogs' and cats' dishes. Under her hand, cream and butter and seasonings transformed even plain old carrots into a succulent treat. Thick sour cream and extra eggs fluffed her waffles. Long after her death, Papa would still beg me for pork hocks and noodles or small-curd cottage cheese "like Vivian used to make." I never thought I got it quite right but he apparently did.

One food I could never replicate for him was the justly famous specialty of Don's grandmother. It was known as Grandma Moats's Hot Sweet Chopped Green Tomato Piccalilli. The tomatoes had to be harvested just before the first killing frost. Then you had to collect red peppers, onions, condiments, spice bouquets, and, of course, mustard and vinegar. Even Mother Douglas did not know the complete list nor the exact proportions, because the recipe was a tightly guarded secret.

When the Douglases lived in Benson, Grandma

Lunch in the field

All fieldwork came to an immediate halt when the picnic lunch arrived. Dad parked his Farmall H as soon as Mother set up the folding table and laid out lunch, crowned of course by a double-decker chocolate cake. (Photograph by J. C. Allen & Son)

Moats lived with them, as did her frail sister whom we called Aunt Belle. From my visits to Don's house as a college student, I remembered the two white-haired women in their dark, practical housedresses, knees spread to support the dishpans of potatoes they always seemed to be paring for dinner. I understood that Grandma Moats had sworn her sister to secrecy about the recipe.

Grandma Moats had not always been so tight-lipped, but as her delicious mix steadily gained fame at home and at church suppers, people constantly asked for it. Papa began to tease that he was going to steal the recipe, market the relish, and gain fabulous wealth. Grandma, a widow concerned about money, began to guard her secret jealously, especially from Papa (or, as time passed, from any possible spies).

Mother Douglas reminisced about the controversy one day as we sat in the sunny kitchen peeling tomatoes we had scalded for canning.

"The relish was sweet and sour, too," she began. "It was too tart for a sauce and too hot. I know there was plenty of red pepper in it. Wonderful with meat, especially pork. And a little bit went a long way. I've seen it bring tears to a grown man's eyes." She almost giggled. "We canned it in pints, and a pint lasted for days even with extra men at the table."

"But you said a whole relish dish of it disappeared?" I prompted.

"Yes. Once at threshing time the men gathered at that long harvest table we used at Benson. The men joked and laughed as they seated themselves—all except for Frank, a quiet fellow who was new to the bunch. My mother and Aunt Belle had helped all morning and I made them sit down with the men. Mother would not sit until she found a place for her precious bowl of piccalilli among the crowding trays of bread and dishes of butter, jam, and cabbage slaw. I brought platters of pork roast, mashed potatoes, baked beans, and tomatoes. In a second, the noise stopped and they all started in."

"You didn't sit down?"

"No, I had just got busy pouring coffee when I noticed a look of real distress on my mother's face. I soon discovered why. The new man had started on her dish of relish, which was near the edge of his plate, and he did not pass it on to the others. He must have assumed it was his side dish. He was eating it like a dish of applesauce, and it seemed to have no effect on him."

"I'll bet Grandma was wild! Didn't she say anything?"

"No, I was afraid she'd choke, but she kept still. He'd have been so embarrassed if he'd realized what he'd done."

Mother Douglas was laughing now, but her quick fingers worked as rapidly as ever. "Then I was afraid Frank would choke," she continued. "He was really gobbling that hot stuff—he must have been brought up to clean his plate!"

"Papa didn't notice?"

"Oh, trust him! But it was too late. Frank had laid down his spoon by an empty dish."

"Now, are you going to tell me that Frank had enough fire in his belly to do the work of two men that afternoon?"

"That's what Papa claimed—said he'd use the story in advertising. His motto would be 'Grandma Moats's Hot Sweet Chopped Green Tomato Piccalilli is energizing and safe in any amount.'"

Her story reminded me of when my friendliness had been tested by two hired men, a Mexican and an Indian, who were with us for two or three weeks. Inspired, I put my small bottle of Tabasco sauce on the table, thinking our food might seem bland. Apparently it did! I had used that same bottle from the time we were first married, measuring exactly ten drops in a celebrated salad dressing. They showered it on meat, potatoes, and vegetables, and sopped it up with bread. When I asked Don to get another bottle on the next grocery order, I told him, only half joking, "If I ever see them put that stuff on my pie, they will never come back, I mean it."

It was feeding the neighbors who came to help and the hired men, of course, that created most of the work in the kitchen. When neighbors were our helpers, there was news and friendly gossip. Sometimes they joked and told stories about the community that I enjoyed, as I waited on them and the children, snatching a bite when I could. Hired men were more a part of the farmers' world, and Don always found a basis of comradeship with his men. I tried to visit with them at meals, but mostly their talk was of the fields and machinery. Still, I remember them best through food. Sometimes I packed up iced tea in a thermos bucket and sandwiches and cake or cookies and rattled out to the field with the toy wagon. The children often trailed along, and a short picnic made a pleasant, albeit dusty, break in the day.

Apple cider time

Above: *Making apple cider involved the whole family. Sis sorted and washed the apples while Ma and Pa ran the cider press and Grandma ladled the fresh cider into barrels. Naturally, the little ones helped as well, sampling the cider to make certain everyone else was doing their job right. (Photograph by J. C. Allen & Son)*

Cream separator

Right: *The cream separator was an essential tool on every dairy farm, and De Laval's machines were known across the country. (Photograph by J. C. Allen & Son)*

To this day I can't see a pork chop without thinking of Red. He was a big, powerful, good-natured bachelor from town who played in a German band all winter and lived on unemployment benefits most of the summer. Don talked him into becoming temporary crew foreman because of an unusual problem.

We had hired two young men from town after rain had delayed the cultivating. They ran the machinery well enough, but the work proceeded very slowly. Don suspected they were taking naps in the sunshine when their tractors were out of his sight, but he couldn't afford to stop his own work long enough to prove it. Their bad habit abruptly ceased when Red joined us. Coincidentally, we noticed a couple of freshly blackened eyes. The arrangement got us over the hump and is the only time I can recall when Don's relationship with his helpers needed strong-arm tactics.

Red was fond of my pork chop casserole. Thus, when he agreed to work Easter Sunday so that we could keep a long-promised dinner date at the Lundgrens', I made this favorite dish for his dinner. I browned eight large pork chops, covered them with raw rice, generous slices of raw onion, and tomatoes, and left them in a slow oven to stew. I assumed that I'd have leftovers ready for Monday. Suffice it to say that Red loved to eat, and we did not begrudge him a single pork chop.

Sometimes hired hands shared more than our food, though. They shared hopes, disappointments, and daily life.

For several years, Andy Larsen lived with his family in one of our houses. His three small children and our kids played together. One day he indicated to Don that he was trying to save to buy a little land of his own. Hearing that, we gave them garden space and paid him extra for odd jobs. During a spree one weekend, he accidently let his wife discover his secret. Once she knew, nothing would do except to turn over the savings to her to squander. Thoroughly discour-

Egg money
Going to town to sell a full basket of eggs and shop for something special always brought a smile. (Photograph by J. C. Allen & Son)

aged, Andy began frequent excessive drinking bouts and sought a job in town.

The following year a lively young fellow asked Don for work so that he could be married to the daughter of a well-respected German farmer just northwest of us. Don offered to supply paint, lumber, and wallpaper for them to decorate a two-room building that had been used as an office before we came. Hank proved to be an excellent farmer and well worth the higher wages he had requested. They stayed only a year before a better job called, but our friendship has lasted.

Old Joe was different. He came to the farm one day in his old Ford pickup, with the door on the passenger side tied shut with rope. His eyesight was failing, and he assured us he never drove over fifteen miles an hour, and then only on the shoulder! We didn't really need a man at the time, but he apparently had nowhere else to go. He eagerly offered to work for us at a low wage that Don promptly raised, as Joe became both useful and trusted. We had assumed he would not handle machinery nor take much initiative. Only later we discovered, through stories he told the children, that he had once been an assistant agent on an Indian reservation and carried considerable responsibility. He proved to be easy with the stock, prompt, and reliable at chores, and he watched out for the children's safety when they followed him about. Finally we felt enough confidence to go to the Twin Cities for a long-postponed overnight with my parents, leaving Joe in charge of the farm. On our return we found that he had sold last year's hay (which he knew we didn't need) to farmers who had come by seeking some. There on the kitchen table lay the money with his careful notations.

Don could remember with fondness a hired man who had been like a member of his family and had taught him to read the newspaper before he started school. But this was my first time of sharing our daily life with a person who had no close family of his own. Joe's discharge from the agency, due to the frailties of age, must have been traumatic for him, but I never heard him talk about it. How lonely and useless he must have been feeling when he turned up at our farm seeking work. His two-year time with us met a real need for him, and he proved to be a contented, useful employee. Eventually he was welcomed into the home of a nephew in South Dakota for his final years.

Perhaps I noticed Joe's loneliness more because I could see Don's circle widening. While Papa and Mother Douglas kept a low profile, seldom even attending church, Don radiated the confidence born of his comfortable upbringing; he was liked and trusted. Often on Saturday evenings, we made popcorn and read aloud or played games with the children. Don, however, sometimes had errands or needed to visit Perry's Barber Shop. That often ended with a shared bottle, but serious drinkers went to Correll, as Appleton always voted dry.

When I occasionally served hot gingerbread with applesauce or chocolate cake and the eternal coffee for one of Don's informal committee meetings, I could see his feeling of belonging through these contacts—and not only belonging. It became clear that people sought out his opinion, people from a wider community, less stratified than the one we had known in the city. (He continually encouraged the merchants of Appleton to admit a big chain store to increase their trade area, but they feared the competition and had to watch the neighboring town of Montevideo grow and thrive instead.)

My work of preserving, preparing, and serving food remained constant, however. I always had some hired help to feed during the crop season—except for our last summer when Don offered the job of hired hand to Anne and Bill. Bill got up early and ran a tractor till noon, Anne worked from noon till late supper. Each was faithfully paid one half of full wages every Saturday night. Anne later went to college, cherishing the knowledge that her daddy had said she "could disc in a dead furrow better than he could."

Life should have been simpler for the distaff side when big machinery replaced some of the hired men and threshing rings. Food was served in much smaller quantities than in the old days—but often at strange hours. Many times when bad weather threatened, but the crop was dry and right for harvest, Don ran our big combine all night. He stopped in for hot lunches or carried sandwiches and coffee with him to keep him safely awake. I had to agree with Mother Douglas, who insisted that headlights on tractors should never have been invented. They robbed farmers of their rightful rest—to say nothing of farmers' wives.

When winter weather was severe, Don arranged with Willy, who was the International dealer and also drove the township plow, to watch for our yard light. If he found it on after a storm, he stopped and plowed us out, knowing I would have roast beef sandwiches ready and lots of hot coffee. Of course Don paid him, but it was the food, I think, that lured him to come so promptly—and it saved us hours of hard work. If the snowfall was especially heavy, Don joined his friend as he went back to plowing out the county roads. They roared through the night. While Willie guided the big blade, Don kept his eyes fastened on the sloping wingblade as it swept the roadside and yelled a warning if an obstruction loomed in the swirling whiteness.

I would snuggle back into bed, thinking of Mother Douglas again and her saying to me as a newcomer that farm people worked hard and deserved the best food and lots of it. I ruefully added to myself—yes, and apparently at all hours!

The Polk County Homewreckers

By Sara De Luca

Household tasks were rarely as celebrated as the farmyard chores. Plowing, milking cows, and threshing often seem to be idealized, whereas laundry, cleaning, and kitchen work are remembered as pure, unadulterated drudgery. In her memoir, *Dancing the Cows Home: A Wisconsin Girlhood*, Sara De Luca writes of the hardships of farming as well as the joys, of the struggles as well as the triumphs. In the end, however, her stories and memories are as rich as the fertile land.

Her memoir tells of growing up on her family's farm near Milltown, Wisconsin. In this chapter, Sara recounts the seemingly endless household tasks with a bittersweet sentimentality. She still feels the ache of tired muscles even now some five decades later—yet at the same time, she fondly recollects aspects of the toil in this light-hearted look back at the way things were.

Aside from church, Mama was never much of a joiner. She had one affiliation—the Polk County Homemakers. She saved her ten-year membership award—a framed certificate representing ten years of monthly meetings devoted to lessons in family nutrition, budget-wise shopping, emergency first aid, home nursing, bread baking, party planning, cleaning, canning, vegetable gardening, slipcovering, stain removal, and various other skills demanded by a family in the 1950s.

The Homemakers' Creed is printed on the back:

We, the Homemakers of Wisconsin, believe in the sanctity of the *home*, the cradle of character, blessed by motherly devotion and guarded by fatherly protection.

We pledge ourselves:

To work for the preservation and improvement of home and community life;

To strive for healthier minds and bodies, and better living;

To promote the welfare of our boys and girls, the nation's greatest asset;

To be true to God and country, and of lasting service to our homes and communities.

"Mama's off to her Homewreckers meeting," Daddy joked the only night of the month when Mama could not be found at home. That fourth Thursday evening she always hurried with the barn chores, scrubbed her arms and neck and face, changed into a dress, nylon hose and pumps, arranged her hair, and applied a dash of powder and some bright, red lipstick. Then she jumped into the car and sped down the driveway, clouds of dust billowing in her wake.

It would be ten o'clock before she arrived home,

Collecting eggs

Doing battle with the hens for their fresh-laid eggs was often a part of the daily chores of any farm "homewrecker." (Photograph by J. C. Allen & Son)

all coffeed up and too excited to sleep. Our parents' late-night conversation funneled upstairs to our bedroom through the hot-air vent, and my sisters and I strained to catch any tidbits that might provoke our interest.

"What was the topic tonight?" Daddy asked, sounding half asleep.

Mama shared the latest word on making beds with tidy hospital corners or removing blood or food stains from cotton, wool, or acetate. Daddy was snoring loudly, long before the lesson was over.

Mama brought home mimeographed "lessons" from her Homemaker meetings. Sometimes she shared them with her daughters. "Last night's lesson was all about housecleaning, using the new products to advantage. You girls are all going to be keeping house some day. And I'm counting on you to help me now as much as you possibly can. You really ought to read this."

I skimmed it, feigning interest.

The Many-Handed Housewife

Spring housecleaning has bitten the dust. The American housewife can keep her household tasks constantly under control by using the modern methods which are now available. She has Big Business to thank for this. Post-war industry has concentrated on the needs of the housewife and supplied us with many "hands" in the way of household equipment. With a whole battery of tools at her command—light weight vacuum cleaners, brooms, brushes, and cellulose sponges of every size and description—the American housewife is turning housecleaning into a very specialized skill.

She can select from a wide range of nationally distributed household products—from gentle soaps and detergents such as Dreft or Ivory Flakes to heavy duty Fels Naptha, Duz, or Oxydol. She has Soilex for her soiled walls and Bab-O for the bathtub.

The new products take so much of the drudgery out of cleaning that the modern homemaker can wear a poplin housedress while she goes about these tasks, looking relaxed and attractive for unexpected visitors. She notes industry's discovery that bending requires 43% more energy than standing straight—and chooses a long-handled dustpan. She

hears that U.S. soldiers do better on the march with a ten minute rest interval every hour—and she rests before she gets tired. She invents techniques: dust mitts for both hands to speed dusting; a small open market basket with handle to carry cans of paste and bottles of polish from room to room. The many-handed woman takes still another tip from industry and does her cleaning day by day instead of letting it pile up on her. Result: a happy housewife and spring freshness in the home all year around.

What a joke, I thought. Mama was a many-handed woman all right. She had eight hands in all, and six of them belonged to her daughters. This lesson was completely useless. Mama was plenty efficient all by herself, using nothing but her own two hands and a bit of elbow grease. She never needed a ten-minute break, and a pair of mittens would have slowed her down.

Some Homewreckers' lessons on basic cooking might have been more helpful. While Mama turned out delicious breads and pastries and could also spread a tasty Sunday dinner, those three squares a day were usually handled in a slapdash fashion. She admitted she wished cooking were a seasonal chore—like breaking sod or whitewashing the barn. Once done, it ought to stay done for a year or so. Those relentless, pesky mealtimes kept sneaking up on her, three times a day, when she was knee-deep in something more important—mending fences, cultivating corn.

When the noon whistle blew in town, Mama raced to the house, fired up the range, grabbed a package of meat out of the freezer compartment of the refrigerator, and beat it with a wooden mallet. She heated the cast-iron skillet to a white-hot glow and plopped in a tablespoon of Crisco, along with the partially defrosted hunks of cow. Oil splattered in all directions. The hot pan sizzled in protest. Those steaks were tough to begin with, harvested as they were from aging Holsteins well beyond their prime. Now they would be served up on our plates, black on the outside, crunchy with ice crystals sparkling within. I was always puzzled why diners would order anything as disagreeable as "steak" when they visited a restaurant and actually had a choice.

A couple of side dishes helped to balance this large dose of protein. There was always bread, of course.

ONE-ROOM SCHOOLHOUSES

"The pioneer children knew how to work with their hands. They lived an active life in the house, in the fields, in the woods. Even though they worked hard, they had much freedom and few restrictions. School was very different. . . . To sit still, in an unnatural position, on a hard bench, staring either at the blackboard or at a book, trying to learn a new language, was a hard task that made heads ache and limbs stiffen."
—Aagot Raaen, *Grass of the Earth: The Story of a Norwegian Immigrant Family in Dakota*, 1950

Schoolroom

Above right: *A one-room country schoolhouse was furnished with everything from a piano to numerous maps, orderly rows of desks to walls of chalkboards, all befitting the single classroom's role as an educational home to the farm neighborhood's children of many ages. (Photograph by G. Alan Nelson)*

Lonely schoolhouse

Below: *The days of the one-room country schoolhouse are all but gone except in the most isolated parts of the country. This empty schoolhouse sits on the prairie, lonely for the sounds of children. (Photograph by G. Alan Nelson)*

And there might be Jell-O or a carrot-raisin salad on the side. Mama might haul out last evening's mashed potatoes and fry them up in the same black skillet that produced our charcoaled meat.

No time was given to pleases or thank yous or complaints; within ten minutes chairs were pushed back from the table, and the room was empty. Only a cloud of oily smoke hung over the kitchen range to remind us that another meal had come and gone.

Cleaning up the dishes became my job from the age of eight until I escaped for good. Mama did not pass any dishwashing lessons on to me, but I'd been observing the routine long enough. I must haul buckets of ice-cold water from the well pump, then heat it on the kitchen range. I must scrape the dishes carefully, saving the scraps for the barn cats. I must dipper the water into my basin, as sparingly as possible. Soap flakes were precious, too. If there were any suds at all, I knew I had used too much. Sometimes I conserved energy as well by skipping the washing process altogether, simply sponging the plates with a greasy, soggy towel. Mama usually caught me taking shortcuts. She despaired for my future. What kind of wife could I be when I was unable to handle even this most elementary household task?

As for cooking, I never graduated beyond Jell-O brand chocolate pudding. I loved to measure out the milk, mix and stir till it was smooth, then watch it come to the boiling point. I stirred and tasted and stirred some more, lifting my kettle just in time as the pudding crawled up the sides and threatened to flow over the edge onto the hot burner. My pudding was always a perfect consistency, never burned or lumpy. I sampled often from my wooden spoon and also ate the skin that formed on the individual serving dishes once I had portioned it out. I was usually too full of pudding to eat a proper meal, and the remaining servings were small, but no one seemed to notice.

The Homewreckers probably talked about child rearing, too. They must have recommended praising children, helping them build pride and self-esteem. "Sara makes wonderful chocolate pudding!" Mama bragged repeatedly. Yet she never offered to teach me further culinary skills. She was just too busy, I guess.

Time was precious so we specialized. Peggy was assistant cook. She also sewed and mended. Susie liked to straighten, mop, and dust. There was nothing important left for me except starching, sprinkling, and ironing—and those endless piles of dirty dishes.

We were all pressed into service on laundry day. Mama scheduled this on Mondays during the summer months but switched to Saturdays during the school year so she would have plenty of help. Beginning right after breakfast, we emptied mounds of soiled clothing from boxes and baskets in the four upstairs bedrooms. We stripped beds down to the mattress ticking. We lifted the barn overalls, stiff with straw and manure, from their pegs on the porch. All were sorted and stacked around the kitchen according to a complicated method based on color, fabric, and aroma. I never quite mastered the sorting rules and was constantly in trouble.

"What are you doing with those piles, Sara?"

"I'm sorting them with my foot. I read somewhere that bending down takes almost twice the energy."

"This job takes all your energy, young lady. I suggest you bend—or squat right down—and work with both your hands. No, not like that! Never put bright colors with pastels especially nothing red. You will turn everything pink with that load, mark my word. And never mix delicates like those underpants in with the denims. Be sure to check for stains—the stained ones get soaked with Rinso in the basin. Be quick now. I'm almost ready for another load of whites." I loathed the basin duty, which included hand scrubbing food and blood spots and other stubborn stains. Since I was less than thorough, Peggy was usually assigned this task.

Usually I ended up with the simple job of rounding up the hose, connecting it to the well pump, and trailing it across the yard and into the enclosed back porch, which served as a laundry room on Saturdays. The water was rusty. Because the well had been sunk so close to the silo pit, the water took on a yellow hue and smelled of silage in the fall. It wouldn't do for the rinse cycle. Both rinse tubs—the same tubs that served for our Saturday night baths—were filled from large milk cans containing clean, clear water that Daddy hauled from town.

Mama supervised filling the machine with the right amount of cold water mixed with hot from a large copper boiler on the stove. She also dumped in carefully measured Oxydol and the first load of whites. We took turns stirring with a wooden stick, fishing the laundry out of its steaming bath, running it

Suppertime
The table was always a time to share the events of the day. (Photograph by J. C. Allen & Son)

through the wringer, rinsing, wringing, rinsing and bluing, wringing again, hauling it out, and pegging it to the clothesline. I didn't mind the morning hours but grew restless and tired by midday, when we started washing towels and colored shirts. By three o'clock we had progressed to greasy overalls and foul-smelling barn pants. The water was disgusting—gray-blue and thick enough to float the bits of chaff and cow manure that agitated to the surface. The heavy snaps and buckles often caught in the wringer, causing it to fly apart and hold up the entire operation while Mama made repairs.

Peggy was rewarded for her speed and skill with a relatively cheery task—gathering in the clothespins and the dry, sweet-smelling laundry. On a bright, breezy day, the fresh clothing smelled of sunshine

and clover. She sniffed and sighed as she passed by. Peggy did not have it quite so good in winter. Mama helped her then. Most of the hanging was done indoors on twine strings strung in the hall and stairwell and through every downstairs room. Only the heaviest overalls were hung out on the line. They were gathered up quite frozen, almost stiff enough to hike in on their own.

Susie and I drained the tubs at day's end. We were revolted to see the cold, soupy water draining from the tubs through the long hose into the backyard. The last of it had to be toted out in buckets, the sludge wiped from the bottom of the tubs and discarded far away, beyond the borders of our tidy lawn. And even though Mama always checked the pockets and demanded that we do the same, there were

Patch work
Being able to patch or darn clothes on the run was an essential skill. (Photograph by J. C. Allen & Son)

Quilting circle

The quilting circle was once the center of farming gossip and conversation. In Lancaster County, Pennsylvania, quilting is still a community focal point among Amish women. (Photograph by Keith Baum)

the inevitable nuts and bolts and screws and God-knows-what-men-keep-in-their-pockets that had to be fished out of the hoses and drains. I was always impressed by the amount of dirt a family of seven could collect in one week's time. Impressed and exhausted.

"There now, doesn't that make you feel good?" Mama exclaimed.

"Sure does," her helpers chorused wearily.

We sat down to Mama's pancake supper, almost too tired to eat. No meat or potatoes were served on laundry day. We didn't mind. It kept kitchen clean-up to a minimum.

The laundry routine was somewhat simpler once we moved to the Milltown farm in 1953 where there was indoor plumbing and hot running water. But except for the filling and draining, we continued to fight with the same old galvanized rinsing tubs, the same pokey wringer machine.

"Those new automatics just can't get your clothes

as clean! They're fine for city folks, I suppose—but you can't tell me they were designed to handle mud and manure," Mama insisted, defending her ancient but dependable equipment. "I'm going to stick with my wringer machine—I don't care what the Home-makers say."

By the late 1950s many of the Homemakers were "working out," earning hourly wages outside the home. The monthly lessons began to emphasize self-fulfillment. They promoted electric appliances for the homemaker, which would free up her time and broaden her choices. Mama was not sure that they were headed in the right direction. But she remained a loyal member of that organization for ten years—until 1959. After that she just couldn't seem to find the time.

That last autumn Mama invited her family to attend the Polk County Homemakers' Musical Revue. The star performer was Mary Jane Manson, a young,

Country church
The country church steeple always stood tall above the fields. (Photograph by G. Alan Nelson)

unmarried home economist, recently employed by the Polk County Extension Office. Mary Jane pranced around the stage, twirling a parasol, singing:

Single gal, single gal,
Around the town she flies,
Married gal, married gal,
Rocks and cradles and cries.
So if you are a single gal,
Single you should stay.
Don't become a married gal,
And dream your life away.

"What a song to offer a group of housewives tied down tight with farms and families!" Mama laughed, humming the catchy tune all the way home.

At the age of sixteen, I thought it was pretty good advice. If I ever did become a married gal, I wouldn't be wrestling with wood stoves and wringer washing machines. No, I'd be one of those modern types featured in the *Ladies' Home Companion*. I could picture myself already, wearing city suits, high-heeled shoes, and little white gloves, waving at my gleaming appliances as I danced out the door.

WASH DAY

Washing clothes

Washing clothes the old-fashioned way meant boiling water over a wood fire, then scrubbing the steaming-hot clothes on a washboard. Clothes never got cleaner, however. (Fred Hultstrand History in Pictures Collection, NDIRS-NDSU, Fargo)

Stationary gas engine

The small stationary gas engine became the farmer's helping hand, providing muscle to power everything from a dynamo to a saw, the water pump to the washing machine.

In search of whiter whites

No one looked forward to wash day, because it was an hours-long job requiring back-straining hard work. The arrival of the gasoline-powered stationary engine helped all that by powering the old washing machine, giving Ma free time to peruse the Breeder's Gazette. *(Photograph by J. C. Allen & Son)*

Electricity

By Jim Heynen

Jim Heynen's stories about "the boys" growing up down on the farm are precious jewels. They show the boys in all their oddity, curiosity, and wonder as they do the things farm boys do—and by chance learn the ways of the world at the same time. There is the time the boys made chickens dance and the time they drank milk straight from a cow; there are recollections of the benefits of peach packing tissues over corn cobs in the outhouse and reminiscences of what can happen on the walk home from school. Collected into the volume *The One-Room Schoolhouse: Stories About the Boys*, these stories are short and sweet, running straight to the point and aimed straight at your heart.

Jim makes his home in St. Paul, Minnesota. He is the author of several other volumes of poetry and stories, including *How The Sow Became a Goddess* and his latest novel, *Being Youngest*.

This story of the boys tells of the arrival of rural electricty and the enlightenment it brought.

The boys remembered the night electricity came to the farm. At least the oldest did, and the others pretended to. Or they'd heard the story so often they thought they remembered it. After a while, it didn't matter who really remembered it and who didn't. They all knew the story.

It was the night the big switch was thrown somewhere at some big dam. This was long after the electrician had spent weeks wiring all the buildings, putting switches on walls where only wallpaper had been, putting a long fluorescent light like the ones they'd seen in town right in the middle of their kitchen ceiling so that the old lantern had to hang on a new hook until the big switch was thrown.

The night of the big switch: that's when all these dead wires and gray light bulbs were supposed to come to life. Could it really work? Could electricity get all the way out here from that big switch at that big dam hundreds of miles away?

A letter had come telling how to get ready for the big night. Five o'clock p.m. on such-and-such a day the big switch would be thrown. Have all switches turned off, the letter said, and turn them on one at a time. As if the big dam couldn't stand to have all of its electricity sucked out at once. Which made sense to the boys. Cows kicked if you tried to milk all four teats at once. And a horse would take more easily to four riders if they didn't all get on at once. Imagine a chicken laying ten eggs in one shot. It made sense.

So the night of the big switch they sat around the kitchen table waiting, switches turned off. Waiting for five o'clock. Then they saw it happen—a light on the horizon where there hadn't been a light before. Then a light in the neighbor's window, about a half-mile away. Then lights popping on everywhere. It looked as if the whole world was covered with fireflies. The new light was not the yellow light of lanterns but the white clear light of electricity. Light clear as water from the big dam, wherever it was.

Holiday lights
The coming of electricity was a reason for celebration, and Christmas was an ideal time to dress the farmstead in colored lights. (Photograph by Dennis Frates)

One of the boys flicked the kitchen switch. And it happened right there. The big switch worked, even here. It was as if the ceiling opened with light. A fluttering fluorescent angel of light. A splash, a woof, a clatter of light. And in one second there was more light in that kitchen than had ever been there. Light brighter than high noon on the Fourth of July. They looked at each other in this new light—every freckle, every smudge, every stringy hair, every ring around the collar clearer than ever. Then they looked around the room—the cupboards, the wainscoting, the wall-paper, the ceiling where the old lantern dangled like a hanged man.

And out of the throat of one of the horrified light-stricken grown-ups came the words, My goodness! Look how dirty this place is!

So the first night of that great fluorescent light they spent washing the walls. Every one of them. Every inch.

That was the story the boys knew. That was the story they would always be able to tell, whether they remembered it or not.

Party line
Party lines were commonplace in the country. The bane of courting youths and anyone else who didn't want all of their neighbors listening in, they often provided live entertainment to the bored and nosey. Many a supposedly private conversation was greeted with a chorus of "oohs" and "aahs" at the most intimate moments. (Photograph by J. C. Allen & Son)

THE COUNTRY STORY

Checkers foes

The back of the general store was often the domain of those with more time on their hands than they knew what to do with. Whittling, pipe-smoking, and checkers games next to the warm wood-burning stove were ideal pastimes. (Photograph by J. C. Allen & Son)

Checking the wares

The best country general stores carried everything—and what they didn't have you probably didn't really need. And if you really did have to have it, they could always order it. This classic country store is stocked with everything from dungarees to mantle clocks, wall coverings to canned goods. (Photograph by J. C. Allen & Son)

State Fair

By Garrison Keillor

Garrison Keillor needs little introduction. He is the host and writer of the public radio show *A Prairie Home Companion,* which is modeled on the radio shows of yesteryear that kept farm families company after a day of hard work.

In addition, Garrison is the author of numerous books, some of which grew out of his radio show and its semi-fictional hometown, Lake Wobegon. Among his books are *Happy to Be Here,* *Lake Wobegon Days, WLT: A Radio Romance, The Book of Guys*, and *Wobegon Boy.*

This piece was originally a radio monologue delivered live at—fittingly—the Minnesota State Fair; it was later collected into *Leaving Home.* The story fondly tells of the adventures of a rural boy making a pilgrimage to the state fair year after year.

It has been a quiet week in Lake Wobegon and it's a great pleasure to be here at the Minnesota State Fair. I've come every year since I was five, and that's more than twenty years. Every August my mother said, "Well, I don't know if I care to go to the Fair this year or not." Nobody had so much as mentioned the Fair, we were too busy canning vegetables and perishing of the heat and the steam from the pressure cooker—a burning hot day and us stripping skins off tomatoes, slaving to put up a hundred or so quarts of a vegetable we were rapidly losing our appetite for. She said, "There's too much work to do and we can't afford it, it's too crowded, and anyway it's the same as last year. I don't see how we can do it. I'm sorry."

It was her way of lending drama to the trip. So we'd come to the Fair, the roar of engines and the smell of grease, and Mother marched around the Home Activities building looking at competitive cakes and jams. One year we shook hands with Senator Ed Thye, and another time we won a roll of linoleum by guessing the number of agates in a toilet bowl. One year

we wandered into the Education building and saw a demonstration of television, an interesting invention: people stood in a crowd and looked at a picture of themselves on a screen. When they moved the picture moved—interesting. Hard to see why you'd want one if you had a mirror, but it was entertaining for a few minutes.

I came with Mother and Dad, and because we were Christians we gave a wide berth to the Midway, where ladies danced and did other things at the Persian Palms and Harlem Revue tent shows. We avoided sin, but it was exciting for me to be so close to it and see flashing pink lights and hear barkers say, in a voice like a talking dog's, "See Miss Roxanne just inside the gate, just beyond that tent flap, she's waiting in there for you, she wants to show you a *good* time," and I tried to see beyond the flap, not wanting Miss Roxanne to be disappointed by my lack of interest in her. It was exciting to hear bands playing slow raunchy dance tunes and to walk past the freak show with the two-headed boy, where the gypsy ticket-seller looked at me with a haughty look that said, *I know things you'll never know, what I've seen you'd never understand.*

Fair ride
Fortunes worth of egg money and allowances were spent at county and state fair midway rides. (Photograph by J. C. Allen & Son)

I loved the Fair, the good and the bad. It was good to get out of our quiet town into a loud place with bad food and stink, music and sex blaring—listen—it's gorgeous. Dad gave me three dollars and I walked around not spending it, just gaping at the sights. Once I saw a sad midget stand and smoke a cigarette, holding his dog's leash, a big dog. Once I saw a man necking with a fat lady behind the Tilt-A-Whirl. He was running the ride. People were getting tossed around like eggs in a blender, and he was putting his hands up her shirt. Once I saw the newspaper columnist Olson Younger sitting in a booth under the sign MEET OLSON YOUNGER. He was puffier than his picture in the paper and more dejected. He sat drinking coffee after coffee and scrawling his autograph on free paper visors. He led a fairy-tale life in his column, meeting stars of stage and screen, eating meals with them, and even dancing once with Rita Hayworth, and he shared these wonderful moments with us through "The Olson Younger Column."

The bad part was that I had to wear fundamentalist clothes to the Fair, white rayon shirt, black pants, black shoes, narrow tie, because we had to sing in the evening at the Harbor Light gospel tent near the Midway gate. We sang "Earnestly, tenderly, Jesus is calling, calling for you and for me," and fifty feet away a man said, "Yes, she is absolutely naked as the day she was born, and she's inside, twenty-five cents, two bits, the fourth part of a dollar." I held the hymnbook high so nobody would see me. I wanted to be cool and wear a T-shirt. In the pioneer days before polyester, a rayon shirt was like wearing waxed paper.

When the service was over, we got one ride on the ferris wheel, rising up over the bright lights into the dark night toward the stars, and falling back into our real lives. On the long ride home I slept, and when I woke up I was in a classroom that smelled of floor wax; Mrs. Mortenson was asking me to explain the Smoot-Hawley Act.

In 1955 my uncle Earl saw an ad for the $2,000 Minnesota State Fair Cake Baking Sweepstakes, sponsored by Peter Pan Flour, and he entered my Aunt Myrna. He didn't mention this to her because he didn't want to upset her. She was a nervous person, easily startled by a sudden hello, and he was right, she made the greatest chocolate angel-food cake on the face of the earth. (To call it devil's food would give Satan encouragement so we didn't.) She also kept the cleanest kitchen in the Christian world. I liked to walk in, say hello, and when she recovered, she sat me down and fed me chocolate angel-food cake. As I ate it, she hovered overhead and apologized for it.

"*Oh,*" she sighed. "I don't know. I ought to throw this out for the dog. It's not very good. I don't know where my mind was—I lost track of how many eggs I put in, and I was all out of the kind of brown sugar I always use." I looked up at her in a trance, confused by the pure transcendent beauty of it, and she cut me a second, larger piece. "My mother was the one who could make a chocolate cake," she said, and then she allowed herself one taste of cake. And frowned. "It's gummy," she said. "It's like pudding."

"No," I said. "It's the best chocolate cake I ever tasted."

"Oh," she said, "your mother makes cake just as good as that."

Once my mother heard that and smiled at me, hopefully, but all my life I've tried to tell the truth, and I replied honestly, "Sometimes she does, but not often."

Aunt Myrna was one of the few truly slender women in town. She set an impossible standard for the others. "She's small-boned," they said, but the truth is that she was so critical of her cooking, which was head and shoulders above everyone else's, that food didn't satisfy her. She was supernatural that way, like an angel. Angels who visit earth don't feed on corn dogs and pizza. Heavenly creatures have low metabolism, a little bite of something perfect is more than enough. Like her cake. An angel visiting Minnesota to do research on sweet corn could go for a week on one thin sliver of Aunt Myrna's chocolate cake.

When, in early August, Uncle Earl got an invitation from the Peter Pan Flour people, none of us was surprised she was chosen, she was so good. She was mad at him when he broke the news; she said, "I can't bake in front of a hundred people. Stand up and make a cake and have them stare at me like I was some kind of carnival freak. I won't do it."

He considered that for a minute. "I was thinking of it," he said, "as an opportunity to witness for the Lord. If you win the bake-off, I'm certain that you get to make a speech. You could give that Scripture

Sideshow

County and state fairs offered a broad world of adventure to wide-eyed fairgoers of all ages. This sideshow awarded $100 to anyone strong enough of fist or fleet enough of foot to stay in the ring fifteen minutes with Charley Cutler's biggest bruiser. (Photograph by J. C. Allen & Son)

Midway lights
The lights of the fair light up many a small-town night and are a highlight of the summer. (Photograph by Jerry Irwin)

recipe, 'Take four cups of 1 Corinthians 13 and three cups of Ephesians 4:32, four quarts of Hebrews 11:1. . . .'"

"I don't know if I would be up to it. . . ."

"I can do all things through Christ which strengtheneth me. Phillipians 4:13."

She practiced for two weeks and baked about forty cakes, most of them barely edible. She was experimenting with strange ingredients, like maple syrup and peanut butter, marshmallows, cherry bits. "You can't just stand up in front of a crowd and bake an ordinary chocolate cake," she said, but we convinced her that hers was good enough. She baked two of them that Friday, both champs. On the big Saturday she packed her ingredients, cake pans, mixer, and utensils in a cardboard box and covered it with a cloth, and they drove to the Cities, stopping on account of car trouble in Anoka and transferring from the Dodge to the bus. The bake-off was at three o'clock.

They arrived at two-thirty. She had assumed the bake-off was in the Home Activities building and then she discovered it was here at the grandstand. Peter Pan Flour had gone all out. The bake-off was part of the afternoon grandstand program, which also included high-wire acts, a big band playing Glenn Miller tunes, and Siberian tigers jumping through hoops of fire. She and twelve other women would stand on stage and bake cakes, and while the cakes were in the oven, Joey Chitwood's Thrill Show would perform daredevil stunts on the dirt track, and Olson Younger the newspaper columnist would judge the contest and award the prize. We helped Aunt Myrna to the stage. She was weak and moist. "Good luck," we said.

I stand here and look up at the grandstand and can see how nervous she must've been. I remember sitting up there in the forty-ninth row, under the pavilion, looking down at my tiny aunt in the green dress to the left of the saxophones while Joey Chitwood's Thrill Show drivers did flips and rolls, roaring around in white Fords. She stood at a long table whipping mix in a silver bowl, my aunt Myrna making a cake. She was mine, my relative, and I was so proud.

And then the cakes came out of the oven. The State Fair orchestra put down their newspapers and picked up their horns and played something from opera, and the radio-announcer emcee said that now the moment had come, and Olson Younger pranced around. He wore a green suit and orange tie and he waved to us with both hands. It was his moment of glory, and he sashayed from one entrant to the next, kissing her, rolling his eyes, and tasting her cake. When he tasted Myrna's cake, she shrank back from his embrace. She said a few words to him and I knew she was saying, "I don't know. I just can't seem to make em as rich as I used to—this isn't very good at all. It's gummy." It was the greatest chocolate cake in the world but he believed her. So she came in tenth.

A woman in white pedal pushers won because, Younger said, her cake was richer and moister. He had a hard time getting the words out. You could see the grease stains from her cake, beads of grease glittered in the sun. Uncle Earl said, "That's not cake, that's pudding he gave a prize to. This is a pudding contest he's running. He wouldn't know chocolate cake if it came up and ate him." And he was right. When Younger waltzed over to give Aunt Myrna her prize, a bowl, you could see he didn't know which way was north. It wasn't fair. She was the best. We waited for her in front of the grandstand. We both felt bad.

But when we saw her coming, she was all smiles. She hugged us both. She hardly seemed like herself. She threw her head back and said, "Oh, I'm glad it's over. But it was fun. I was so scared. And then I just forgot to be."

"But it wasn't fair," I said. She said, "Oh, he was drunk. It was all whiskey cake to him. But it doesn't matter. It was so much fun." I never saw her so lighthearted and girlish.

That night an old man came forward at the Harbor Light gospel meeting. He was confused and may have been looking for the way out, but we latched onto him and prayed for him. When he left, he seemed relieved. He was our first convert and we were thrilled. A soul hanging in the balance, there in our tent. Heaven and hell his choice, and he chose heaven, with our help, and then Dad lent him busfare.

That night, I said to my mother, "This is the last time I wear a rayon shirt, I hate them." She said, "All right, that's fine." I said, "You're not mad?" She said, "No, I thought you liked them, that's all."

I went up in the ferris wheel for a last ride before being thrown into seventh grade. It went up into the stars and fell back to earth and rose again, and I had a magnificent vision, or think I did, though it's hard to remember if it was that year with the chocolate cake or the next one with the pigs getting loose. The ferris wheel is the same year after year. It's like all one ride to me: we go up and I think of people I knew who are dead and I smell fall in the air, manure, corn dogs, and we drop down into blazing light and blaring music. Every summer I'm a little bigger, but riding the ferris wheel, I feel the same as ever, I feel eternal. The combination of cotton candy, corn dogs, diesel smoke, and sawdust, in a hot dark summer night, it never changes, not an inch. The wheel carries us up high, high, high, and stops, and we sit swaying, creaking, in the dark, on the verge of death. You can see death from here. The wind blows from the northwest, from the farm school in Saint Anthony Park, a chilly wind with traces of pigs and sheep in it. This is my vision: little kids holding on to their daddy's hand, and he is me. He looks down on them with love and buys them another corn dog. They are worried they will lose him, they hang on to his leg with one hand, eat with the other. This vision is unbearably wonderful. Then the wheel brings me down to the ground. We get off and other people get on. Thank you, dear God, for this good life and forgive us if we do not love it enough.

Livestock judging

Beyond the sights and rides of the midway, fairs also serve a serious purpose in the livestock, handicrafts, and food judging. Much pride depends on the awarding of the blue ribbon. (Photograph by J. C. Allen & Son)

Combine demolition derby

Rather than let the old combine rust away in a back pasture, combine demolition derbies offered the perfect outlet for all of a farmer's frustrations for every time the machine broke down. This contest of agricultural gladiators took place at the Minnesota State Fair in the 1970s before a packed grandstand. (Minnesota Historical Society)

RADIO WAS A WINDOW TO THE WORLD

By Orlan Skare

Orlan Skare was raised on a farm near Willmar, Minnesota, in the 1930s. He has started writing down memories of his farming youth to pass on to his children and future generations.

The long-awaited purchase of a radio opened up a whole new world for my family on our rural farmstead in the early 1930s. Suddenly we had daily news, Dad could hear weather and crop reports in early morning, and Mom could listen to Ma Perkins or Judy and Jane in the afternoon.

For younger brother Elmo and me, radio really began after school with Jack Armstrong, Captain Midnight, and Little Orphan Annie. I'm sure many seniors could still hum the advertising melody by the sponsor of Jack Armstrong:

"Won't you try Wheaties, the best breakfast food in the land.

"Won't you buy Wheaties, they're whole wheat with all of the bran.

"They're crisp, they're crunchy, the whole day through. . . . Jack Armstrong never tires of them and neither will you.

"So . . . just buy Wheaties, the best breakfast food in the land."

Evening programs were designed to appeal to the whole family. Fibber Magee and Molly, Amos and Andy, and Fred Allen brought humor, and the Lux Radio Theater brought drama.

But it was programs like Inner Sanctum, The Shadow, The Green Hornet, and Gangbusters that would rivet family members to their chairs. Inner Sanctum had a creaking door that was particularly scary to a couple of small boys alone in a creaky house while the parents were out milking.

Radio has a quality that TV doesn't have. Radio, depending only on narration and sound effects, forces the listener to form constantly changing mental images. I like to think that this helps young listeners to develop creative imaginations.

Radio days
The invention of the radio brought entertainment to the farm, along with weather forecasts and commodity prices. Suddenly, a whole new world was opened to rural families. Early radios were powered by stacks of batteries; the arrival of electricity made listening to the radio as easy as plugging into the wall socket and turning the dial. (Photograph by J. C. Allen & Son)

Our farm didn't have electrical power in the 1930s, so our radio was powered by batteries. Our first radio had three bulky batteries. The A battery was a wet cell, similar to those that automobiles use today, but the B and C batteries were dry cells, also quite bulky. The total battery package was probably larger than the radio itself, even though the early radios were large because of the huge array of vacuum tubes and condensers.

These batteries were quite expensive for depression-era budgets, and relatively short-lived. The result was that as the batteries began to lose power, listeners' chairs inched closer to the radio, with the whole family eventually joined head to head in order to pick up the ever-weakening signal.

Could this be the point where the "family togetherness" concept of rural families got its start?

The Meaning of It All

"Those who labor in the earth are the chosen people of God, if ever He had a chosen people, whose breasts He has made His peculiar deposit for substantial and genuine virtue."
—**Thomas Jefferson,** *Notes on Virginia,* 1785

Those who have never lived on a farm often wonder why farmers do it. Why get up at some ungodly early hour every day and toil long into the night just for fields and animals that don't say thank you? Why take on a business that you can't leave for more than a day before having to get back home for chores? Why stake your livelihood on a continually fluctuating agricultural market? Why live so far away from the energy and excitement of the city? What value could you possibly get out of such a life?

Indeed, many farmers have had to scratch their heads and ask themselves what the value is.

In trying to answer that question, the writers of the following selections describe the intangible rewards of farming—little details that instead of cushioning the pocketbook, satisfy the soul.

Ultimately, if you need to attach a value to farm life, you probably would not understand it anyway.

"Autumn Memories"
Left: *Artist Charles Freitag captures all that's best about farm life on a rich autumn day. (Apple Creek Publishing)*

"His First Lesson"
Above: *Life on the farm was all about planning ahead for tomorrow, whether that meant canning vegetables for the winter months or passing knowledge on to the next generation, as this John Deere plow advertisement reminded.*

The Time I Quit Farming

By Gordon Green

Canadian Gordon Green wrote about the subject nearest to his heart: farming. His essays and stories appeared in agricultural magazines for generations, and many of his books were also focused on his own experiences on the farm. Among his publications were *A Heritage of Canadian Handicrafts*, *Goodbye Little Town*, *A Time To Pass Over: Life With a Pioneer Grandmother*, and a memoir recounting the life and times of his own father, *The Faith of Our Father: The True Story of a Farmer Who Made His Religion a Way of Life*.

This story, which first appeared in *Farm Journal* in May 1958, is classic Gordon Green, offering insight into the strong family values that making farming that life it is.

I can't say I blamed the children for not wanting to do chores with me on that February morning after the storm. The cold nibbled at my feet as I left the sheepskin rug beside the bed. When I tried to get the kids up, they only made comfortable little moans and curled deeper into the covers.

Downstairs, the waterpipes were frozen and the discouraged day struggled through the snow-smothered windows. A county snowplow down the road kept losing its roar in the drifts.

When the children finally got down into the kitchen that morning, their protests came near to mutiny.

"This is pure Siberia!" said our 12-year-old Sydney. "We *work* like Siberia and it *looks* like Siberia!"

His younger sister started in. "Other people just have to worry about getting to the bus. But not us! We have to feed pigs and cows and silly old hens that don't even bother to lay eggs."

I thought that was being pretty mean to the old man, and I said so. "All you have to do is to feed the chickens, Miss Huffy!" I said. "Now let's get your mitts on!"

So amidst tears that nearly froze to their cheeks, they went to the barn with me that awful morning. There were three of them: Marielle of the chickens, Sydney of Siberia, and the one whom we call Chief Big Fellow because he's a head taller than I am.

We kicked our way through the drifts, shoveled out the barn doors and somehow got the job done. But when we were trying to follow our own step marks back to the house again for breakfast, and I had supposed the rebellion to be over, the Big Fellow began to talk.

"Pretty stupid to go through all this agony when you could have a nice comfortable job in the city. Or do you like all this extra worry and no cash?"

That was the unkindest cut of all. Because the truth is, we never do seem to have as much money as our neighbors.

At first I thought it was because our operations were so small. We had only a small flock of hens, a couple

Abandoned farmhouse

The end of a dream: An abandoned farmstead surrounded by green "volunteer" crops left over from seasons past. (Photograph by Rick Schafer)

of Springer spaniel females, a few cows and a garden that kept us eating. But now we had hens by the hundreds and dozens of Springers and a big herd of cattle. Besides pigs, sheep, ducks, geese, goats, turkeys, Persian cats, chinchillas and even rabbits and hamsters in season. Some of these made our living; some were mostly for fun. Yet we never showed much of a profit.

I had never claimed our farm was altogether practical. But until that morning I wouldn't have believed my family could be so unforgiving about it. It was my wife who shook me hardest.

"Why couldn't we be happy with just a nice home?" she asked. "Why don't we sell the farm?"

I pushed my breakfast aside and put on my cap and windbreaker.

"We could keep our house, darling," she went on, "but we could get a real good price for the farm now. And your friends in town have been after you a dozen times to work for them."

I didn't listen. She followed me to the door. "What do you get out of all that slaving?"

It was a question to which I gave a lot of thought that morning.

Before noon that day, a real estate man rapped on the barn door.

"I don't thank my wife for this," I told him, as he looked for a clean place to sit. "She could at least have given me a little time to think it over."

The real estate agent was a gay, sharp little fellow. "Take all the time you want," he said. "Only remember that nine years ago you bought your 40 acres for only $1,000."

It annoyed me to discover how much he knew about my private affairs. "When I want to sell, I'll let you know."

"We're offering $500 an acre. Cash!"

I took a step toward the door, but he stayed where he was. "Let's look at it this way," he said. "You're the last farmer left. City people are coming in so fast it's only a matter of time before you'll have to quit."

"I was here first."

"They can pass laws and tax you out." He edged in closer. "You know as well as I do that the only way to make money out of farming these days is to sell your farm for more than you paid for it. All that stuff about the joys of country life! Why I've got half a hundred farms aching to be sold!"

"I'll think it over," I promised.

We had lamb stew that night for supper, a meal my wife always makes when she wants to sign the peace. So I had to postpone giving her the scolding she deserved for putting the real estate agent on my trail. Besides, I hadn't quite decided the right reply to her question.

What *did* I get out of my farm?

I took the question with me to the barn that night. Well, one thing sure, I got a lot of work out of it. Other men on my road get up to catch the eight o'clock bus. I start the chores at six. For them the work day ends with supper (they call it dinner). For me there's an hour or more of work in the barn.

I know what it's like to get up every two hours on a frosty March night to search the sheep yard for new lambs. Or to wait up through the cold dark hours to watch a sow on the brink of maternity.

And with the work comes muss. In the summer the big lawns all down our road are neat and well-barbered. We have no lawn, only a huge rambling yard where the dogs dig, the geese squat and the children build feed-bag tents. Where on wash day the rooster proclaims himself cock of the walk from the clothes pole, and the pigs have made their own farm pond and the pony scratches his rump on a trellis once intended for roses.

Nor is the muss confined to the stables and the yard. We go into the house with animal husbandry still stuck to our boots and our pants cuffs full of chaff. And in the kitchen there is all too often an orphan lamb to dart out from his nook behind the stove and cast aspersions on the wife's clean floor. Or a runt pig, or chilled chicks.

I get a lot of worry out of my farm, too. I worry about frost, thaws, rain, drought, hail, storms and the rumors of storms. I worry about the rising price of hay and the sinking price of beef. And should there be an ailing animal on my place, my supper means little to me. Even one of lamb stew.

I'll admit, I complain pretty loud about such trials—so loud, perhaps, that my wife may think they overwhelm me. But for all its tribulations, the labor of farming has given me a satisfaction I have never found in any other occupation.

I like the thousand little things about a farm which can stop a man's heart in mid-beat and make him remember ever after. The trust of well-fed animals. The soft neighing of a mare to her exploring colt.

Sunset
The sun sets on a farm as storm clouds rise above. (Photograph by Willard Clay)

The sounds of the woods on the wild spring nights at mapling time and the smell of the fire-pink steam which lifts from the boiling sap. The power and the glory of a young bull as he blats and paws the earth to announce that he has now outgrown his age of innocence. The child-like swelling of pride which you can't quite hold back when one of your gleaming animals wins the judge's nod and a bright ribbon at the fair.

The smell of sun in a small boy's hair at berry picking time. The delighted cries of a little girl in a spring orchard as she peeks through clenched fingers at a bright bug or a tree toad or some other trophy of a child's eternal quest for something younger than itself.

I like the way the farm teaches my children about creation.

A few weeks ago there was quite a commotion at one of the neighboring homes. The center of the excitement was a cardboard box that the good lady of the house was trying to hide. But for all the precautions, a five-year-old boy managed a peek.

"Don't know why they're all excited," he said. "Just the cat having kittens."

That enlightened boy, I am glad to say, started his education on my farm.

All right. So it's a religion with me. But how does a man explain such a thing to his wife or to the real estate agent she sicks on him?

But why should I bother to try? Already there were people down the road who wanted to pass some kind of law that would prevent a rooster from crowing before seven in the morning. And twice in the last week our sheep had congregated on a neighbor's back

porch. We might hang on another two or three years perhaps, but eventually our farm would have to succumb to the same law which had made it a farm. One kind of life must cease so that another might thrive.

It would be hard to say goodbye to the animals, I thought. One never knew what kind of people they would go to. But there was no use fighting the inevitable, especially when the family wasn't willing to fight with you. I decided to sell out.

Back at the house I still cherished the hurt the family had handed me and I didn't give them the satisfaction of knowing that they had won. I said nothing about it at all, but the next time I was in the city, I dropped in to see the real estate man and made the deal. Afterward I dropped around to see my friend in the feed business. Then at supper that night, I told the family.

"The farm is sold. We're slightly rich. I hope you're satisfied."

There was a sudden shocked hush, as if a funeral had unexpectedly come around the corner. "No!" my wife said finally. "You wouldn't!"

I was surprised at her. "But you wanted it this way! You were the one who sent the real estate man, weren't you?"

I thought she was going to cry. "But I didn't send him! I—I just called up to see how much the land might be worth. I didn't tell him to see you!"

The children had stopped eating too. "But what will we do with all the animals, dad?" Sydney asked.

"Sell them. What else?"

"Not my horse, you won't!"

"And not my chinchillas!"

The Big Fellow took a little more time to give me his opinion. "You might have asked me," he said. "I never did say that I didn't like farming. It was just that I didn't like the way we were doing it here and now."

And as I listened to them scolding me for being so impetuous, I saw that it was not as I had thought at all. Sure, my family had protested against the battle of the farm. They had protested it bitterly, just as I

"The Passing of the Old West"
Flocks of birds fly south above the ghost of a prairie farm in this painting by artist Francis Lee Jaques. (James Ford Bell Museum of Natural History)

had. But like me, they loved it just the same. It had taken this to make them realize it.

I felt a little ashamed, and very, very happy. We had a half gallon of ice cream a little later and a box of chocolates for mother. And next day I called on the real estate man again.

"Some of these bigger farms you have on your list," I said. "Some of these places just aching to be sold—how about showing me a few?"

So the animals will only go to a new place, not to new owners. Not 40 acres this time, but 200, and every acre as beautiful as the combined hands of God and man can make it. Just the thought of it makes me feel breathless and a little guilty. Have we any right to expect so much?

And the money it will take—the money, the money! We may be the rest of our lives paying on the mortgage.

Which is why I am out in the barn now writing this as I wait through the cold dark hours with a lantern under my knees, beside a sow approaching the brink of maternity.

"Farming, particularly, has invested not just its trust, but its faith in every religious sense you can imagine into divine machinery. . . [and] a part of us venerates those old machines, as if they were saints' relics in old churches."
—Bill Holm, "The Virgin on the Farmall—The Venus in the Chevy," from *Landscape of Ghosts*, 1993

Ghosts
Obsolete thrashing machines sit out their days perched on prairie hilltops like bizarre agricultural sculptures. (Photograph by G. Alan Nelson)

Tax Rebate

By Patricia Penton Leimbach

Patricia Penton Leimbach is farming's Erma Bombeck. Like Bombeck, she is a sage philosopher on the trials and tribulations of everyday life. She writes with a sharp pen about the joys and troubles, the hard work and humor, the meaning and value of rural living.

Leimbach was raised on a fruit farm near Lorain, Ohio. Alongside her husband Paul, a fourth-generation farmer, she has run End o'Way farm in Vermilion, Ohio, for more than four decades.

It is through her writing that Leimbach has become one of the best-known farm women in North America. For many years, she authored the weekly "Country Wife" column in the Elyria, Ohio, *Chronicle Telegram* newspaper. She also has three books to her credit, *A Thread of Blue Denim*, *All My Meadows*, and *Harvest of Bittersweet*, all of which are filled with wit and wisdom culled from her firsthand knowledge of everything from raising puppies to driving farm tractors.

In this essay from *All My Meadows*, she does her accounting for another year on the farm.

"Hey, make me up a list of what you earned last year," hollers my husband from the next room where he's winding up his six weeks' dalliance with the income tax.

Well, let's see. What did I earn last year? A skilled homemaker should be worth at least $8 an hour. (If you're not skilled after twenty-four years, when would you be?) She invests about twelve hours a day. Of course, I wasn't here every day and Sundays were light. . . . Say 300 days at $96 a day. That's $28,800 to start with. And then a farmer's wife has supplementary tasks to lengthen most of her days.

I went to work with my thinker and my eighth-grade math and I drew up my list.

Amount earned:

Skilled homemaker	$28,800
Labor foreman (equally skilled)	3,200
Tractor driver (mediocre)	1,600
Truck driver (fantastic skill)	1,600
Computer operator	3,000
Purchasing agent (reputation—"Scotch")	3,000
Sales clerk, real estate agent, phone operator, social arbiter (gracious, knowledgeable, witty)	2,400
Total	$43,600

I laid it on the bookkeeper's desk and left. In a calculated few moments there was a roar.

"That's not what I wanted!"

A world of gold
The sun shines through the gold-tinged autumn leaves of farmyard maple trees. (Photograph by Dennis Frates)

"But you asked me what I earned. I thought my estimate was conservative, considering my education and experience and all."

"Would you please make me up a list of what you actually *got*," he said in exasperation.

"Ohhh, what I actually *got*. . . . Well, that's something else. . . ."

Much later I slipped in and laid my second list on his desk:

Payment Received for Services Rendered:

sunrise over the valley about 300 times (No failure
    with the sun. I was absent a few times.)
sunset over Schmalz's barn
a picture frame of barn siding
picnics in the pasture in May
two dogs working a woodchuck hole
rain coming across the potatoes in August
new peas, June 10
first sweet corn, July 15
new potatoes, August 10
a banana cream pie baked from scratch by a son on a
    Sunday morning
swamp buttercups in May
rural free delivery
an oriole in the pear tree
hot buttered rum by a hearthfire in a blizzard
a wrought-iron kettle restored by a son
lunch alone with my honey on weekdays
sons coming in to supper from working with their
    father
a golden gingko tree in October
little kids in leaf piles
Teddy with a bucket loader filled with firewood
impromptu visits with neighbors
walking down the road on a starry night
bare branches against the moon and the winter sky
wheat emerging under snow
more love, support, concrete assistance, and encour-
    agement than I deserved

Total value: Incalculable.

Haystack
Haystacks presented hours of fun to farm children everywhere. The different permutations of games to be played in the hay were endless. (Photograph by J. C. Allen & Son)

And to it I affixed the following note:

I found it impossible to assign a value to these things, and I suppose it's just as well. If the IRS figures a way to tax our real wealth, we'll be bankrupt. As it is, I don't suppose the IRS will be much interested. Label it "Left After Taxes." No matter how you slice it, "Payment Received" exceeds "Amount Earned."

Christmastime
Sis hangs her stocking with care above the fireplace on the night before Christmas. (Photograph by J. C. Allen & Son)

"Say what you will about the general usefulness of boys, it is my impression that a farm without a boy would very soon come to grief. What the boy does is the life of the farm. He is the factotum, always in demand, always expected to do the thousand indispensable things that nobody else will do."
—Charles Dudley Warner, "Being a Boy"

The old fishing hole
Right: *Dad jumps off his trusty John Deere to help Junior, who has snagged a turtle at the old fishing hole in this painting by artist Walter Haskell Hinton. (Deere & Company)*

Sunset
Overleaf: *The sun sets on another day. (Photograph by Willard Clay)*

"Verily there are things no man can take from you, and among these are recollections and remembrances, and in your reflective years you will be happy or sad according as your recollections are pleasant or otherwise."
—"The Rural Philosopher," quoted in A. C. Wood's *Old Days on the Farm*, 1918

Permissions

"The Land Remembers" from *The Land Remembers* by Ben Logan. Copyright © 1975 by Ben T. Logan. Reprinted by permission of Frances Collins, Literary Agent.

"The Kitchen" from *Growing Up In The 40s* by Jerry L. Twedt. Copyright © 1994 by J. L. Twedt; copyright © 1996 by Iowa State University Press. Reprinted by permission of Iowa State University Press, Ames 50014.

"And God Said: 'Let There Be Red'" from *Landscape of Ghosts* by Bill Holm, with photographs by Bob Firth. Copyright © 1993 by Bill Holm. Reprinted by permission of the author and Voyageur Press.

"Privies" from *The American Farmhouse* by Henry J. Kauffman. Copyright © 1975 by Henry J. Kauffman. Reprinted by permission of the author.

"The Specialist" from *The Specialist* by Charles Sale. Copyright © 1929 by Charles Sale. Reprinted by permission of Dwight and Laura Sale, Specialist Publishing Company, 109 La Mesa Drive, Burlingame, CA 94010. *The Specialist* and its sequel, *I'll Tell You Why*, can be ordered for $6.00 each from Specialist Publishing.

"Big Load" from *From the Hidewood: Memories of a Dakota Neighborhood* by Robert Amerson. Copyright © 1996 by Robert Amerson. Reprinted by permission of the Minnesota Historical Society Press.

"Roger's Rules for Restoring a Tractor for Fun and Profit" by Roger Welsch. Reprinted by permission of the author.

"About Cows" from *About Cows* by Sara Rath. Copyright © 1987 by Sara Rath. Reprinted by permission of the author.

"Death of a Pig" from *The Second Tree From the Corner* by E. B. White. Copyright © 1947 by E. B. White. Copyright renewed. First appeared in *Atlantic Monthly*. Reprinted by permission of HarperCollins Publishers, Inc.

"Food and Those Who Ate It" from *Eggs in the Coffee, Sheep in the Corn: My 17 Years as a Farmwife* by Majorie Myers Douglas. Copyright © 1994 by Majorie Myers Douglas. Reprinted by permission of the Minnesota Historical Society Press.

"The Polk County Homewreckers" from *Dancing the Cows Home: A Wisconsin Girlhood* by Sara De Luca. Copyright © 1996 by Sara Hellerud De Luca. Reprinted by permission of the Minnesota Historical Society Press.

"Electricity" from *The One-Room Schoolhouse* by Jim Heynen. Copyright © 1993 by Jim Heynen. Reprinted by permission of Alfred A. Knopf Inc.

"State Fair" from *Leaving Home* by Garrison Keillor. Copyright © 1987, 1997 by Garrison Keillor. Used by permission of Viking Penguin, a division of Penguin Putnam Inc.

"The Time I Quit Farming" by Gordon Green. Reprinted by permission of *Farm Journal*.

"Tax Rebate" from *All My Meadows* by Patricia Penton Leimbach. Copyright © 1977 by Patricia Penton Leimbach. Reprinted by permission of the author.

Charles Freitag's paintings are reproduced by permission of the artist and Apple Creek Publishing, 4444 1st Avenue NE, Cedar Rapids, Iowa 52402.

Raymond L. Crouse's paintings are reproduced by permission of R. L. Crouse Inc. Farm Art USA, 112 East 4th Street RD, Greeley, Colorado 80631-9529.

"Deere in the Barnyard"

Artist Raymond L. Crouse's painting of a forgotten Johnny Popper left to the forces of nature evokes the passing of a way of life on the farm.